LĪHUʻE

LĪHU'E

ROOT AND BRANCH OF A HAWAI'I TOWN

Pat L. Griffin

KAUA'I HISTORICAL SOCIETY
ESTABLISHED 1914

Publication of this book was made possible by

BANK OF HAWAII

GOODALE FAMILY FUND

KAUA'I VISITORS BUREAU

PACIFIC FUNDS LLC

STRONG FOUNDATION

The Kaua'i Historical Society and the author are grateful for their support to further knowledge about the rich details of Hawai'i's past.

ADDITIONAL FIGURE CREDITS

Photos without captions are credited as follows: The frontispiece image was taken by *Garden Island* photographer Harvey Tam. It is in the Kaua'i Historical Society's collection of his work. The quilters, p. xi, were photographed by William J. Senda, Kaua'i Historical Society. "Greater Akialoa," p. 2, is by Frederick W. Frohawk, *Aves Hawaiiensis*. The sketch of sugarcane and grinders on p. 3 and the train *Paulo*, p. 64, are by the author. The American Factors, "successors of H. Hackfeld" card, p. 38, is from an October 1918 letterhead, Hawaiian Sugar Planters Association archives. Stamp, p. 104, is from the collection of Andy Bushnell. The cream bottle on p. 184 was donated by Marion Penhallow. The Nawiliwili Transportation token, p. 192, is in the collection of Reginald Gage. The *Filipino News* flag, p. 209, is from a collection of the newspapers in the Kaua'i Historical Society archives. The camphor can and rice cooker, p. 218, were purchased at Yoneji's and reside in the author's kitchen. The children, p. 323, came to Līhu'e with the E. K. Fernandez circus in 1933. The stuffed animal display, p. 324, is by W. J. Senda, in the Kiyoto Okimoto collection. Lihue Store, p. 325, is in the Grove Farm Homestead Museum archives. All photos not otherwise credited were taken by the author. The proverb on p. 371 is by Mary Kawena Pukui in *'Ōlelo No'eau;* photo is by Ray Jerome Baker, Kaua'i Historical Society.

PUBLISHED BY KAUA'I HISTORICAL SOCIETY

P. O. Box 1778 • Līhu'e, Hawai'i 96766

Library of Congress Cataloging-in-Publication Data

Griffin, Pat L., author.

Lihu'e : root & branch of a Hawai'i town / Pat L. Griffin.

pages cm

Includes bibliographical references and index.

ISBN 0-9703293-9-3 (alk. paper)

1. Lihue (Hawaii)--History. I. Title.

DU629.L54G75 2014

996.9'4--dc23

2014032545

PRINTED IN THE UNITED STATES OF AMERICA

Coordinated by University of Hawai'i Press

Designed by Julie Matsuo-Chun

CONTENTS

CENTRAL LĪHU‘E

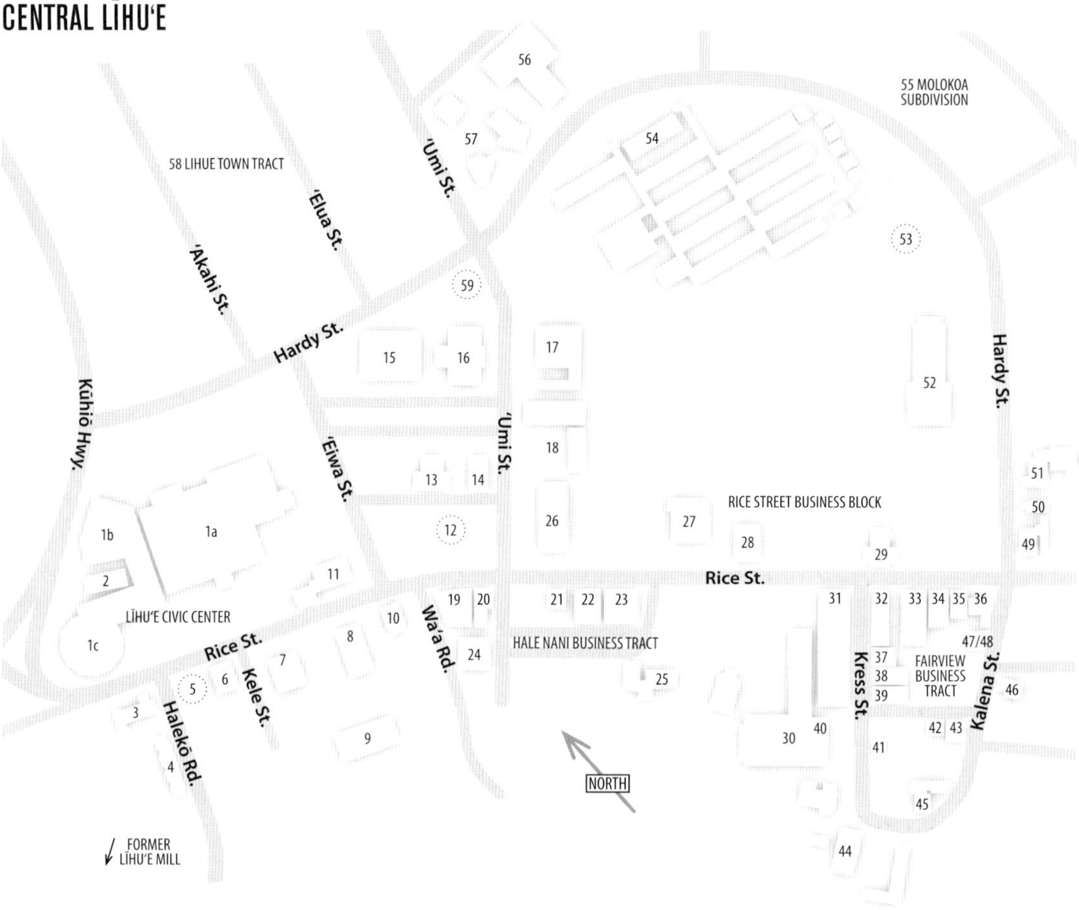

1. Līhu‘e Civic Center (Originally Lihue Shopping Center)
    - 1a. Pi‘ikoi Building
    - 1b. Kapule Building
    - 1c. Mo‘ikeha Building
2. Hawaiian Telcom
3. Central Service Station
4. Halekō Duplexes
5. Isenberg Monument
6. Bank of Hawaii
7. U.S. Post Office
8. First Hawaiian Bank
9. Lihue Plantation Building
10. Chevron Station
11. Kaua‘i Museum and Annex
12. County Lawn
13. Historic County Building
14. County Building Annex
15. Hawai‘i State Building
16. Former Courthouse
17. Former Police Station
18. Lihue Health Center
19. Lihue Missionary Church
20. Prosser Realty and Kiibo
21. Hale Nani Studio
22. James Licke, Esq.
23. City Liquor
24. Aloha Furniture
25. Tensho-Kotai-Jingu-Kyo
26. Lihue Plaza Building
27. Watumull Plaza
28. American Savings Bank
29. Hale Kauai
30. Rice Shopping Center
31. S. H. Kress & Co.
32. Kawakami Store
33. Royal Theater
34. Waimea Garage
35. Filipino News
36. The Yoneji Building
37. Barbecue Inn
38. Robert's Jewelry
39. Kauai Realty
40. William Hyde Rice, Ltd.
41. Hamura Saimin
42. KQNG Radio
43. Kauai Electronics
44. Lihue Christian Church
45. Kauai Palms Hotel
46. Tanaka Plumbing
47. Flowers Forever
48. Lihue Fishing Supply
49. Motel Lani
50. International Longshore and Warehouse Union (ILWU)
51. Salvation Army
52. Kaua‘i War Memorial Convention Hall
53. Tennis Courts
54. Elsie H. Wilcox Elementary School
55. Molokoa Subdivision
56. Lihue Public Library
57. St. Michael and All Angels Church
58. Lihue Town Tract
59. Art in Public Places Sculpture

PREFACE

This study was conceived as a thirty-two-page walking tour of the three central blocks in Līhu'e Town. It was to take its place in the Kaua'i Historical Society's touring series, which follows that format. To be honest, I knew from the outset that the subject deserved a more studied treatment. I expected the work to stretch to forty-eight pages, maybe even sixty, but that idea too exploded as I uncovered one rich detail after another about the growth and development of Līhu'e, a town both representative of and uniquely different from others in Hawai'i. Combined with the images that recall the past in ways no thousands of words can match, the result is the volume you now hold.

The book expanded despite a comparative shortage of documentation about Kaua'i in the standard regional libraries and archives. Ethel Damon's 1931 history of Kaua'i, the two-volume *Koamalu,* has remained one precious resource for all of us who seek to glimpse the island's past. She painted a compelling picture of a certain segment of the population, the "Pioneers on Kauai" whom her subtitle describes, though her lack of source documentation and the destruction of many of her primary sources hobbles some attempts at further research. And her focus on an elite group, the prevalent approach of her era, ignores the contributions of many others.

Today, most social historians understand that the past is both more complex and more interesting than highlights of a founding generation and its most prominent citizens can provide. People who were once written out of the record have important stories to tell about the development of a place, if only we can uncover them. Land records and newspaper articles help. The reality that Līhu'e is primarily a twentieth-century place has also added the advantage of oral histories to shine glimmers of light on the subject.

But by increasing the historical focus to a broad population, we run the risk of losing the distinction between the elemental and the incidental. Think about each of our days: in the time it has taken you to read the three paragraphs above, Līhuʻe inhabitants have collectively performed more tasks (and dreamed more dreams) than an entire library could archive. How do we pick and choose the salient events to record, the ones that help interpret that past for the present? That's a historian's task, and the future itself will determine our successes and shortcomings.

Līhuʻe is a sturdy town, a practical town. No one would describe it as a beautiful town, though it has its share of beautiful buildings. Because it never suffered decline—a wrinkle in time that suspended change and allowed another generation to restore a charming, period "village"—different eras each contributed their own unique elements to the whole. Līhuʻe today is a patchwork quilt of styles and designs and attributes. The result may not have produced an aesthetic masterpiece; the magnificent poetry of Kauaʻi lies elsewhere. Līhuʻe remains a prosaic place. Yet it is also a town to celebrate. The power of Līhuʻe is palpable. In its reach lie the major port and airport for the island, its largest hospital, only institution of higher learning, most concentrated commercial center, and the seat of government. There is a story to tell here about who we are as a community on Kauaʻi. Līhuʻe remains its heart. I hope this history does it honor.

ON THE USE OF THE HAWAIIAN LANGUAGE

This text is guided by the *Hawaiian Dictionary* and *Place Names of Hawaii.* In accordance with current Kauaʻi Historical Society convention, it utilizes *kahakō* and *ʻokina* for Hawaiian words, locations, and possessives. The exception is personal names, which are written in the form that people were originally given; as my honored Hawaiian language *kumu,* Ilei Beniamina, once admonished, we should not presume to change a name gifted to a child by its parents. Those "children" include companies such as Lihue Plantation. Of course, if a name is used in a direct quotation, it is copied exactly, with the diacritical marks, hyphens, or any other symbols utilized in the original source. The result is that the same word may be spelled two or more ways within a single paragraph.

Following are abbreviated translations of Hawaiian words as they are used in the text. Far richer and more complete entries are included in the Pukui and Elbert *Hawaiian Dictionary.*

ahupuaʻa	land division, usually stretching from upland to ocean
ʻāina	land
ʻakahi (ʻekahi)	one (numerical)
aliʻi	chief (not gender specific)
aliʻi ʻaimoku	chief of a *moku*
aliʻi nui	high chief
hānai	adopted or foster child
hau	*Hibiscus tiliaceus,* a true hibiscus, one of the "canoe plants" brought by Polynesian voyagers, with a multitude of uses for its wood, bark, and sap
hoʻike	to show (for students, a test)
ka poʻe kahiko	the people of old

kahu	honored attendant, guardian
kama'āina	native born
kalo	taro
kamani	*Calophylium inophyllum,* a large hardwood tree brought to Hawai'i as a canoe plant, its wood prized for structures and calabashes; many uses also for its blossoms, fruit, seeds, leaves, and bark
kaukau ali'i	lower-ranking chief
kāula	seer, prophet
koa	*Acacia koa,* endemic tree, largest in Hawai'i, prized for its wood
ko'i	adze
kuhina nui	very powerful, principal advisor to the king; originated in the monarchy period
kukui	*Aleurites moluccana,* canoe plant with a multitude of uses for its oily nut, bark, and flowers; easily detectable in forests by its pale green leaves
kumu	teacher
lauhala	leaf of the indigenous *hala* tree, *Pandanus tectorius* (screwpine), used in plaiting for mats, baskets, hats, and other such items
lū'au	young *kalo* tops and a Hawaiian feast at which they were always served; anglicized as luau
mahele	portion or division; the Great Mahele formally divided the lands of Hawai'i and established private ownership of them.
ma kai	(frequently written as *makai)* toward the ocean
maika'i	good
maile	*Alyxia oliviformis,* a flowering plant endemic to Hawai'i, with fragrant leaves (the *maile* on Kaua'i is particularly celebrated)
ma uka	(frequently written as *mauka)* toward the inland or mountains
mele	song or chant
moku	section, district, island
mo'olelo	history, traditions, legends and lore
nei	this here
'ōhi'a	*Metrosideros polymorpha,* endemic tree, most commonly with bright red blossoms, common in Hawaiian forests

ʻokana	district or subdistrict, usually composed of several *ahupuaʻa*
ʻolēʻolē	small conch shell
ʻoli	chant (not accompanied by dance)
pāʻina	feast, luau
pau hana	finished work
pāʻū	woman's long-flowing skirt, commonly worn by equestrians in parades
pono	just, righteous

Quilters. William J. Senda, Kauaʻi Historical Society

ONE

A MILLENNIUM CONDENSED

The past is a foreign country:
they do things differently there.

—L. P. Hartley, *The Go-Between*

Līhu'e Town began around a sugar mill and grew to become the most important urban center on the island by force of geography, institutions, and personalities who seized on its potential over the past century and a half.

Līhu'e forest, ca. 1910. Ray Jerome Baker, Hawai'i State Archives

The heart of Kaua'i is young. Some towns may bustle upon foundations as ancient as human life itself in Hawai'i. Not so Līhu'e. The island's county seat is barely a century and a half old; no buildings within the central core of the town are known to predate the twentieth century.

In ancient times *ka po'e kahiko* chose to live close to the rich ocean and along the lush valley streams in this part of the Puna District.[1] For hundreds of years, even the trailways that traversed the island passed near Kilohana crater rather than through the land once known as Kalaiamea, the place we identify today as the Līhu'e plain.[2] That belonged to the forest birds in their *kukui, koa, hau,* and other native bowers, and to the things upon which they fed, and to the other crawling, burrowing, living creatures that contributed to the life of the land. Humankind visited only sporadically.

The death of Kamehameha the Great in 1819 became the catalyst for the region's transition. Within two years Kamehameha's heirs moved to ensure that Kaumualii, the ruler of Kaua'i, would never challenge their dominance. They kidnapped him and his royal son and removed them to O'ahu, where both were restrained by marriage to Kamehameha's favorite wife, the powerful *kuhina nui* Kaahumanu. Kaua'i remained passive until Kaumualii died in 1824, then rebellion by some Kaua'i *ali'i* erupted on the island's west side. Brief and unsuccessful, it was met by Kaahumanu's warriors with a repressive brutality that

When Keopuolani, the sacred wife of Kamehameha I, died in 1823, missionaries and other foreigners attended her burial on Maui along with her son Liholiho (King Kamehameha II), his wives, and many *ali'i.* Kaikioewa, using a cane, second from left, marched in the procession with his wife, Keaweamahi. He was appointed Kaua'i governor in 1825. William Ellis, Mission Houses Museum Library would reverberate through the nineteenth century. According to American missionary Samuel Whitney, men, women, and children were vindictively slaughtered, their bodies left as "food for hogs and dogs."[3] Kaua'i *ali'i* were dispossessed of their holdings whether they had taken an active part in the rebellion, remained innocent of any participation, or supported the Kamehameha dynasty. Many were deported; others simply disappeared. Kaua'i's lands were redistributed among the foreign *ali'i*.

A governor loyal to the Kamehameha dynasty, Kaikioewa (1765–1839), was sent to rule Kaua'i. Although he settled at the royal center of Waimea, Kaikioewa made frequent sojourns around Kaua'i, erecting homes for his convenience at various stopping points. After Ladd and Company began planting sugarcane at Kōloa in 1835, the aged Kaikioewa did the same: "Cane continues to be planted by Kaikioewa daily," wrote manager William Hooper to the firm's Honolulu office in 1838.[4] The governor also experimented with sugarcane in cooperation with entrepreneur William French in the Waimea area. Additionally, he ordered a home and large Christian meeting house to be constructed in the Puna District on the east side of Kaua'i, where he may have begun to plant cane as well.[5]

Kaikioewa's plans for the region are lost; he died at Kōloa during the mumps epidemic of 1839. By that time, however, the population concentration and the level of activity around Līhu'e had already convinced Hawai'i's Christian missionary brethren to establish a Kōloa outstation there, more or less midway between Kōloa and Kaua'i's other royal residence and ancient hub, Wailua. They sent "one of the most brilliant minds in the Mission," the Reverend Doctor Thomas Lafon, to build a home and open a school in the Līhu'e region.[6] He spent two years at the post in energetic labor before leaving the mission—and the Hawaiian Islands—forever.

After Kaikioewa's death and Lafon's departure, Līhu'e languished. Its rebirth after 1849 would be motivated by decidedly Western influences. The increasing involvement of Americans in the Hawaiian government, the Great Mahele land division, the lucrative Western market opened by the California gold rush, and the promise of successful sugarcane cultivation in Hawai'i would all conspire in Līhu'e's emergence.

The cataclysmic process of assigning ownership of the lands of Hawai'i, the Great Mahele, changed forever the traditional relationship of Hawaiians to the land. On Kaua'i it compounded the dislocation begun by the 1824 revolt. Edward Joesting described the result:

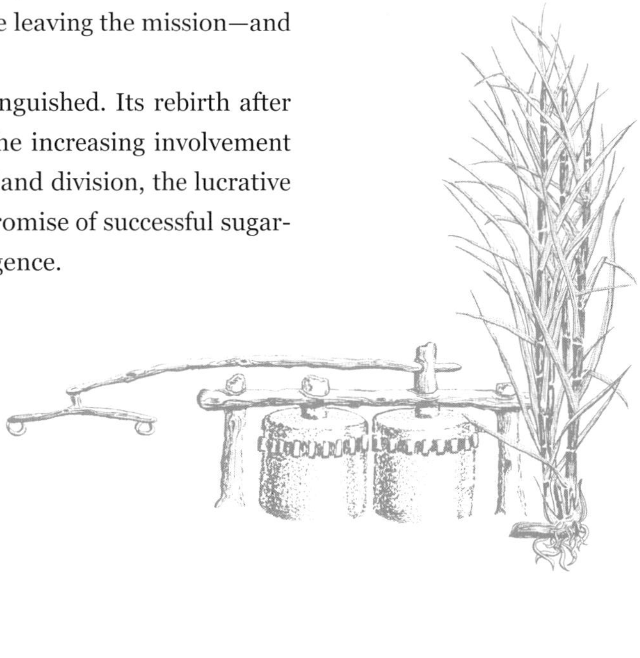

> Many persons with blood ties to the Kamehameha line or with high connections in the monarchy made no attempt to prove their claims. They simply applied for parcels of land and were granted fee-simple ownership. Victoria Kamamalu, a granddaughter of Kamehameha, received over 51,000 acres of Kauai land. The Native Register, compiled as documentation during the Mahele, is evidence of the vast amount of land taken from the people of Kauai and given to others.[7]

OPPOSITE PAGE
Victoria Kamamalu (1838–1866), a granddaughter of Kamehameha the Great, gained title to more than 51,000 acres of Kaua'i lands in the Mahele. Charles Weed, Hawai'i State Archives

Among nine-year-old Kamamalu's Mahele land grants was the large section of Kaua'i known in ancient times as Hulē'ia, an *'okana* that comprised part of the Puna District. Within this parcel were the more than two thousand acres that she, through her father Mataio Kekuanaoa, sold to Henry A. Peirce and Company in 1849. The sale included what is today the Līhu'e town core. A decade later, after ownership of the struggling Peirce and Co. sugar plantation changed, the business was renamed Lihue Plantation Company.

Lihue Plantation mill and pond, ca. 1880. Grove Farm Homestead Museum

Lihue Plantation quickly earned a reputation for innovation, efficiency, and aggressive growth. It dug the first irrigation ditch in Hawai'i's sugar industry and introduced the first steam power. Over the next century the company purchased or leased lands well beyond its origins—acreage at Ahukini, Hanamā'ulu, Wailua, Keālia, Moloa'a, and Princeville.

In the early years, when speed was measured by the pace of oxen pulling a loaded cart, laborers lived close to their work. The hamlet of Līhu'e grew around the mill, which was positioned in the Nāwiliwili Stream valley. Many Hawaiian workers lived in the nearby settlement of Pua Loke, but their declining numbers could not fulfill the needs of this labor-intensive industry. Seeking remedies, planters founded the Royal Hawaiian Agricultural Society in 1850 with a primary purpose of finding workers. From the mid-nineteenth century into the early twentieth, plantations relied on a succession of immigrant laborers—Chinese in 1852, Japanese in 1868, Portuguese and Gilbert Islanders in 1878, Germans in 1881, Puerto Ricans in 1900, Koreans in 1902, Filipinos in 1905, Spaniards in 1907. They were imported to plant, hoe, harvest, operate the mill, and perform the other tasks necessary to make sugarcane a profitable venture in the islands.

Līhu'e quickly expanded well beyond a wide place in the road. In 1876 the plantation

Lihue Plantation store, 1865. Kaua'i Museum

The mill and edge of Līhu'e village, 1890s. Severin, Hawai'i State Archives

moved the company store to the coalescing hamlet from its original location in front of Koamalu, the manager's home (on the *mauka* side of today's Kaumuali'i Highway where Aloha Church is now located). The building was set on rollers and hauled by oxen down one steep, muddy side of Nāwiliwili Valley, past the mill and up the other to what is now the parking lot on the Rice Street side of the civic center. By 1880, Līhu'e was considered the most important town on the island; in 1888 it boasted several stores, two schools and a livery stable.[8] Two years later enough travelers passed through the area to justify the establishment of a full-fledged hotel on the main road between the village and Nāwiliwili.

The population of greater Līhu'e grew 150 percent in the 1890s, then expanded another 150 percent in the following decade, claiming 4,434 residents in 1900 when Hawai'i became a U.S. territory. By 1913, Lihue Plantation Company accounts recorded over 1,300 laborers, and 1,600 by the end of World War 1. Neighboring Grove Farm plantation, though smaller, registered similar growth.[9]

PREVIOUS PAGE
Līhu'e, 1924, looking from the mill toward the ocean.
Hawai'i State Archives

Among the benefits of becoming a U.S. territory, beyond enough optimism to encourage considerable entrepreneurial activity, was an infusion of federal funds to develop ports and roads. Given its central location and commercial vitality, Līhu'e Town was an obvious choice in 1905 to be selected as the island's county seat, and by the end of the decade government officials had determined the need to construct an imposing new county building to house government affairs in the center of town. In 1912 the County bought a five-acre tract of land from Lihue Plantation along the main road to Nāwiliwili, now named Rice Street but then listed generically on most maps as "government road" and colloquially called the main street. It contracted the prominent Honolulu architectural firm of Ripley and Davis to design an impressive new headquarters. The plantation also utilized Ripley and Davis to sculpt a new commercial center at the main crossroad to reflect the plantation's prosperity and further transform Līhu'e from haphazard village into substantial town. In addition, it sold to the Bank of Hawaii a half-acre lot diagonally across the street from the parcel the county government purchased for its new building.

By 1916, Līhu'e's main intersection—some would argue it was Kaua'i's main intersection—was bounded by the Tip Top theater and commercial building on the northwest, the Lihue Store on the northeast, and a memorial to Paul Isenberg, the nineteenth-century mastermind of much of Lihue Plantation's success, on the southeast. Duplex houses claimed the fourth side of the intersection. They ran downhill toward the mill (as well as elsewhere in the neighborhood) and were constructed primarily for employees of European origin. To the west of the village, *mauka* of the mill, the plantation erected a grand new manager's house at Koamalu. With the exception of the lava-rock Isenberg memorial, all of these buildings, as well as the county building, were constructed of reinforced concrete, a material that helped convey the message of strength and stability in Līhu'e.

The duplexes contributed one of many residential areas in and around town. The plantation established workers' camps in several other nearby locations. Along the main road on the Nāwiliwili side of the county building and lawn it carved out fourteen exclusive house lots. Some of those accommodated plantation management, others were sold to independent professionals who had begun to populate the growing town. An advertisement in the local paper promised that future homeowners of these lots would be "within five minutes' walk of post-office, bank and store, fifteen minutes from church, private and public schools."[10] It also guaranteed "permanent water rights, excellent soil, good drainage." Situated as it was, "right in the heart of Lihue," this well-to-do section was dubbed "Elite Street" by locals.

The story of Līhu'e in the twentieth century is the story of sugarcane receding as urbanization advanced. The road from Nāwiliwili passed by the exclusive residential homes along Rice Street, then angled to the left at the county building. The Grove Farm homestead is at left, and rows of houses in a Lihue Plantation camp can be seen at right. 11th Photo Sec., Hawai'i State Archives

From its early days in the sugar business, Lihue Plantation had commissioned the Honolulu-based H. Hackfeld and Company to serve as its factor, or supplies and purchasing agent. The ties between the two companies were strong. Paul Isenberg, Lihue Plantation's former manager and a guiding force in the company's success, became Hackfeld's managing partner in 1881. The overlap between companies resulted in the Hackfeld partners and their family members owning enough stock in Lihue Plantation to give Isenberg outright control of the business at the turn of the century.[11] But World War I brought an end to the sixty-year-old Hackfeld and Co. It was incorporated by new owners as American Factors, Ltd.; four years later, having already received a significant share of the plantation's stock with the Hackfeld takeover, it purchased enough additional shares to gain majority ownership of the Lihue Plantation.

In the 1920s and 1930s, Lihue Plantation concentrated commercial enterprises along the road running north of Lihue Store and Tip Top, now Kūhiō Highway. The telephone company, automobile dealerships, soda-making firm, newspaper, theater, dentist, insurance agency, and other establishments set up shop in what became the town's central

THE ESTABLISHMENT OF NĀWILIWILI HARBOR

Harbors and ports have long been lifelines to settlements. In Kaua'i's historic period Capt. James Cook originally touched land at Waimea, Kōloa landing dominated the whaling era, and Ahukini landing at Hanamā'ulu Bay was the shipping point for Lihue Plantation. The completion of Nāwiliwili Harbor in 1930 brought the bulk of shipping and passenger traffic to the Līhu'e area. The U.S. Army Corps of Engineers had recommended developing Nāwiliwili as an all-weather, deepwater harbor in 1909–1910. Plantations distant from Līhu'e balked, and the Territory proved hesitant to provide the funds necessary to match a federal subsidy until 1917, when the Hawai'i Legislature voted for a $200,000 bond issue. Two years later, after Congress appropriated funds, an impatient G. N. Wilcox, owner of Grove Farm plantation, bought the entire block of territorial bonds to get the project moving. His determination, with assistance from the Chamber of Commerce, shipping companies, and others, carried the project to conclusion despite many fits and starts along the way.[12]

Nāwiliwili at the turn of the century. Hawai'i State Archives

LEFT *Passengers arrived and departed by sea until the advent of air travel.* Theodore Bissell, Hawai‘i State Archives

BELOW *Voyaging and canoe-paddling traditions meet modern ships at Nāwiliwili.* Harvey Tam, Kaua‘i Historical Society

Looking toward Rice Street on Kūhiō Highway's commercial strip in 1939. The popular Lihue Theater and Garden Island Motors are at left. William J. Senda, Kaua'i Museum

business district, though workers' houses would intermingle with commercial buildings in this neighborhood for many years. Between the main intersection and the county building along Rice Street were a few other supervisors' cottages, the Lihue Plantation's headquarters, and recreational centers—a two-lane bowling alley and a social hall on one side of the street and a bandstand, later replaced by the library (now Kaua'i Museum), on the other. Behind that was a ball field and tennis courts, with an armory and stables in back of the county building.

In an effort to stimulate the economy during the Great Depression of the 1930s, President Franklin Roosevelt's administration instituted many back-to-work programs across America and its territories, which precipitated pronounced government spending on Kaua'i. Federal funds financed jobs throughout the 1930s to construct many of the roadways still in use today. A federal public works project, for instance, provided money to

S. H. Kress and Company, Līhu‘e. William J. Senda, Kiyoto Okimoto

cut a road *mauka* of the mill (now part of Kaumuali‘i Highway). Until that time all traffic had proceeded down and around the mill via the original oxen path later named Halekō Road. The Territory of Hawai‘i also engaged in construction projects, completing an office building next to the county building in 1930 and a courthouse to its rear late in the decade. In 1939, on Rice Street in Līhu‘e, the federal government dedicated the first stand-alone U.S. Post Office building on Kaua‘i.

As the major landholder in the area, Lihue Plantation had historically driven the town's planning and controlled decisions about what businesses could set up shop there. But the land directly across the street from the county building and Elite Street houselots was not owned by the plantation; the family of William Hyde Rice held title to it. That property included his homestead, a dairy, and the Lihue Hotel. The plantation's exclusiveness was dramatically challenged in 1937 with the decision by William Hyde Rice, Ltd., to sell its dairy land along the main street to the national "big box" of its day, S. H. Kress and Company. Local businesses soon followed. The result was a second commercial district that emerged beyond the plantation's developmental control. After World War II the historic Rice estate across from the county building was also sold and the buildings demolished. On that land, too, entrepreneurs opened business establishments, as they gradually did along the strip once occupied by the grand homes farther down Rice Street.

In the 1960s, Lihue Plantation, guided by its parent company American Factors (later known as Amfac), embraced the concept of urban renewal by radically redesigning the town core. Almost everything in the square block around Lihue Store was demolished to make way for the area's first mall. The plantation constructed its new headquarters across the street from the museum; displaced tenants rebuilt elsewhere in town. On Hardy Street, a secondary road that curved behind the civic and shopping centers, county funds subsidized a convention hall, and the State built a new regional library, a three-story government office building, and a public health complex, all of which were clustered around the 1950s-era police station and elementary school.

The metamorphosis also included a residential component. Unionization after World War II had ended the old paternalistic system of plantation-provided housing, and in the late 1940s and early 1950s Lihue Plantation had made fee-simple lots available for worker-owned residences in the Isenberg tract *mauka* of the Kūhiō Highway business district and elsewhere beyond Līhu'e. Fifteen years later the plantation harvested its last crop of sugarcane on land between Hardy Street and Ahukini Road and subdivided it into the Molokoa subdivision. The project coincided with a demographic shift in town. After more than a generation of decline, Kaua'i's population in the 1960s was again on the rise. The postwar generation was also busy creating the baby boomer generation, and their desire for in-town living opportunities in a home of their own provided a ready market for Amfac's Molokoa product.

Disposition of productive agricultural tracts signaled a major shift for many plantation owners' long-held philosophy that one's wealth is in one's land. It was replaced by a new reality of being land poor, and American Factor's evolution reflected that change. The corporation transformed many of its real estate holdings from burden to asset by utilizing them as a commodity for development and sale. In the 1970s, Lihue Plantation's influence in the town it built virtually disappeared after Amfac sold nearly 40 percent of Līhu'e's commercial property to freewheeling entrepreneur Harry Weinberg. Parcels included the Lihue Shopping Center, lots on both Rice Street and Kūhiō Highway, and the industrial

Līhu'e experienced dramatic urban renewal with the replacement of the half-century-old Lihue Store by the Lihue Shopping Center, 1964.
Kaua'i Historical Society

park at the northeastern edge of town. After Grove Farm, the sugar plantation turned development company, opened Kukui Grove Center at Puhi in 1982, many retailers left Lihue Shopping Center and moved into the new mall. Five years later the county government purchased the older shopping center from Weinberg's company HRT, Ltd., and converted it into a civic center as a solution to its pressing need for additional office space. Today, a significant portion of central Līhu'e is dedicated to government affairs, which in the twenty-first century promise to require still more space. Police, Civil Defense, and the

judiciary have already moved out of the town core and into massive complexes near the airport. The U.S. Post Office plans to do the same.

At the dawn of this century, Lihue Plantation, by then a subsidiary of Chicago-based Amfac/JMB Hawaii, announced plans to close. America Online founder and *kamaʻāina* Stephen M. Case bought almost 19,000 acres of Lihue Plantation land in 2001. Case added that acquisition to the 23,000 acres on Kauaʻi he already owned, having previously purchased neighboring Grove Farm, whose lands stretched from Līhuʻe to the Maluhia tree tunnel and south to Poʻipū. The two former plantations were consolidated under the name Grove Farm Company, Inc., making it the second-largest private landowner on Kauaʻi (Robinson Family Partners owns approximately 51,000 acres). Its twenty-first-century holdings surround the town of Līhuʻe and nearly rival the vast ownership of Kauaʻi *ʻāina* that the Mahele land grants conferred upon Victoria Kamamalu a century and a half ago.

Līhuʻe to Nāwiliwili, 2006.
Timothy T. DeLaVega Photo, County of Kauaʻi

TWO

THE POWER BEHIND THE TOWN

There are no endings. If you think so you are deceived as to their nature. They are all beginnings.

—**Hilary Mantel,** *Bring Up the Bodies*

It's gone now. Pulverized. The stripped-raw land awaits twenty-first-century reinvention. But for 160 years the Līhuʻe mill stood as the physical manifestation of Lihue Plantation's dominance in the region.

Lihue Plantation factory. John Wehrheim, Kauaʻi Historical Society

The significance of Lihue Plantation, from the time of the Great Mahele in the mid-nineteenth century to Hawai'i's statehood in the mid-twentieth, is difficult to overstate. Henry A. Peirce, William Little Lee, and Charles Reed Bishop were three entrepreneurial travelers who ventured to Hawai'i from the northern United States and set the wheels of development in motion.

Henry Augustus Peirce.
Kaua'i Historical Society

THE FOUNDERS

Henry Augustus Peirce (1808–1885), a Massachusetts-born trader, merchant, diplomat, and sporadic Hawai'i resident, was on his way to China after selling a shipload of wares in the gold-driven boomtown of San Francisco when he spied the land above Nāwiliwili Harbor. Intrigued by its potential, Peirce convinced Honolulu associates William Little Lee and Charles Reed Bishop to invest in the development of a sugar plantation on Kaua'i.[1] The deed for the land was signed by Lee and recorded on December 5, 1849. Their business was named Henry A. Peirce and Company. The partners quickly began the process of clearing land and planting cane; by August 1851 the first crop was mature and ready to mill.[2] After early indications of success, and the plantation manager's assessment of "the finest looking field of cane I had ever seen," blight, drought, rot, labor shortages, and overall inexperience soured Peirce's enthusiasm for the business.[3] By 1859 he had sold his interest in the plantation and moved on to other pursuits, many of them based on sea rather than land.

Before he turned sixteen Peirce had joined the crew of the merchant ship *Griffon,* on which his brother was shipmaster. In 1828 he quit the ship when it docked in Honolulu, and between the late 1820s and 1847 he clerked for, owned, and co-owned the mercantile firm that would become C. Brewer and Co.[4] Not that he stayed put: during that time, Peirce continued voyaging and trading around the world, from the east and west coasts of the United States to South America, Hawai'i, Russia, and China. In 1838 he married Susan Thompson in Boston and after 1850 settled down on elegant Beacon Street for some years with her and their two children while he continued his international business activities.

Peirce, a dedicated American expansionist in the Pacific, added diplomatic activities to his entrepreneurial ones. Between 1856 and 1869 he acted as consul for the Kingdom of Hawaii at the ports of Portland, Maine, Portsmouth, New Hampshire, and Boston.[5] In 1869, President Ulysses S. Grant appointed him U.S. minister to the Hawaiian Islands. After Kalakaua was elected king in 1874, he accompanied the monarch to Washington,

Henry Peirce was among the men who traveled to Washington with King Kalakaua in 1874 to secure a reciprocity treaty between Hawai'i and the United States. Seated: John O. Dominis, Kalakaua, and John M. Kapena. Standing: Henry Peirce and Luther Severance. Bradley and Rulofson, Hawai'i State Archives

D.C. While there Peirce was instrumental in negotiations for the Reciprocity Treaty of 1875, a deal that would prove the impetus for sugar's surge as the economic and social driver in Hawai'i. Three years later Kalakaua appointed him Hawai'i's minister of foreign affairs, an assignment that lasted only a few weeks before the king dismissed and replaced his entire cabinet. Peirce returned to Boston in 1883, then lived his final days in San Francisco.

William Little Lee (1821–1857) put his Harvard Law School training to immediate use after arriving in Hawai'i on October 12, 1846: less than two months later, on December first of that year, the twenty-five-year-old native of Sandy Hill, New York, was appointed judge on O'ahu and made a member of the Privy Council by King Kamehameha III. He soon became chief justice of the Superior Court (1848), then chief justice of the Supreme Court of the Kingdom of Hawaii (1852). He was also elected to Hawai'i's House of Representatives (1851) and became the chancellor of the kingdom under King Kamehameha IV (1855).

William Little Lee. Hawai'i State Archives

Lee played a significant role in shaping Hawaiian government structure on Western models. In 1847 he drafted legislation that outlined the duties of the judiciary (executive and legislative duties had been completed before his arrival). His work on the Board of Commissioners to Quiet Land Titles—the land commission for the Great Mahele—would establish private land ownership based on Western traditions as well.

In 1851, while Lee was on a three-month tour of the islands for his land commission duties, his wife Catherine stayed with James Fowle Baldwin Marshall and his wife Pattie at the Līhu'e plantation. Marshall, who had purchased an interest in Peirce and Co., "went to Lihue as resident partner after the first field of cane had been planted, where [he] aided in putting up the buildings and machinery." Catherine Lee described the plantation as "a tract of twenty five hundred acres of well-wooded, well-watered land with between two and three hundred acres of sugar cane ready for grinding this month. Eighty native laborers are now employed upon it and a large number of coolies or Chinese operatives are expected in a short time."[6]

Lee characterized her husband as someone who put in "as much labor as half a dozen people ought to *prudently*." That work ethic, and perhaps his tireless, hands-on efforts to assist victims of the 1853 smallpox epidemic, led to a resurgence of the tuberculosis from which he had sought escape when he left New York. William Little Lee died in 1857 at the age of thirty-six. His wife returned to New York and married Edward Youmans in 1861, but she retained both a personal and a financial interest in the Līhu'e plantation. Known as a brilliant personality, she utilized assets Lee left her, in part, to help support her second husband's *Popular Science Monthly* magazine.

Charles Reed Bishop. B. F. Howland, Bishop Museum

Charles Reed Bishop (1822–1915) accompanied his friend William Lee to Hawai'i. Their destination was Oregon Country, where Lee planned to practice law and Bishop to survey land as the United States and Great Britain worked out boundary divisions there. When the ship arrived in Honolulu Harbor after 236 often harrowing days' sail, the friends decided to travel no farther.

Bishop's formal education ended at eighth grade, although he gained experience with animals and agricultural equipment on his grandfather's farm, where he lived after being orphaned at age four. He also worked as a clerk and bookkeeper, ran a post office and lumber yard, and became a shrewd judge of character.

During his first years in Hawai'i, Bishop clerked for the U.S. consulate, was appointed a commissioner of customs, and became secretary of the Royal Hawaiian Agricultural Society, which Lee had founded and served as president. He also began to invest in land, both in the Līhu'e venture and at Hāmākualoa, Maui, in 1849. In 1853, Bishop opened a general store with William Aldrich. Five years later they established the Bank of Bishop and Company (it was then literally what it is now named, the First Hawaiian Bank), and he became a privy councilor, a member of the House of Nobles, and treasurer of the trustees of Queen's Hospital. For the next half century Charles Reed Bishop brought his considerable acumen to banking, real estate, agricultural, government, educational, and eleemosynary endeavors.

Bishop probably met the fifteen-year-old Princess Bernice Pauahi in 1847. They married on June 4, 1850, and honeymooned on Kaua'i. By all accounts their marriage was a lifelong love match. After she died in 1884, Bishop served as trustee of her immense estate—the princess, as heir to the lands of the Kamehameha dynasty, was sole owner of 353,000 acres in the Hawaiian Islands—fulfilling her will to establish Kamehameha Schools with a portion of her wealth. He also gradually contributed much of his own personal fortune, the equivalent of 22 million 2013 dollars, to charitable works and organizations. Bishop remained loyal to his wife's memory and the Hawaiian monarchy; he left the islands forever in 1894 after Queen Liliuokalani was dethroned, and he lived the remainder of his twenty-one years in California.

THE EARLY YEARS

As contemporaries in America continued their inexorable expansion across the continent, settlers in Hawai'i sought similar opportunities in the islands. By the 1830s, sandalwood had given way to whaling as Hawai'i's major economic driver, and sugar, cotton, silk, and sago palm were among the crops being explored for their agricultural potential.[7] The decline of whaling that followed the discovery of petroleum in 1859 intensified the search for new products, and the outbreak of the American Civil War shortly thereafter proved a boon for Hawai'i sugar producers, who supplied the growing West Coast population and the Northern states when the South's products were embargoed (between 1861 and 1864 sugar prices in the United States rose from four cents to twenty-five cents a pound).[8]

Immigrants from the United States were not the only pioneer planters. The man who would lead Lihue Plantation to prominence, Paul Isenberg, was German. The other two men who became closely associated with driving the growth of Līhu'e and its environs, William Hyde Rice and George Norton Wilcox, were born in Hawai'i, the children of missionaries. Their parents had been sent to the islands in the second quarter of the nineteenth century by the Boston-based American Board of Commissioners for Foreign Missions to

Lihue Plantation mill, 1865. John Valentine, Grove Farm Homestead Museum

educate and Christianize the Hawaiian people. The ABCFM had prohibited its missionaries from owning land in the islands or operating private, for-profit businesses there. That changed in the 1850s when the board deemed the Hawaiian mission strong enough to provide its own governance. They expected missionary families to become self-supporting in Hawai'i and provided impetus by granting many of its mission station lands to the missionaries who had lived and worked on them. As an alternative the board offered to pay the expense of those who wished to return to New England. Most of the missionaries chose to stay in Hawai'i, as did their children (including the Rices and most of the Wilcoxes), and many took successful advantage of the shifting use and transfer of lands throughout the islands.[9] In 1863, after a twenty-one-day debate, the Hawaiian Evangelical Association voted to assume full responsibility for their work and their livelihoods: "The mission has been, as such, disbanded and merged into the community."[10]

A striking aspect of nineteenth-century Līhu'e photos is the barrenness of the landscape. Before the plantation era, forests covered much of Līhu'e. Catherine Lee described a lush scene at the Marshall home in 1851:

> Principally *kukui* or "candle nut" trees, from the nuts of which the natives obtain their oil, bread-fruit, *ohia*, or the native apple, *koa*, the Island

> mahogany, and a very few orange trees and cocoa-nuts. The under-growth consists of arrow-root, ginger, sandal wood, bamboo, and a variety of shrubs to me unknown. In the way of fruits we have the ohia, guava, pine-apple, papaya, banana, oranges and cocoa-nut.[11]

Mary Rice had similar reflections of the area being "densely wooded," with even the field of Halo, the first on which Lihue Plantation's cane was grown, "left partially standing in trees with the cane growing between and around the trees."[12]

By the time James and Pattie Marshall departed, the effects of the plantation on the land were already in evidence. "I shall feel sorry to leave Koamalu, for it is a beautiful spot, and I feel much attached to the country about us," Marshall wrote to his mother at the end of 1853, adding that he had watched the plantation emerge "from the time when it was a howling wilderness till now, when its fields are moving with cane, its pastures filled with cattle, & roads & buildings in every direction mean the presence of civilization & enterprise."[13]

By the 1870s, little was evident of the wooded land Lee and Rice had described. Writing in *Koamalu,* Ethel Damon accused "two improvident generations" of having "literally devoured" the forests of Līhu'e. She wrote that Hawaiians called one Westerner who came to live in the area, representative of many, "Mu-ai-laau, Worm-that-eats-wood, so insatiable were the demands of trade and so ravaging their effects on the neighboring forests."[14] Those forests were destroyed to provide firewood for whaling, sugar boilers, and other industry—sometimes even cut and shipped to Honolulu for that market's use—but also cleared to plant crops and despoiled by introduced animals.

G. N. Wilcox initiated basic reforesting efforts at Grove Farm when he began to replant a dying *kukui* grove with Australian ironwood in the early 1870s. At neighboring Lihue Plantation, Paul Isenberg was also aware of the need to protect the watershed and conserve or restore forest resources. In 1882 he included among his German recruits a forester to develop a reforestation program.[15] By 1906, Grove Farm and Lihue Plantation had reforested more than 650 acres in the Līhu'e area. In 1909, Grove Farm planted another 20,000 trees, and two years later the *Garden Island* noted in a front-page story that several thousand ironwood and eucalyptus trees had arrived for Lihue Plantation's "constant campaign of tree-planting."[16] The paper urged other plantations to "profit by following this very commendable policy." Early in the twentieth century the Territory of Hawai'i formed the Bureau of Agriculture and Forestry, which aided in the reforestation effort as well.

FOLLOWING PAGE
The mill after 1876. Lihue Store (on the horizon above and to right of the mill) was moved that year from the front of the manager's house to the crossroads of the budding hamlet. A. A. Monsarrat, Hawai'i State Archives

EXPANSION

Lihue Plantation purchased land at Ahukini in 1866 and added 17,000 acres at Hanamā'ulu in 1872. Five years later, after Wilcox traveled to Scotland to acquire a mill for Grove Farm, Paul Isenberg bought it from him and installed it at Hanamā'ulu. Isenberg succeeded in the transaction by extending Grove Farm a more advantageous grinding contract at Līhu'e than he had previously proffered; he sweetened the purchase offer by putting Wilcox's brother Albert in charge of planting and milling the cane at Hanamā'ulu.[17] Then Isenberg leased an additional 30,000 acres in Wailua.

The plantation's land expansion proved auspicious. Sugar exports had grown more than twenty-fold between 1857 and 1874, but depressed prices in the United States and that country's import duties stalled progress in Hawai'i.[18] The long-term triumph for the future of sugar in the islands occurred in 1875, when Hawai'i and the United States signed a joint trade agreement to allow sugar and certain other Hawaiian goods duty-free import into the country. The Reciprocity Treaty went into effect in 1876, the year before

The mill at Hanamā'ulu, 1918. Kaua'i Museum

Lihue Plantation mill, 1918, before consolidation with the Hanamā'ulu mill. William J. Senda, Grove Farm Homestead Museum

the mill was constructed at Hanamā'ulu. Within five years the twenty plantations operating in Hawai'i had increased to sixty-three. The number of plantations peaked in 1890 at seventy-three, then began to decline as companies failed or merged under the control of the commercial agents called factors. With the improvement in transportation and mill technology, Lihue Plantation shut down the Hanamā'ulu mill in 1920 and consolidated several pieces of its machinery at the Līhu'e factory.

What benefited the planter economy in the fourth quarter of the nineteenth century came at the expense of Hawaiian traditions of place, family, and culture. In exchange for allowing duty-free imports from Hawai'i, the Reciprocity Treaty gave the United States

SUGAR: THE FINAL REFINEMENT

The Lihue Plantation factory's final product was not the end of the production business. In 1906 a cooperative of Hawaiian sugar companies, including Lihue Plantation and Grove Farm, organized the California and Hawaiian Sugar Refining Corporation. Except for a small refinery in Hawai'i for sugar to be used in this market, raw sugar was shipped, via specially fitted Matson Liners, to Crockett, California, for refining, packaging, and distribution. The cooperative members sold their interests to Alexander and Baldwin in 1993, which then sold a majority interest in C&H to others late in that decade.

The C&H refinery is positioned on the Carquinez Strait, near San Francisco, California. private collection

Kilipaki camp, ca. 1900. Originally constructed for Gilbert Islanders, the camp, in foreground, later housed other groups of plantation workers. The growing Līhu'e village and store are on the horizon, and trains hauling cane to factory can be seen center right. Grove Farm Homestead Museum

rights to Pu'uloa (Pearl Harbor), when it was revised a few years later, and also effectively rendered Hawai'i a commercial satellite.

The changes to the population in Hawai'i were as dramatic as the conversion of its landscape. When Lihue Plantation was founded at mid-century, 98 percent of the people in the islands were Native Hawaiians, and they still comprised about 85 percent when the Reciprocity Treaty was signed in 1875; by 1900 that number had plummeted to one quarter of the population. An inverted birth-and-death ratio and outmigration contributed to the precipitous decline of Native Hawaiians in their own country. More significant statistically was the effect of imported labor on the total population. The overall number of people in Hawai'i climbed from 84,000 in 1850 to 154,000 in 1900, a 183 percent increase. Population figures on Kaua'i were even more startling. Its 7,670 people in 1850

Despite the tsunami of immigrant labor brought to Hawai'i after the Reciprocity Treaty, Hawaiians did not completely disappear from community life: in 1906, five-eighths of the 1,036 voters on Kaua'i were Hawaiian. Nor were they absent from plantation life: here, Enoka, Kaaihue, and Lekua prepared a pig at Grove Farm for a *pa'ina* to celebrate Charles Wilcox's birthday in 1903. At far right is Sam Wilcox, Charles's father. Belle Dickey, Grove Farm Homestead Museum

increased 270 percent to 20,734 in 1900. By 1920 the population of Kaua'i had further jumped to 29,438.[19]

The demographic shift in Hawai'i's people was immediately apparent on plantations. When the Reciprocity Treaty was signed, Hawaiians supplied two-thirds of the workforce; by the overthrow of the monarchy in 1893, more than two-thirds of the workers were Japanese. In his investigative report to the U.S. secretary of state about America's involvement in the overthrow, Special Commissioner James H. Blount observed that the Reciprocity Treaty had precipitated "an intoxicating increase of wealth, a new labor system, an Asiatic population, an alienation between the native and white races, an impoverishment of the former, an enrichment of the latter." In 1913 the influx of Asians was apparent in the mix of Lihue Plantation's 1,308 laborers: 685 Japanese, 208 Portuguese, 140 Filipinos, 111 Koreans, 55 Puerto Ricans, 45 Americans, 32 Chinese, 20 Hawaiians, 12 Spanish.[20]

The newcomers from around the globe who arrived by the thousands needed shelter. Plantations supplied it mostly by constructing clusters of housing in camps, which typically were placed near their occupants' work and segregated by ethnic group and time of entry to Hawai'i. Labor historian Edward Beechert observed, "The total lack of adjacent communities had forced the plantations to create their own communities and provide them with the necessary services."[21] So grew Līhu'e.

WATER POWER

The Hawaiian word for wealth, *waiwai,* is a doubling of *wai,* meaning both "water" and "to earn or deposit." Water certainly played a defining role in the creation of Lihue Plantation's wealth. Some have argued that the prosperity of the entire sugar industry in Hawai'i was directly attributable to irrigation, which Lihue Plantation was first to implement

The mill pond, 1915.
Ray Jerome Baker, Kaua'i Historical Society

successfully with the construction of a ten-mile-long ditch in the 1850s that brought life-giving water to the fields.[22] Even before then, with the construction of the mill, the founders had dammed adjacent Nāwiliwili Stream for a pond to utilize water power rather than the more typical oxen to turn the imported Chinese granite millstones. A few years later, Lihue Plantation was the first in Hawaiʻi to harness steam to grind its sugarcane, a procedure that led to the drying and burning of bagasse, the post-milling cane trash.

The plantation electrified its factory in the 1910s, rendering the pond, if not water power, obsolete. It utilized Waiahi Stream to drive the turbines to turn the generators in a hydroelectric plant about eight miles from town. From there high-tension lines carried the electric current to a Kapaia substation, then to the mills at Līhuʻe and Hanamāʻulu. It also brought electricity to the town. According to the Kauai Board of Supervisors' minutes book, the county fathers voted on February 5, 1913, to give the plantation permission to "erect pole lines for distributing power for lights along roads in Lihue." Six months later the *Garden Island* waxed poetic about Līhuʻe's new incandescence: "Born of nothing—it leaps to life and in the short space of one second of time lives a thousand lives—dies a thousand deaths and still lives on."[23] In a presentation to the Kauaʻi Historical Society the next year, Mary Girvin Rice described the mill pond as "soon to be done away with." Tracks were eventually laid and trains crossed the former pond area, but the government highway that would traverse it and realign the main transportation route *mauka* of the mill was not constructed until the 1930s.

THE SUMMIT OF THE PLANTATION'S POWER

Electricity was only one of the broad changes that Līhuʻe experienced in the first third of the twentieth century. Hawaiʻi became a U.S. territory in 1900, and Līhuʻe Town was chosen as the county seat of Kauaʻi five years later. The public and private investment that followed expanded the dynamics of the town beyond its plantation roots.

William A. Lydgate (1909–1998), the son of Rev. J. M. Lydgate, wrote in his memoirs about the Kauaʻi of his youth as "an age of innocence," beyond the reach of social unrest, a "simple, orderly" era; he recalled that the impact of World War I on Kauaʻi was minimal.[24] Others in Līhuʻe, with its large German population, church, and language school, would have disagreed. By 1917, when America entered the war, anti-German hysteria was rising. Loyalties were questioned, blameless people lost jobs, and the German school in Līhuʻe was ordered closed.

A greater blow was aimed at H. Hackfeld and Company. Hackfeld had served as Lihue Plantation's agent since its early days. After the United States entered the war, the government declared Hackfeld to be owned by "enemy aliens." Its German assets were seized, and the company was reorganized under different ownership as American Factors, Ltd.[25] (The B. F. Ehlers store, named for cofounder Heinrich Hackfeld's nephew and also controlled by the Hackfeld and Isenberg families, was renamed The Liberty House.) H. Hackfeld and Company had held equity in Lihue Plantation before the war. In 1922, as American Factors, it acquired a controlling interest; the plantation remained its subsidiary thereafter.[26]

Despite the ownership shifts, work and expansion at Lihue Plantation continued. It had become majority stockholder in Makee plantation before the United States entered World War I. Between the world wars, after Caleb Burns became manager of both plantations, Lihue bought out Makee entirely. The latter's shareholders adopted a resolution to accept Lihue Plantation's offer "to purchase all the property, assets, rights and claims of every description owned by Makee Sugar Co. for the sum of $3,279,308.91 as of Sept. 1st, 1934."[27] Makee was dissolved, its mill dismantled, and many of its parts reassembled to expand the Lihue Plantation factory.

German ship captain Heinrich Hackfeld (1816–1887) established a ship chandlery and general store in Honolulu in 1849. It expanded to a trading house that imported supplies for plantations and exported their main product, sugar. Although Hackfeld retired to Germany, the firm continued to flourish in Hawai'i until World War I, when H. Hackfeld and Company assets were liquidated, acquired by other investors, and renamed American Factors. Hawai'i State Archives

The Līhu'e factory after consolidation with Makee plantation. Kaua'i Historical Society

With the acquisition of Makee, Lihue Plantation's land ownership extended far up the east side of Kaua'i, deep into the Kawaihau District. Its reach was even broader. Grove Farm, whose lands stretched west across the Līhu'e District, had long contracted with Lihue Plantation to grind its cane. Nearby Kipu Plantation, operated by the Rice family from 1907 to 1942, also hauled its sugarcane crops to the mill to be ground.

By the time Kipu ceased its cane operations, Hawai'i had plunged into World War II. If the December 7, 1941, attack on Pearl Harbor came as a shock, the cognizance of impending war had been widely shared. By mid-1941, one chronicler of the war in Hawai'i wrote, a multitude of defense preparations were under way and "Kauai was humming like a very disturbed hive." When war exploded, martial law was declared. The governor quickly instituted blackouts in homes, on roads (along with strict curfews), and in factories, where nighttime unloading of cane could be a filthy, steamy affair with every crack and window shut and papered over. Gasoline, tires, and some staple foods were rationed with varying degrees of success to control supply and demand. Plantation workers and equipment were also loaned to the military for island defense efforts. Acres of buildings and cane land were leased for military use, other acres to truck farming, where students sometimes assisted in the fields.[28] Managers' wives, women of the Mokihana Club, and others performed myriad duties, from driving in mobile corps to serving in dispensaries and canteens, to providing first aid training and even childcare assistance.[29] Some parents with the ability to do so shipped their children to mainland relatives in an effort to move them out of harm's way.

The outbreak of hostilities exacerbated an already existing plantation labor shortage. Because that work triggered deferment as an "essential occupation" (and plantation officials who sat on draft boards took full advantage of the exemption), many Filipino workers who longed to fight against the country that had invaded their homeland were prevented from joining the military. For more than a year Japanese Americans were also prohibited induction, their obstacle being "morale reasons." Both groups quickly found ways to join the war effort by aiding civil defense. In the spring of 1942 the Kauai Volunteers, a home front militia comprising mostly Filipino plantation workers, was organized and trained under the command of Lihue Plantation office manager Paul Townsley. The Japanese community formed the Kauai Morale Committee and began the volunteer Kiawe Corps to clear brush, string barbed wire, and perform other patriotic services.[30]

The camouflaged Lihue Plantation factory from Hoʻomana Road, 1943. Charles Procter, Kauaʻi Museum

Camouflaged factory from Halekō Road. David Alexander

Nearly 160,000 Japanese—37 percent of the population—called the islands home at the outbreak of World War II. On Kaua'i the percentage was even higher. The Territory resisted official commands for wholesale Japanese internment, though Shinto and Buddhist priests, teachers, and others in positions of consular authority (a total of less than 1 percent of the Japanese population in Hawai'i) were detained. Like the German school in World War I, the Japanese-language schools were shut down, and without the priests no one was on hand to conduct traditional burial services or counsel issei who had relied on their religious leaders.[31]

Every person who lived through the war has personal memories about that time of confusion, fear, and dislocation.[32] Some who worked at Lihue Plantation recall that, having grown up with their Japanese neighbors, they absolutely believed in their loyalty. Others don't want to discuss a painful past, though one Japanese employee in the plantation's administration offices during the war remembered accountants obscuring their work when she walked by.

THE POSTWAR ERA

Lihue Plantation introduced mechanical harvesting in 1941 and transitioned totally to mechanized cane cutting by the middle of the war in 1943. The move was enabled by increased industrial capabilities and motivated by the combination of chronic labor shortages and escalating worker unrest. World War II only temporarily halted the two-decade-long unionization efforts in Hawai'i. After war's end the territory-wide sugar workers' strike and resulting unionization meant a rise in wages that further pressured the plantation to accelerate labor-saving machine use.[33]

Mill engine tenders Victoriano Castro (left) and Julian Espiritu perform off-season cleaning of Number 3 engine cylinder, Mill A, 1959. Kaua'i Historical Society

Revenues from sugar plantations were a major but not exclusive component in American Factors' increasingly diversified portfolio. During World War II its president, H. Alexander Walker Sr., had been given the awesome power to control distribution of food, materials, and supplies to civilians in the islands. Afterward, the company's wholesale goods included a broad range of groceries, liquor, drugs, building materials, and clothing. According to "Diversity, Inc.," a 1946 corporate brochure, American Factors was supplying "virtually every retail grocer throughout the territory," and it had become the General Electric distributor in Hawai'i as well.[34]

The bull gears in Mill A are taken apart in halves for inspection and cleaning by machine shop workers Ernest Koerte and Tak Yoshinaka, 1959. Kaua'i Historical Society

American Factors' strength as a commodity supplier for the islands weakened in the 1950s, when national supermarket and retail store chains entered the market. Social and political changes were also affecting the corporation. The Democrats won control of the Hawai'i Territorial Legislature for the first time in 1954, which shook up the major landowners' long-held Republican dominance of political affairs. Mainlanders had also begun investigating Hawai'i companies for possible lucrative investments. Two of them, Harry Weinberg and Howard Bucher III, bought enough stock to gain seats on the American Factors board, and by 1962 investors outside the state owned more than half of the company's stock.[35] Because sugar played an increasingly fragile role in the prosperity of American Factors as well as in the islands themselves, the company president and head of Hawaiian

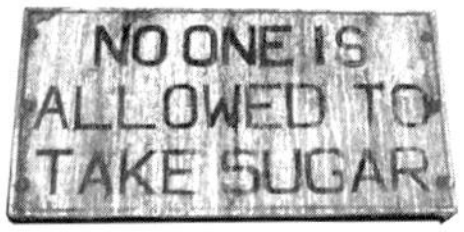

Sugar Planters Association, C. Hutton Smith, declared, "'The sugar industry is fighting a battle for survival,' and the people of Hawaii must face up to this fact."[36]

Neighboring Grove Farm was also evolving in the postwar years. That plantation had existed almost as long as Lihue Plantation. As soon as foreigners could buy land in Hawai'i, Warren Goodale purchased the property speculatively; he sold it for a profit in the same year, 1850, to J. F. B. Marshall, who had moved to Kaua'i to manage Lihue Plantation. When Marshall left the islands in 1854, he engaged Hermann Adam Widemann "to take charge of my dairy, & cultivate my land."[37] Widemann bought Grove Farm in 1856. He struggled with the business of sugarcane for eight years before leasing the plantation to George Norton Wilcox, who competently completed irrigation ditches and began to accomplish successful harvests. In 1870, Wilcox bought the plantation from Widemann, by then a Supreme Court judge and political figure in Honolulu. It is G. N. Wilcox's name that has been associated with Grove Farm since.

Although the Grove Farm story is tangential to this center-of-town history—it had no ownership in the urban core of Līhu'e—its association with Lihue Plantation and its influence in the greater district was substantial (Grove Farm's Ha'ikū lands stretched beyond Mt. Kahili and the tree tunnel leading to Kōloa). Wilcox combined the knowledge gained from his father's upbringing in a Connecticut farming family with industrial and technical advances he learned during studies at Yale's Sheffield School, and he brought the best of both to the operation of his plantation.[38] Throughout his career he was known as independent, innovative, and forward thinking in his business, agricultural, and personnel practices.

Label on Grove Farm sugar bag. private collection

After G. N. Wilcox died in 1933, the company relocated its headquarters from the grounds of his homestead on the west rim of Nāwiliwili Valley, where it had existed since the 1850s, to a new administration building at Puhi. After World War II the increasing importance of efficiency of scale in the achievement of operational success led Grove Farm president Gaylord Wilcox to conclude that the company must expand or fail. Expand it did: it bought Koloa Plantation, which effectively doubled Grove Farm's acreage and gained it a mill of its own. The challenge became how to transport sugarcane cost-effectively from the *mauka* lands to the mill with a mountain between the two. Engineer and Grove Farm operations manager William Moragne (he would later become manager and a company vice president) devised a plan to utilize surplus military equipment to tunnel through Hā'upu Ridge. The work was successfully completed in 1949. Three years later the Kōloa factory was grinding 70 percent of Grove Farm's crop, with the remainder, from Līhu'e lands,

Grove Farm built the first hollow-tile homes on Kaua'i. Designed by W. M. Moragne and constructed by plantation carpenters, these were built in Puhi, 1937–1938. Peter Tupas is walking in front of the house at right. Grove Farm Homestead Museum

still processed at Lihue Plantation. The *Wainiha* locomotive pulled the last load of Grove Farm sugarcane to the Līhu'e mill on September 24, 1957. In 1958, for the first time in its long history, Grove Farm's processing became completely independent, with all of its cane ground at Kōloa.[39]

The profits derived from more acreage and its own factory proved short lived, the end simply postponed. In the early 1970s, the Grove Farm board of directors, deciding there was little future for sugar in the islands, leased its Līhu'e cane lands to Lihue Plantation and the Kōloa lands and mill to Alexander and Baldwin's McBryde Sugar Company. Grove Farm transformed itself into a land leasing and development company until selling its assets to Stephen M. Case in 2000.

FROM FIELD TO FACTORY

Among the many changes that occurred during the postwar period was the Hawai'i sugar industry's transition from trains to trucks. In 1881, Kilauea had become the first plantation on Kaua'i to initiate a railroad system to haul its cane from fields to mill; at the time, Lihue Plantation was employing a thousand oxen for its heaviest labor. (In an era of little wastage and lots of manure, the company pioneered the practice in Hawai'i of fertilizing fields).[40] By May 1888, Paul Isenberg was convinced of the value of train transport and expressed his impatience to convert to the new conveyance in letters from his Bremen home to family in Līhu'e:

> Things have changed since Paul [his son, D. P. R. Isenberg] was a little boy at Lihue. It all shows how necessary a railroad is. But Carl [Isenberg, his brother, who was then plantation manager] is against it, because he has never seen one used for plantation hauling. And the owners of Lihue are against it, Mr. Bishop

Lihue Plantation fully converted from train to truck hauling in 1959. Kaua'i Historical Society

> feeling that it would mean financial ruin. However, with the Wailua land for 24 years yet, I cannot give up the idea of a railroad. What I wanted to do was to lay it first to Hanamaulu and then add a new section every year. Some day it must be done.[41]

Trains at Lihue Plantation were finally inaugurated in January 1892, and they proved successful enough for Isenberg to write three years later, "I am glad that George Wilcox is satisfied with the railroad to Grove Farm. I wish it could have been put in years ago."[42]

The last of the steam-driven locomotives was retired in 1951, having been gradually replaced by diesels, some of them 32-ton behemoths that could pull fifty-one loaded cars to the mill. By then, however, train transport was already becoming a thing of the past. The Lihue Plantation board of directors voted in May 1956 to transition completely from trains to trucks for hauling cane. Studies by plantation staff and their consultants, Belt Collins, cited as reasons for the change safety issues and increasing costs of both new equipment

Despite their advantages, trucks did not always guarantee solutions to train-related safety issues.
Kaua'i Historical Society

At 3:10 A.M. on September 25, 1959, factory shift engineer Frank Rosa (second from left) and shift workers began to unload the final haul of train-transported cane. Kaua‘i Historical Society

and maintenance of existing stock and tracks. Three years later the plantation's annual report noted that, with the conclusion of the 1959 harvest season, "hauling cane over our railroad system comes to an end. We are the last plantation in the Islands to give up the railroad . . . the end of an era."[43]

The last train-hauled cane car was unloaded at the Lihue Plantation factory on September 25, 1959, at 3:10 A.M. Like the landscape of the region and the heritage of its inhabitants, the sounds of Līhu‘e had changed dramatically over the previous century. Lowing cattle and clip-clopping horse hooves yielded to hissing steam, piercing whistles, rhythmic chugging, and the occasional metallic screech of wheel on track. The twentieth century introduced rumbling vehicular noises and the electrical dissonance that the population takes for granted today.

Noise was an issue for residents of Kapa'a in January 1958 as they debated the preferred route for the big Kenworth trucks to travel from the plantation's Kealia fields to the Līhu'e mill. Noise, dust, and traffic dangers all came under scrutiny at the public meeting, though Lihue Plantation representatives David Silver and Joe Orrick assured the community that all three nuisances would be less with trucks than trains. They told the crowd that the company planned to drive empty trucks on public roads. However, since general roadway traffic would slow the loaded big rigs down on the public thoroughfare, they presented four proposals for exit points from Kūhiō Highway onto haul cane roads, where the trucks could travel down to the mill unimpeded. Work on the haul cane road system had already begun near the mill. The company's 1956 annual report announced the dredging of 387,000 cubic yards of coral from Nāwiliwili Harbor to be used for road construction.

Train cars remained plentiful in the mill yard through the 1950s. Kaua'i Historical Society

OPPOSITE PAGE
A photo captured the moment on June 17, 1958, when water began to sluice cane to Mill B for processing. Kaua'i Museum

In 1959 the company began dredging additional coral off Kapa'a to supply forty-four miles of roads in the Kawaihau District.[44]

The plantation's railroad department numbered ninety-five men in 1951. Eight years later, after that last cane car was unloaded at the factory, the department was rendered obsolete. Even in the final year of use, the trains' impact had significantly diminished: 70 percent of the company's gross cane tonnage was already hauled by truck. Lihue Plantation's 1959 annual report described the year's truck-driven harvest as a "very satisfactory operation" and praised the drivers "who have handled these new units so efficiently."

When Lihue Plantation was discussing Kealia-to-Līhu'e routes in 1958, twelve harvesting trucks were in service (by 1964 there were twenty-five in the fleet). They were capable of hauling 21-ton loads, as compared with the trains' 4 tons per carload. The trucks were big, too big to access the factory on Halekō Road. As a solution, the company transferred its unloading station offsite, a half mile *mauka* of and 90 feet higher than the factory. The 1,613-

The plantation's factory yard changed substantially after haul cane trains were retired and the trucks delivered their cargo a half mile *mauka* of the plant. Kaua'i Historical Society

THE SWOPE HERITAGE HAWAIIAN SUMMER SCHOOL

Thirty-two days before Lihue Plantation retired its trains, Pan American Airways introduced jet liner service to Hawai'i. A week before that, on August 17, 1959, Hawai'i had been admitted to the union as America's fiftieth state. Easier travel combined with the possibility of exploring the newest and most exotic edge of the nation brought waves of visitors and led to tourism's emergence as the largest economic driver of the state. People came for many reasons; one enterprising Texan began bringing students to Kaua'i in 1962 as part of the Swope Heritage Hawaiian Summer School. A 1963 "Swope girl," as the local boys dubbed the female students, fondly remembers her six-week experience of boarding at Kapa'a School, taking classes in the morning, going to the beach or on other excursions in the afternoon, and attending the occasional dance offered of an evening—properly chaperoned, of course. Almost 130 students from ten states (though the majority were Texans) attended the 1964 session, along with five students from Oshima, Japan, a Kaua'i sister city. One of the outings available to the students was a mill tour.[46]

By the time of the Swope excursions, tours of the plant were a routine part of business. Lihue Plantation had integrated them into operations while trains still hauled cane and before the unloading station was moved off premises. The November 1956 issue of the *Lihue Plantation News* reported, "Word has finally reached the Garden Island Publishing Company office that our de luxe tour of the factory is quite the thing." The article quipped that the four newspaper women who toured the plant could now "advise visiting mainlanders and even neighbor island visitors about the marvels of a modern sugar cane factory."

A factory visit for students in the Swope Heritage Tour, 1964. Harvey Tam, Kaua'i Historical Society foot flume system it constructed to carry the cane from the unloading and cleaning facility to the mill was the longest in Hawai'i. Its task was assisted by the motive power of 15 million gallons of water per operational day (and by the occasional worker who had to climb up and untangle a mess when the flume became clogged with cane). The water-driven flume transport system was replaced in 1983 by a 60-inch-wide rubber-belt conveyor system built on top of the old channel and used until the plantation closed.[45]

The section of the flume most visible to the public, the part that crossed over Kaumuali'i Highway, was erected on December 30, 1957, although the four-month "Aloha" sugar workers strike in 1958 pushed its inauguration to June. For nearly fifty years the flume reminded those who passed under it of the industry that had created Līhu'e. The rusting, defunct structure stood as a shadow of the past for five years after the plantation harvested its last field of sugarcane; it was dismantled and removed in 2005.

REINVENTION AND DECLINE

While American Factors was remaking the Līhu'e town core in the 1960s, the corporation was transforming itself into an acquisitional dynamo. In 1967, when Henry Alexander Walker Jr. took the organization's helm, Amfac, Inc. (the name adopted in 1966) was a $150 million company. Its board of directors

Lihue Plantation mill, 1966.
Hawaiian Sugar Planters' Association archives

instructed Walker to expand Amfac and to diversify its holdings beyond sugar and beyond Hawaiʻi.[47] To fulfill the charge, Amfac was listed on the New York and Pacific Coast stock exchanges and swelled to a broadly diversified conglomerate. Within three years Amfac operations in the continental United States accounted for more than half its employees and revenues; by 1973 the revenues outside Hawaiʻi had jumped to 71 percent.[48] *Time* magazine profiled Amfac in a July 1972 article as the "biggest and fastest growing Hawaii-based company," noting forty-two acquisitions in four years and almost quadrupled revenues. Amfac chronicler Frederick Simpich Jr. described the conglomerate of that period:

> The goods Amfac makes or sells would fill a mail-order catalog and require an appendix for such items as shiploads of sugar and molasses, wool and wheat . . . tract homes and townhouses . . . quiche lorraine and cherries jubilee . . . frozen french fries and apple turnovers. . . . Add to these debentures, mortgages, and investment opportunities ranging from savings accounts to ownership to feed-lot cattle, all in multimillion-dollar dimensions.[49]

Amfac continued to balloon, with $1.3 billion sales in 1976. In 1981 it was listed on the London Stock Exchange, and two years later the corporation expressed its Pacific interests by moving several of its administrative offices to San Francisco. But Amfac's debts mounted, and when it experienced losses in three of the next five years the company reversed course and began "paring itself down to its Hawaiian roots."[50]

JMB Realty Corporation of Chicago bought Amfac in 1988. As Amfac/JMB Hawaii Inc.—it became a limited liability corporation a decade later and finally Amfac Hawaii LLC—the company explored numerous restructuring strategies. It sold off land on various islands, including former Makee plantation acreage in the 1998 sale of the Kēalia *ahupuaʻa* and 1,400 acres of Waipouli-Kapaʻa farm land north of Wailua River early in 2000. Nevertheless, the company remained mired in debt, $120 million of which, between 1989 and 2002, it blamed on its agricultural operations.[51] One of them, Oahu Sugar Company, closed in 1995 and another, Pioneer Mill on Maui, in 1999. Lihue Plantation (and Amfac/JMB's other Kaua'i plantation, Kekaha Sugar Company) struggled along until 2000, despite the crippling loss of arable acreage and late-century drought conditions.[52]

November 17, 2000, marked the last official day of a century and a half of Lihue Plantation operations. That afternoon horns sounded a dirge as the Amfac haul cane trucks began their doleful parade to honor the part the plantation had historically played in so many lives—in the life of Līhu'e itself. People lined the streets to pay their final respects. The sense of loss rippling through the community was coupled with concern about unemployment. Closure of Lihue Plantation and its Kekaha Sugar Company sibling put four hundred men and women out of work, almost half the island's agricultural labor force and the largest farm worker layoffs in Kaua'i's history.[53] Many had spent decades at Lihue Plantation. Some had followed parents into work there. A few were third generation with the company.

Four years after the factory closed and an auction disposed of considerable equipment, files and machinery still lay as if workers had simply walked away for a long, dust-filled moment.

The plantations closed, but considerable cleanup remained. Vehicles and other moveable assets were auctioned at an event attended by hundreds of people, a mix of nostalgic onlookers, souvenir seekers, and bidders from businesses hoping to find reusable equipment bargains. Amfac/JMB sold most of the remaining Lihue Plantation land to Steve Case in 2001 and entered into Chapter 11 bankruptcy the next year.

THE FINAL GOODBYES

Neither the factory site nor a still-functioning power plant on the property was included in the 2001 Lihue Plantation land sale. A deal to build the power plant and to supply

electricity to Kaua'i's electric company had been forged in the 1970s, when a national oil crisis, gas rationing, and a significant rise in the price of fuel made alternative forms of energy generation attractive. One alternative to oil was bagasse, a biofuel that had historically been utilized in the Hawaiian sugar industry.

Electricity had begun to supersede pond-generated and steam power at the factories early in the twentieth century. McBryde Sugar Company formed the Kauai Electric Company in 1905 to create a hydroelectric plant on the Wainiha River. It provided power to its mill and gradually to the south, west, and north sections of the island. Lihue Plantation followed in 1913 with Waiahi Electric. It electrified the Līhu'e region and eastern part of Kaua'i. The two operations merged in 1960 under the Kauai Electric Company flag; Connecticut-based Citizens Utilities Company purchased Kauai Electric in 1969.[54]

The amount of electricity generated by the plantations was once significant. In 1957 the Hawaiian Sugar Planters' Association had boasted that Hawai'i's twenty-seven sugar

OPPOSITE PAGE
Power plant stacks viewed from the forced draft fan.

The bagasse storage building was completed in 1964. Kaua'i Historical Society

The factory in 2006, prior to the power plant being dismantled and shipped to the Philippines. The cooling tower was positioned along Halekō Road (to the right of the quonset hut) at the factory's entry; the tall powerhouse was adjacent to the bagasse storage building at the rear. Timothy T. DeLaVega Photo, County of Kaua'i

The defunct cooling tower and power plant. Timothy T. DeLaVega Photo, County of Kaua'i

mills generated enough electricity to "light up every home in the islands at one time."[55] Four Kaua'i plantations routinely sold surplus power to Kauai Electric, with Lihue Plantation providing more than half that total amount. But many of the plantation power plants were aged and required upgrading by the 1970s. Given projected increases in customer demand, Kauai Electric was also approaching capacity and nearing the need to build a new generation plant.[56] If Lihue Plantation could cost-effectively build a new, bagasse-powered plant, it might acquire another income source for the plantation while supplying a portion of the local utility's energy requirements.

The bold graffiti artists who climbed a third the way up the mill stack to create their work had precious little but rusted metal for standing support.

Though successfully constructed, the expensive plant "was never a money maker" for the plantation, remembers former Amfac Sugar Kauai manager Lyle Tabata, "it was a burden."[57] According to Tabata, Kauai Electric wouldn't accept all the supply the plantation could provide. Rather, it bought only enough kilowatt-hours to fulfill the basic contract—enough for Lihue Plantation to make its loan payments to boiler manufacturer Foster Wheeler, but not enough available power beyond that amount to deliver reinvestment profits to the plantation. The result, Tabata said, was that the plantation "struggled and struggled to make a go" of sugar farming. After Lihue Plantation shut down its sugar operations, Amfac renegotiated to continue the power plant for a couple of years until the utility's new gas turbine generator came on line. Shortly before the plantation concluded its service to the utility at the end of 2002, Citizens Utilities sold Kauai Electric to a locally formed nonprofit entity, the Kaua'i Island Utility Cooperative.

First Farmers Holding Corporation, an agro-industrial cooperative in the Philippines, bought the power plant in 2006 and applied to Kaua'i County for a demolition permit for the boiler and powerhouse buildings, the condensation storage tanks, and the cooling tower. The next year First Farmers, with Foster Wheeler engineering and construction company, carefully dismantled the structures and shipped them to Talisay City in Negros Occidental, where they used the equipment to upgrade their existing bagasse cogeneration facility.[58] First Farmers anticipated that the addition would quintuple its existing power-generating capacity to 25 megawatts, with hopes that 40–60 percent of the total could be sold to the region's electrical system. The buyers recognized the challenges they faced to bring sophisticated equipment on line that had been out of operation for half a decade, and they knew that their purchase was missing important accompanying technical information.[59] Despite the difficulties, First Farmers successfully retrofitted the system, which enjoys a second life today in an active, offshore sugar industry.

The Līhu'e factory itself sat vacant for years in Kaua'i's damp, verdant, subtropical climate. Or not quite vacant: squatters invaded the old buildings, casually furnishing their lairs and throwing "all their garbage down a caged (as in open air) elevator shaft, leaving it to rot and seriously stink up that whole area of the building, right next to where they slept."[60] Graffiti artists tagged and retagged vertical spaces; joy seekers shot out windows; petty thieves pilfered their way through the lab and other business offices. Nature, too, had its way: metal corroded, wood rotted, and vegetation strove to triumph over all.

Pacific Funds LLC bought both Lihue Plantation and Kekaha Sugar Company factories and the land beneath them in 2005. According to attorney Jonathan Chun, the buyers had "no definitive plans for the two sites."[61] Nearly fourteen acres are zoned for general industrial activities, but the parcel is a complicated blend of terrain features: 40 percent or more is located in a flood zone; Nāwiliwili Stream runs through a portion of it; decades of industrial use resulted in ground contamination. Discussions between the owner and the County led late in the year to a Kaua'i Planning Department white paper about the site's renovation or redevelopment. It recognized that the mill, "like most sugar mills on Kauai is the central point of the town," and suggested that "the shells of the existing buildings are in good condition." It concluded that industrial zoning was no longer compatible with the site's surroundings and that a mix of commercial and residential usage was an appropriate alternative, noting that "being located in the hub of the hub of the entire island increases the amount of development options for the site."[62] The study outlined the potential for a partnership whereby some percentage of the property would be turned over for county use in exchange for the government's assistance if hazardous ground cleanup became necessary. While explorations of possibilities were under way, the mill was resold to Lihue MS LLC.

The deterioration and demolition of the mill in the first years of the twenty-first century told the most visible tale of the plantation's death, but the web of roads and ditches that crossed its land have suffered similar decay.

In January 2011 work began to clear debris and conduct asbestos abatement on the grounds, though notice was given that cleanup would "not involve removal of mill buildings."[63] During that year, however, consultants hired to assess the buildings returned the verdict that, beyond the structures' advanced deterioration, asbestos had been integrated in construction and insulation materials throughout the plant, precluding the possibility of reuse of any portion of the buildings. The County issued demolition permits for all buildings on the parcel. Asbestos mitigation began in January 2012, followed by the razing of the structures themselves. The two mills, boiling house, sugar bin, and molasses tanks all disappeared under the assault. (Occasionally during the process a detectable aroma of sweet molasses reminded pedestrians of the old days of factory operations, when that smell could permeate the entire town.) By the end of the year, only the bagasse warehouse near Kaumuali'i Highway, the 167-foot-tall smokestack, and the

Lihue Plantation factory site, November 12, 2012.

façade of the electric shop fronting Halekō Road remained. On January 15, 2013, the stack, too, bit the dust, and in the next months the last of the old buildings disappeared. According to the owner's representative, the next steps in the process are to conduct a brownfield study to assess possible environmental contamination from the long industrial use and to allow the scraped land to settle for about three years.[64]

Future use for the mill site remains unclear. The new identity for this "hub of the hub of the entire island" and the contributions it can make to the town that Lihue Plantation endowed with life will reveal themselves in the fullness of time.

With the demolition of the plantation factories at Līhu'e, Kekaha, and Kōloa, Kaua'i's connection to its sugar past grows more abstract. In Līhu'e the street that curves around the old mill site is still named Halekō (Cane House) Road, and the Isenberg Monument

Looking from Grove Farm railroad right-of-way toward the mill, May 2005.

November 2012.

March 2013.

at the head of the street reminds passersby of one of the industry's nineteenth-century giants. Beyond central Līhu'e, Grove Farm Homestead Museum on Nāwiliwili Road provides visitors a glimpse of the life-that-was for plantation owner G. N. Wilcox and his family.

Fortunately, four artifacts in the museum's collection are providing a tangible link to the former mill site and its past: its collection of Kaua'i haul cane locomotives. The Grove Farm locomotives were listed on the Hawai'i Register and the National Register of Historic Places in 1979. Before Lihue Plantation announced its closure, Grove Farm obtained a railroad right-of-way terminating directly across from the mill. It laid 1,800 feet of original, 30-inch track on which it provides a "moving" interpretive exhibit: once a month it fires up a locomotive to haul a couple of cars now occupied by passengers rather than piled high with sugarcane.

Lihue Cemetery, January 2004. Generations of men and women who spent their working lives in the sugar industry later rested in the shadow of the Lihue Plantation mill stacks.

NAITO

THREE

THE TOWN CORE

Make big plans; aim high in hope and work, remembering that a noble, logical diagram once recorded will not die, but long after we are gone will be a living thing, asserting itself with ever-growing insistency.

–Attributed to **Daniel H. Burnham,** architect and urban planner

The Līhu'e town core encompasses the Kaua'i seat of government, commercial activities, and hints of the era when sugar was king on Kaua'i. Bold thinking about town planning at several points in its development contributed to the multidimensional place that exists today.

The town in transition, 1966. Kaua'i Museum

Līhuʻe's distinction as the crossroads of the island began in the area defined today by the circumference of the "round building." It is properly known as the Moʻikeha Building, named to honor the first *aliʻi ʻaimoku* of Kauaʻi, whose voyages between Hawaiʻi and southern Polynesia have long been celebrated in Hawaiian *moʻolelo*. Today it and the rest of the complex serve as administrative headquarters of county government. The mayor's offices are located here, along with the departments of public works, planning, parks, housing, elderly affairs, waste management, taxation, finance, and personnel. The county attorneys work in this civic center, and the citizenry visits for drivers' licenses, camping permits, meetings of boards and commissions, and any number of other public engagements.

COMMERCE AT THE CROSSROADS

For the hundred years before the County of Kauaʻi purchased this property and transformed it into a home for the island's government operations, the land and its buildings served as the retail center of Līhuʻe and Kauaʻi. The original Lihue Store was moved to the site from the front of the Lihue Plantation manager's home in 1876, a warehouse was later

Lihue Store ca. 1913. The post office was located through the doorway at the right front corner of the building. The top of the store's warehouse is visible, back left. A young *kamani* tree, Japanese *toro* lantern, and *torii* gate beautified the main Līhuʻe corner. The original lantern disappeared during World War II, but the gate now stands in a garden at the rear of the civic center. Kauaʻi Historical Society

The concrete Lihue Store in 1919. Billed as Kauai's Emporium, it helped secure Līhu'e as the heart of Kaua'i. William J. Senda, Kaua'i Historical Society

added, then a new wood frame building erected after 1890. The post office and a few independent businesses, including a tailor and a coffee shop, occupied space within. The Bank of Hawaii opened its first branch in the islands within the commercial complex in 1903.

By 1912 the store was inadequate for the needs of the flourishing community, and the plantation contracted the well-connected Honolulu architectural firm of Ripley and Davis to replace it. The new Lihue Store was a three-story, 25,330-square-foot, reinforced concrete building promoted as the "most elaborate store building in the Territory outside of Honolulu." It boasted an electric elevator to the furniture department on the second floor "for the convenience of handling the immense amount of freight which is to be transferred from one point to another," the *Garden Island* reported that October. By the next March the paper extended the elevator's benefits to shoppers, who could use it to "cover the entire store with ease and comfort." The store's refrigerated meat market, which contained perishables such as fish, butter, and ice cream, opened adjacent to the main building.[1]

Labeled "Kauai's Emporium," the new Lihue Store served a far greater customer base

Lihue Store Japanese department. Over the years other shopping choices were available outside the town core. Yukimura's, for instance, was popular in Kilipaki Camp across from the mill. Kapaia also contained a thriving community with small stores, as did Nāwiliwili. William J. Senda, Kauaʻi Historical Society

than plantation employees—by 1920 two-thirds of its patrons were not affiliated with Lihue Plantation—and it was appreciated beyond the shores of rural Kauaʻi. A *Honolulu Star-Bulletin* article in 1920 gushed, "An invariable compliment paid to the store by women visitors from the capital city of the Islands is: 'Why you can get anything here that you can get in Honolulu.'"[2] The article described the layout of "this wonder of country stores" as being

> in the form of a cross, thereby dividing the floor space into four separate and distinct divisions. In one division are drygoods, dress goods, shoes and men's furnishings. . . . Another department contains hardware. A third contains all the goods usually found in a first class grocery, and a fourth a completely stocked Japanese department including stationery, also a thoroughly up-to-the-minute soda and ice cream fountain and a compete stock of drugs.

Kauai's Emporium was not the only retailing choice for residents, of course. Numerous small establishments independent of the plantation operated around the area over the years, outside the central business block in Līhu'e. In addition, traveling salesmen circulated through the islands and set up temporary displays to market their wares. One of many examples of the practice is illustrated by a 1923 *Garden Island* article that announced the arrival at the Lihue Hotel of Irving Watson, who represented the Manufacturer's Shoe Co., of Honolulu. The salesman had brought "a variety of the latest styles in footwear," including the newest rage, the "King Tut" sandal, "done in brocade, satin and metal cloth." A newspaper advertisement fifteen years later announced that well-known Hawai'i retailer McInerny's had booked into the Lihue Hotel for a week-long showing of shoes, gowns, lingerie, hats, cosmetics, and accessories, along with a tailor to take made-to-order measurements for men's suits.[3] Also, as the pages of the then-weekly *Garden Island* attested in its "society" news, residents with the means to do so routinely hopped interisland steamers to Honolulu for shopping and socializing. And ads regularly appeared in the newspaper to "Order It By Mail!"—the "it" being everything from Rexall drugs to luxury goods, though local merchants complained about the mail order practice then as they do now. A 1912 *Garden Island* comment in support of local businesses queried:

> Are you one of the mail order fiends? . . . Don't be a sucker any longer. Look about you; visit the local stores, and see how their goods and prices compare with those of the big stores. . . . Your home merchants let you see the goods before you pay for them; while the mail-order house makes you pay before you see.[4]

Nevertheless, one *kama'āina* mother, Edith King Wilcox, remembered that in the 1940s and 1950s she ordered clothing for her three girls from New York's Best and Company. Holbrook Goodale, working at Kīpū on his grandfather's ranch, ordered his cowboy attire from Montgomery Ward. Reporter Mike Ashman's wife Doris also recalled ordering clothes from the Ward's and Sears catalogues, though more frequently she sewed most of the children's clothing. "The boys usually wore nothing but home-sewn malos that, in the early years, were worn over cloth diapers," Ashman recalled.[5]

The round building, which was conceived primarily to provide office space for professional services, replaced Tip Top, the companion building to Kauai's Emporium. Old-timers remember the original Tip Top well. A century ago the place that became the *mauka* end of the shopping center accommodated stables. In 1913 the wood-framed Lihue Store building was temporarily relocated there before work began on the concrete store across

FOLLOWING PAGE
The Tip Top replaced Lihue Plantation stables. Kiyosuke Imizo, head stable man, is on horseback at left. The plantation's administration building (behind the cistern) and the town's bandstand can be seen in the background. Kaua'i Museum

the street. Once Lihue Store was completed, a new structure emerged at this location that would trump everything previously built on the site.

Also designed by Ripley and Davis, the Tip Top building was constructed of reinforced concrete in a style designed to complement the store. It served to further cement the intersection as an elegant crossroads of commerce, the center not simply of Līhuʻe Town but of the entire island. When it was completed late in 1916, the *Garden Island* declared:

Regular patrons enjoyed their own shaving mugs at the Tip Top barber shop. Mary Moragne Cooke

> The new Tip Top building in Lihue contains, besides the pretty theater and its various accessories, a shoe store, a double cafe, a barber shop, a furniture display room, a tailor shop and the photo establishment of J. Senda. Other enterprises will open up in the building shortly. The place seems destined to become quite an addition to the business center.[6]

Many other businesses called the Tip Top home over the years, among them Mokihana and Deluxe beauty salons, the Lihue Barber Shop, Isonaga Jewelry, Hawaiian Life Insurance and First Insurance companies, and physicians Samuel Fujii, Richard Haruki, and W. Boyden. Organizations such as the Masonic Lodge, Hawaii Medical Services

The V-J Day Parade to celebrate America's victory over Japan in 1945 followed a standard route between the Tip Top and Lihue Store. Parades turned at the corner and concluded at the County Building. William J. Senda, Kauaʻi Historical Society

Association, and the Chamber of Commerce operated there too. In 1920, following a new Hawaiian Sugar Planters Association policy during that paternalistic era, the plantation took over management of the theater and began to "furnish and censor" the movies. The first "talkies" on Kaua'i arrived there a dozen years later.[7]

THE LIHUE SHOPPING CENTER

The landmark Lihue Store thrived for a half century, with renovations and replacements such as a new warehouse built behind the store in 1938 and a new meat market in 1941. In July 1952 the Līhu'e store and its branches at Hanamā'ulu and Keālia became Kauai Stores, Ltd. Seven years later it added Koloa Store to the mix, bought from Grove Farm Co., Ltd.[8] But by 1960 the changing concepts in land-use practices prompted American Factors and its Lihue Plantation subsidiary to rethink the town core. In January 1961 it announced a "general plan for the best use of lands in and around Lihue," with a new shopping center, an industrial park, and housing subdivisions, including a "low-cost" component.[9] What followed was a dramatic reinvention of Līhu'e.

Most Americans now take the era's mall format for granted: an island of shops grouped along a central pedestrian walkway with large "anchor" stores at either end, the whole surrounded by an ocean of parking spaces and easy highway accessibility. They

Conceptual sketch of the Lihue Shopping Center, designed by John Graham and Company. Earle Duff, Kaua'i Museum

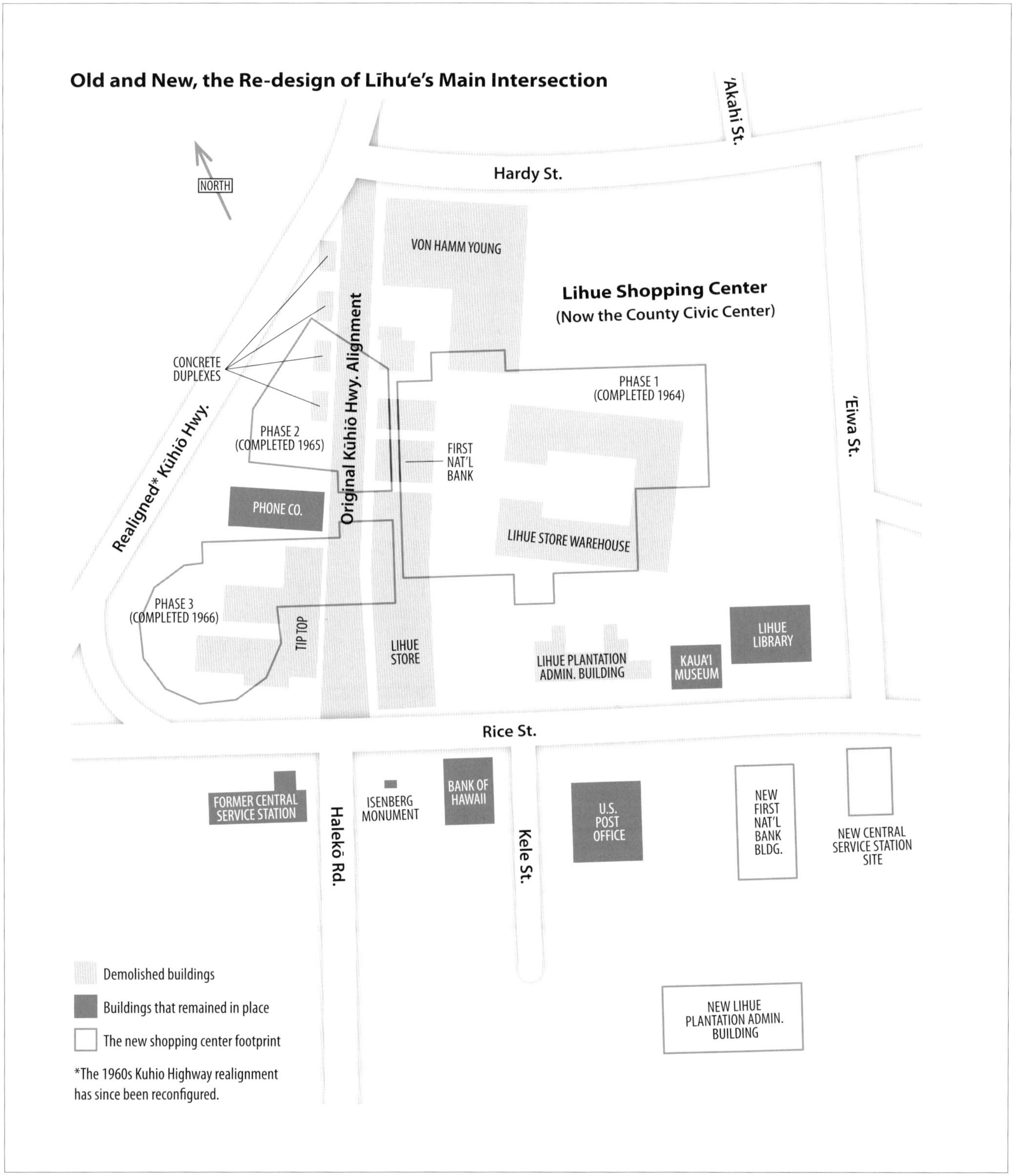
Old and New, the Re-design of Līhu'e's Main Intersection
NORTH
'Akahi St.
Hardy St.
VON HAMM YOUNG
Lihue Shopping Center
(Now the County Civic Center)
CONCRETE
DUPLEXES
Original Kūhiō Hwy. Alignment
PHASE 1
(COMPLETED 1964)
'Eiwa St.
Realigned* Kūhiō Hwy.
PHASE 2
(COMPLETED 1965)
FIRST
NAT'L
BANK
PHONE CO.
LIHUE STORE WAREHOUSE
PHASE 3
(COMPLETED 1966)
TIP TOP
LIHUE
STORE
LIHUE PLANTATION
ADMIN. BUILDING
KAUA'I
MUSEUM
LIHUE
LIBRARY
Rice St.
FORMER CENTRAL
SERVICE STATION
Halekō Rd.
ISENBERG
MONUMENT
BANK OF
HAWAII
Kele St.
U.S.
POST
OFFICE
NEW
FIRST
NAT'L
BANK
BLDG.
NEW CENTRAL
SERVICE STATION
SITE
NEW LIHUE
PLANTATION ADMIN.
BUILDING
Demolished buildings
Buildings that remained in place
The new shopping center footprint
*The 1960s Kuhio Highway realignment
has since been reconfigured.

turned on its head the traditional downtown style of shop-lined streets with the occasional department store providing a commanding presence along the way. Malls emerged with the development of suburbs after World War II and the increasing dominance of automobiles as the primary mode of transportation. One of the first, completed in 1950, was Seattle's Northgate, designed by John Graham, Jr. (1908–1991).[10]

American Factors hired Graham to design the Lihue Shopping Center. He had already achieved celebrity in Hawai'i as the designer of the monumental Ala Moana Shopping Center. Atop the Ala Moana office building on the *mauka* side of the mall's parking lot, he created (and patented) America's first revolving restaurant, La Ronde.[11] John Graham knew a good thing when he conceived one. Commissioned to design the Space Needle for the Seattle World's Fair, he created at its top the Eye of the Needle, a 1960s, revolving "entertainment restaurant" sensation that became a must-have feature on at least one fashionable address in cities around the country. Graham also designed Hawai'i's first high-rise luxury resort, the Ilikai, in Honolulu. The Lihue Shopping Center shared with the Honolulu projects Graham's trendy use of native coral rock façades on exterior walls;

Coral rock veneer is applied during Phase 1 construction in 1964. The old concrete Lihue Store, not yet demolished, can be seen in the background.
Kaua'i Historical Society

An expectant public awaits the opening of the Phase 1 of Lihue Shopping Center, June 13, 1964. Kaua'i Historical Society

the 60,000 pounds of coral stone needed for the Kaua'i project were obtained from Grove Farm.[12]

Construction of the Lihue Shopping Center proceeded in three phases. The first and largest phase included a grocery market and the main store, along with two parking lots and the necessary sewage treatment plant to serve the entire project. Moody-Sellen, a joint venture by the Walker-Moody Company of Honolulu and John Sellen Contractors of Seattle, won the bid as general contractor for the project. Shortly thereafter the old First National Bank (now named First Hawaiian Bank) and the Von Hamm-Young auto dealership buildings crumbled under the wrecking ball. Over the next year a new retail complex emerged.

Woolworth's opened in 1965 with the completion of Phase 2. Harvey Tam, Kaua'i Historical Society

Excitement surrounding the completion of Phase 1 in 1964 rivaled the launch of the Kauai's Emporium a half century before. Great crowds enjoyed the festivities at the grand opening of the Food Center in June. (Three years later Foodland took over the space, that market's first outer island venture. It would later be replaced by Big Save.) That October thousands joined in a week-and-a-half-long opening celebration for the new Lihue Store, formally known as the Kauai Stores. The *Garden Island* dedicated ten pages to the event, including the publication of a floor plan that indicated the location of clothing, housewares, sporting goods, electronics, and other departments in the store.

The old concrete store was razed in November, and construction began on the center's

The Food Center behind Kauai Stores was the first component of the shopping center to open. Kaua'i Historical Society

The Tip Top was demolished in 1965 to make way for Phase 3 of the shopping center complex. Work progressed around the telephone company building, which remains disguised but in place to this day. Kaua'i Historical Society

Phase 3 under construction. Kaua'i Historical Society

second phase. In that section F. W. Woolworth Company, the well-known five-and-dime, opened its first outer island store in Hawai'i. Woolworth's celebrated with a three-day event in October 1965 that again attracted overflow crowds. The 27,000-square-foot space contained a restaurant, clothing, fabrics, housewares, film processing, a book nook, and all of the other goods that characterized the chain nationwide.

The previous June, Tip Top had been demolished to prepare for the third and final phase of the Lihue Shopping Center. It included construction of the round building and the adjoining two-story section that fronted Rice Street across the pedestrian breezeway from Lihue Store. It was completed in October 1966, and Sears Roebuck and Company moved the next year from its Rice Street location across from the county building into a ground-floor space facing the parking lot. In addition to serving as a catalog order and pick-up center, Sears featured appliances and aloha wear in the space now inhabited by the county's building division.

Several longtime Tip Top tenants signed leases for space in the new center. Others constructed their own establishments in the neighborhood. The Ota family, who operated Ota's Bakery and Restaurant at the Tip Top and also the popular Ota's Sweet Shop in its own building next to the Lihue Theater on Kūhiō Highway, constructed a motel and restaurant on 'Akahi Street that is still in operation today. During the planning commission hearing on the Ota's request to rezone their residence and build the commercial structure, their attorney described the forty-seven-year-old cafe and bakery, which employed

OPPOSITE PAGE
A moment in time: Phase 1 of Lihue Shopping Center has opened but, clockwise from left, the Lihue Store, Tip Top, telephone company, and a couple of concrete duplex houses still stand. The old road is still being used, but the new highway has been completed. At the top of the photo is a segment of the Līhu'e mill, with its new bagasse plant and the flume elevated over the highway to the sugarcane unloading area a half-mile away. Sean O'Neil, Kaua'i Historical Society

fifty-six people, as "the Times Square, the Fort-and-King [center of downtown Honolulu] of Lihue, where almost every visitor meets his Kauai friends."[13] The Otas carried the name Tip Top to their new location.

Another entrepreneur to build his own establishment was William Junokichi Senda. As a budding photographer in 1913, he had purchased the Go Kan Gallery at Kapaia before moving to the second floor of the Tip Top three years later. When the post office, which had been located on the ground floor for some years, completed its own stand-alone building in 1939, Senda moved into that space. In 1950 his son George graduated from photography school in Los Angeles and, with daughter Akiko, the operation became a multigenerational affair. With the planned demolition of the Tip Top, the Sendas bought and built on property across from the new shopping center at the Nāwiliwili-side corner of Hardy and 'Akahi streets. They also leased space to Koichi Isonaga, who relocated his jewelry store and remained a tenant for four decades. First Insurance reestablished itself on the next block of Hardy, at the intersection with 'Elua Street, in a building now owned by the YWCA.

HRT, Ltd., Harry Weinberg's company, bought the Lihue Shopping Center in 1974 and maintained the operational status quo until 1982. At that time, the tenant roster included a mix of national chains, local retailers, and professional and organizational offices. The main level was occupied by Foodland, Woolworth's, Kenny's Restaurant, American Security Bank, Tad and Mary's, Lads and Dads, T and T Jewelry House, Pua Lani Florist, Apollo Travel, Dean Witter Reynolds, Towne House Beauty Salon, Sun Systems, Phone Mart, Finance Factors, and Sears. The signature space formerly occupied by Lihue Store (Amfac Inc. shut down all of its Kauai Stores in 1980) became a Gem's department store. The second floor of the center housed the *Honolulu Advertiser* Kaua'i bureau, HMSA, Matson, the Office of Hawaiian Affairs, Security Title Corporation, Wallace G. Rezentes, CPA, Clinton Childs Realtors, State Farm Insurance, Atchison Insurance, Taylor-Hughes and Associates, psychiatrist Thomas Morelli, dentists Charles Taba and Richard Haruki, and the Kaua'i County Department of Public Housing. The lower, "basement" level contained Lihue Washerette, Judy's Okazu and Saimin, Weinberg's HRT management office, and the Legal Aid Society of Hawaii.

The 1982 opening of Kukui Grove Shopping Center, a thirty-five-acre mall developed by Grove Farm in Puhi, shifted retail dominance west of the town core. The Amfac-owned Liberty House department store moved into the mall as its front, anchor tenant (Liberty House was bought by Federated Department Stores, Inc., in 2001 and became Macy's). Many Lihue Shopping Center businesses followed. Among them, Sears and Woolworth's

became anchors at the opposite end of the mall from Liberty House (Woolworth Corporation closed its thirteen Hawai'i stores in 1997, and its space was later leased to an expanding Sears, which itself closed at Kukui Grove in 2013). Locally owned Tad and Mary's boutique and the national Phone Mart filled smaller spaces in the interior (both of them have since been replaced by different retailers as well). Other Lihue Shopping Center tenants found locations elsewhere, including some professional services that would later seek space in the Kukui Grove business district across Nāwiliwili Road from the mall.

The departure of so much concentrated retail activity may have robbed the town core of its commercial vitality, but it created a real estate opportunity for the county government, which had been exploring options for needed office space. In 1987, Kaua'i County purchased the Lihue Shopping Center and consolidated many of its departments into the one location. The County named the back section, the former Woolworth's, the Kapule Building. The front segment that included the round building was designated the Mo'ikeha Building. Eventually Gem's left the premises and the County renovated that space to suit government activities. That original and largest phase of the shopping center was titled the Pi'ikoi Building. Only Big Save, which replaced Foodland at the back of the complex, remained as an independent, rent-paying, commercial operation in the civic center. It also closed after QSI, Inc., doing business as Times Supermarkets, bought the Big Save Value Centers in 2011.

ABOVE, LEFT
When Kukui Grove Shopping Center opened in 1982, much of the commercial vitality drained away from central Līhu'e.

ABOVE, RIGHT
Līhu'e civic center, 2012.
Casey Riemer Photography

HAWAIIAN TELCOM

Obscured among government operations in the civic center is a private, stand-alone building owned by Hawaiian Telcom. The Kauai Telephonic Company was organized by Grove Farm plantation owner George Norton Wilcox less than four years after Alexander Graham Bell and partners founded the Bell Telephone Company in Connecticut. Wilcox, William Hyde Rice, and Dr. Jared K. Smith signed the request for a corporate charter from the Kingdom of Hawai'i in 1880.

The first phone line stretched between the Grove Farm homestead on the road to Nāwiliwili and the Kōloa home of Dr. Smith, the island's only physician at that time, and it connected each stockholder who resided along the way. A line was next extended to Keālia, with connections branching off to investors living north of Līhu'e, including Makee plantation manager G. H. Dole and later to Z. S. Spalding. In 1891 additional capital was raised to run service from Kōloa to Waimea and from Keālia to Hanalei. The system covered the entire island in 1907, with 170 subscribers paying a hefty fee for service, the 2013 equivalent of about $120 a month.[14] By 1914, Kaua'i could boast 600 aerial line miles (nearly eighty miles from one end to the other), providing connections to 214 telephones around the island. Among the connections were those to the offices of the county attorney, sheriff, auditor, and clerk in the new county building.[15]

Men originally served as the switchboard operators, but women quickly began filling

G. N. Wilcox's Grove Farm homestead was a fairly simple compound in 1886, shortly after the first phones were introduced to Kaua'i and connected his property to the doctor's in Kōloa. Margaret Girvin Gillen, Grove Farm Homestead Museum

the role. In addition to connecting one party to the phone number of another, they provided numerous other services when asked, such as the time of day, the nearest doctor's phone number, and information about ship arrivals.[16] Questions early in the twentieth century about what constituted appropriate behavior on the telephone presaged similar morality debates about Internet usage early in the twenty-first. In April 1921, Governor C.J. McCarthy signed House Bill No. 290, "An Act to Prohibit the Use of Obscene or Lascivious Language over Telephone." Punishment for offenders who were convicted of "'cussing' the operator" was an astonishing $100 fine (equivalent to almost $1,300 in 2013), three months imprisonment, or both.[17]

The Hawaiian Telephone Company building in 1966 had changed little since it was constructed in the 1920s. Its front façade was "modernized" after the shopping center was built around it. Hawaiian Telcom

Expansion of phone service continued rapidly and, in 1921, Lihue Plantation sold Kauai Telephonic the commercial lot adjacent to the Tip Top, thereby assuring of Līhu'e's status as the "wire center of the island."[18] Associated Engineers of Honolulu drew up the building plans for a two-story, fireproof structure with a classical, flat-roofed design of reinforced concrete to nicely complement in style and scale both the Tip Top building next door and the Lihue Store across the street.

Public telephones and the business office in the new building were located on the first floor. The switchboards were housed at the back of the second floor, and two offices were available for lease in the front. One was occupied by Dr. S. Y. Chang, a dentist—and later a member of the County Board of Supervisors—who also maintained an office in Kapa'a. A basement was used for storage.

By the time the building was constructed, Līhu'e had been electrified, and the phone company recognized a marketing possibility as demand for electrical appliances grew. According to a contemporary *Garden Island* account, the phone company contracted with Hawaiian Electric Co. to sell the latter's home appliances and wiring supplies directly to Kauaians "as cheaply as they can purchase in Honolulu."[19] The article explained that, by utilizing part of the new building space to sell electrical equipment, it could generate additional revenues necessary to improve telephone service.

In 1929 Mutual Telephone Company acquired the Kaua'i company, described at the time by the *Garden Island* as "the oldest telephone company in the islands, and possibly

ABOVE, LEFT
Switchboard operators Kum Sin Pak Hasegawa, Connie Kinney Grube, and Margie Panui, ca. 1950. Hawaiian Telcom

ABOVE, RIGHT
Switchboard operators and other staff, 1970: Eleanore Paia, Rose Dahle, Carole Fujimoto, Alexa Blacksted, Emmaline White, Laka Kaohelaulii, Irma Tanigawa. Standing, Roy Miyake, Asa Okamoto, Josephine Cup Choy, Susan Dias George Senda, Hawaiian Telcom

the oldest in the United States."[20] Its name was changed to Hawaiian Telephone Company in 1954, then to GTE Hawaiian Telephone Company, and after that to Verizon Hawaii, Inc. In 2005 the Carlyle Group, a Washington, D.C.–based private equity group, purchased the Hawaiʻi assets of Verizon Communications and formed Hawaiian Telcom, Inc., the largest phone company in the state. Late in 2008, and more than a billion dollars in debt, Hawaiian Telcom filed for bankruptcy protection, citing "increased competition, economic volatility and its failure to meet capital expenditure needs." The company successfully emerged from bankruptcy in 2010, having restructured without Carlyle and reduced its debt to $300 million. Profits rose the following year as increasing sales of high-speed Internet service offset the decline of landline customers. In December 2012, Hawaiian Telcom acquired Wavecom Solutions (originally Pacific Lightnet). The acquisition brought the company an interisland fiber optic network and several new voice and data services geared primarily to small and medium-sized businesses.[21]

Throughout the changes of name and ownership, the original building has remained in place, though it no longer holds retail operations or personnel. It serves now as an automated telephone exchange, housing the equipment switches for Līhuʻe and the "toll room," where most of the island and long-distance toll-line connections are made.[22] The building's original rectilinear form is still detectable from the rear of the building at the Kūhiō-Kaumuali'i highway interchange. Within the civic center, however, the little-noticed structure has been disguised by numerous remodeling jobs and "facelifts" that make it all but unrecognizable as a 1920s, neoclassical testament to the growth of the twentieth century's communications age on Kaua'i.

ISENBERG MONUMENT

Paul Isenberg's story is reminiscent of those of several successful nineteenth-century industrialists in Hawai'i and America, men who emigrated from another country and, by virtue of energy, talent, intelligence, determination, and luck, accumulated great wealth as they changed the world around them. Isenberg remains a towering figure not only in the history of Līhu'e but in the development of Hawai'i itself.

Paul Isenberg (1837–1903). Kaua'i Historical Society

Heinrich Paul Friedrich Carl Isenberg was born in Dransfeld, Germany, in 1837, the son of a Lutheran pastor. After dropping out of school he became apprenticed to a farmer, then managed a small estate before being recruited to Hawaiʻi on the basis of his knowledge of European farming practices. Isenberg arrived in October 1858 after a 186-day voyage caretaking three pairs of sheep only to arrive in an environment radically different from his expectations. "What an empty tiresome world this is!" the lonely twenty-one-year-old wrote to a friend in Honolulu four months later.

> I have never been so cast adrift. . . . Never before have I been so unhappy. . . . Dear Father and Mother, after all they have sacrificed, and thinking, as I did myself, that I should find it so pleasant here! The life here was painted in such alluring colors and such fine promises were made me! And what did I find? They did not even have work for me and packed me off to the hot desert side of the island where I was not wanted either.[23]

Hanna Maria Rice Isenberg (1841–1867). Kauaʻi Historical Society

Shortly before Isenberg penned those plaintive words, manager William Harrison Rice had hired him at Lihue Plantation, and his world soon brightened. A robust, striking man with a facility for languages—he spoke fluent German, English, and eventually Hawaiian—Isenberg must have set many young hearts aflutter; in 1861 he won both heart and hand of Rice's oldest child, Maria.

Those were precarious days for Hawaiʻi's five plantations, but Paul Isenberg had grown steadfast in the belief that a prosperous future lay ahead for sugar in Hawaiʻi. Only "because of the urgent arguments of young Isenberg the plantation was not abandoned in 1861," wrote historian Bernhard Hörmann.[24] By the time William Harrison Rice died the following year, Isenberg had enlarged the groundbreaking irrigation ditches his father-in-law had pioneered and shown such industry that he was an obvious choice to take over as manager of Lihue Plantation. He then set about transforming it into one of the largest, most successful operations in Hawaiʻi.

Isenberg also formed or invested in many other enterprises. In 1871 he and two partners purchased Koloa Plantation from Dr. Robert Wood when he retired to America. Isenberg became manager of that plantation as well. Ten years later, with his brothers Carl and Otto as well as three of the Wilcox brothers, he erected a mill at Kekaha (headed by Otto, who was a trained sugar boiler). It ultimately consolidated with two sugar-growing efforts on the west side of the island to become the Kekaha Sugar Company. Also in 1881,

Isenberg became managing partner in the prosperous firm of H. Hackfeld & Co., General Commission Agents and Ship Chandlers.[25] There he rose to new heights of entrepreneurial brilliance. With G. N. Wilcox, Hackfeld began a business to harvest guano at Laysan Island, the predecessor of the Pacific Chemical and Fertilizer Company. Under Isenberg, Hackfeld also experimented with vanilla and coffee in Kona and invested in Benjamin Dillingham's O'ahu railroad.

The firm continued as the commercial agent for several plantations in Hawai'i and acquired land and capital through occasional failures. One example was the 1885 foreclosure of Pioneer Mill Co. on Maui, in which Isenberg acquired a half interest, the balance a decade later. As corporate biographer Frederick Simpich Jr. concluded, "Thus Isenberg assembled the lands of Pioneer, molded the present-day plantation, and unwittingly provided Amfac with the thriving resort site of Kaanapali."[26] Paul Isenberg became Hackfeld's president in 1899.

Perhaps the most extraordinary aspect of Isenberg's success is that he moved back to Germany in 1878 and for the next twenty-five years *commuted* to Hawai'i. After Maria

Kekaha Sugar Company was a consolidation of two sugar enterprises and the mill founded by the Isenberg and Wilcox brothers on the west side of Kaua'i. Grove Farm Homestead Museum

Rice died of tuberculosis in 1867, leaving him a widow with two young children (Dora and Paul Jr.), he had taken the long journey back to Germany to visit family and friends. There he met and married Beta Glade. Life in the islands was unhappy for Beta, and after a few years she convinced her husband to return to live in the land of their birth.[27] Isenberg regularly returned to Hawai'i, however, both for his business activities and to fulfill his responsibilities in the House of Nobles, to which King Lunalilo had appointed him in 1872.

When he moved to Germany, Paul Isenberg left his brother Carl as manager of Lihue Plantation. He also asked his youngest brother, Pastor Hans Isenberg, to relocate

Dora and Hans Isenberg.
J. J. Williams, Kaua'i Historical Society

permanently to Kaua'i in 1887 to serve as pastor of the Lihue Lutheran Church and minister to the German laborers on the plantation.[28] Hans Isenberg later became president of Lihue and Koloa plantations, serving in that capacity in addition to carrying on his duties as pastor. With his wife Dora, a *kama'āina* born in Līhu'e (she was William Harrison Rice's granddaughter, Paul's daughter, and Hans's own niece), he continued Paul Isenberg's legacy of a flourishing sugar business within a prosperous community. The first great concrete building period of Līhu'e Town occurred in his administration.

Paul Isenberg was not indifferent to the welfare of either the workers in the islands who had made his businesses a success or of the health of his Lutheran religion in Hawai'i. He wrote to authorize a charity fund in Līhu'e "for all laborers, including Chinese and Japanese, who have grown old in the service of the plantation"; he deviated from many colleagues of his time by considering the Japanese desire for their own Japanese doctors natural; and he defined a ten-hour workday as including commute time to and from the job. To celebrate Hackfeld's fiftieth anniversary in 1899, he and partner J. F. Hackfeld donated the funds to establish a Lutheran church in Honolulu and presented thirteen charities with $1,000 each.[29]

On January 16, 1903, Hawai'i was grieved to learn that Isenberg had died of a ruptured appendix that day in Germany. His death "was a shock of immense proportions to a community that regarded him as almost Herculean," wrote Frederick Simpich.[30] To honor his memory, businesses around the territory closed and flags were lowered to half-staff. Ethel Damon wrote in *Koamalu* that after his death "hundreds of his Kauai friends brought together, of their own wish and initiative, half dollars, quarters, dollars, what they could, to be wrought into the bronze portrait which they placed in the center of his Lihue garden."[31]

HALEKŌ DUPLEXES

Across Halekō Road from the Isenberg memorial stand the last four remaining houses of what was once Lihue Plantation's fifty-dwelling Camp Site I. The two-story duplexes were constructed between 1910 and 1918 of eight- to twelve-inch thick concrete walls, an extremely early, rare adaptation of the material for residential use.[33] The second floor of one of the structures extends over the entry porch, and a shed roof covers a single story porch on the other three. They were designed with living and cook rooms downstairs, the sleeping quarters upstairs accessed by an exterior stairway. Each was equipped with a

DEDICATION OF THE ISENBERG MONUMENT

To honor the memory of Paul Isenberg, a memorial park was established at the corner of Rice Street and Halekō Road. A monument with his bronze portrait was placed there and dedicated with great ceremony on his birthday, April 15, 1904. Of the event, Ethel Damon effervesced:

> Since under Paul Isenberg every Lihue harvest had ended with a luau, so, very characteristically, Hawaiian women themselves prepared a real Hawaiian feast for this occasion also. Again they laughed at the deluge of rain which fell the day before. And again the day itself dawned with blue skies. One most unexpected and touching part of the hookupu was the arrival of Paul Isenberg's many Chinese friends, who came to the ceremony bearing pyramids of small cakes, strings of firecrackers and a baked pig slung on a pole. William Hyde Rice had charge of the luau preparations for over two thousand guests and took a keen interest in it all. For days the Hawaiians were busy with preparation of ti leaves and bundles of various sorts to be baked in an imu, or ground oven. Many outsiders came to watch the process of baking, sitting on piles of lumber in the lumber yard, for the feast was made ready there on the hill opposite the old plantation store. After the rain, clean beach sand was strewn everywhere over the muddy paths. Long tables were laid and more than six hundred people, of all colors and creeds, sat down at one time. How many there were in all, no one ever knew. But it was a feast to satisfy the heart of every true Hawaiian.[32]

ABOVE *Paul Isenberg's son, Daniel Paul, eulogized his father's life at the monument's dedication. Grove Farm Homestead Museum*

RIGHT *The luau that followed served an untold number of guests. Outside the* hale lū'au: *Lottie Jordan, Mabel Wilcox, Emily Rice, William Hyde Rice, Miss Kreutzmann, Elsie Wilcox. J. L. Hjorth, Grove Farm Homestead Museum*

Construction of the reinforced concrete housing for German plantation workers began in 1910, an early and rare expression of that material for domestic use. Other structures were added between these four duplexes in the early 2000s, which created a nonhistoric appearance of townhouses. Nancy Bannick, Hawaiʻi State Archives

concrete stove that included an oven and iron top-plates. Shared privies and washhouse were set behind the houses.

The building style and cultural aesthetics of these houses testify to the significant German influence at Lihue Plantation: in 1893, 93 percent of the plantation's forty-one supervisors were German. The first German workers had arrived in 1881 at the instigation of Heinrich Hackfeld, an experiment that coincided with ongoing kingdom-wide efforts to secure a solid source of workers from somewhere in the world for the labor-intensive business of farming sugarcane. Paul Isenberg's hand was strong in the effort. Already living in Bremen, Germany, he acted as the agent for the initial recruitment of German workers. Of the 1,200 men, women, and children who traveled to these far isles between 1880 and 1900, almost half were sent to either Lihue Plantation or Grove Farm.[34]

According to the *Honolulu Star-Bulletin,* the house design for these duplexes was not universally appreciated. An article in the newspaper's 1920 centenary issue noted:

> What was considered an ideal building plan for plantation homes was put into effect at Lihue several years ago, but has since been abandoned, because of the objection of Japanese mothers. This was the construction of two-story concrete houses. Several were built, and they are distinctive objects in the

There were concrete duplexes on both sides of Rice Street as well as along Kūhiō Highway and Halekō Road until the Lihue Shopping Center precipitated the remake of the town core. One of the remaining houses along Halekō is visible, far right. private collection

> plantation landscape today, but the laborers' wives complained that it was impossible to keep their children from climbing to the upper floor and falling off the balconies. The management took heed and will build no more.[35]

By then the plantation had decided to congregate its workers in camps centrally located at Līhu'e and Hanamā'ulu. Their stated reasons, according to the article, were that the non-European workers "prefer to dwell in communities, and moreover the management finds it far easier to supervise central camps than isolated dwellings."

All of the remaining Camp Site I concrete duplexes except the four still standing were demolished in the 1960s to make way for the rebuilding of central Līhu'e. These last structures were converted by the plantation for commercial use, with carefully conceived landscaping around the buildings that included plants originating from the countries of many of Hawai'i's immigrant groups.

Tenants gradually changed after Harry Weinberg's HRT, Ltd. bought this property along with the shopping center and a considerable amount of other Līhu'e real estate in 1974. Owners of Casa de Grillo restaurant, the final enterprise operating there, abandoned the premises after Hurricane 'Iniki stormed through Kaua'i in 1992. Islanders watched the structures deteriorate through the rest of the decade until only the thick walls

The celebration of diverse religions that were part of the plantation fabric was still appreciated in 1966. Both Buddhist and Christian shrines were added to the garden behind the Halekō Road structures, which were converted to commercial use. Bishop Shjitsu Ohara of Honpa Hongwanji Mission of Hawaii donated the bronze statue of Amida Buddha. Yoichi Watada designed the pagoda-temple shrine, constructed by the plantation. From left, Clinton Childs, Lihue Plantation administrative assistant to the manager; David Ballie Jr., assistant manager; Rev. Ryosho Kondo, minister of Lihue Hongwanji Mission; with Kapa'a ministers Sekikaku Takesono, Shoyu Kitajima, and Kakue Asaoka. Kaua'i Historical Society

Father Matthew Alencastre, dean of Catholic churches on Kaua'i, blessed the Christian shrine in the landscaped garden. Dora Jane Isenberg Cole donated the bust of Christ. It had been brought from Germany around Cape Horn by Hans and Dora Isenberg and was displayed at their home, Molokoa, for many years. Nancy Bannick, Hawai'i State Archives

remained, and they too were crumbling into memory. When reconstruction began in 2001 (ownership transferred to the Harry and Jeanette Weinberg Foundation after the death of Harry Weinberg in 1990), it substantially altered the configuration of the row. Today, the buildings enjoy new life, but the infill between the century-old structures has created a nonhistoric, townhouse-like appearance to originally detached duplexes.

A charming ornament to the one-time concrete workers' houses is the ornate horse trough located at the top edge of the row of structures. It stands as a testimony to the civic pride of Līhu'e's pioneer builders a century ago. Plantation president Hans Isenberg and his wife Dora bought the marble water trough in Italy during their around-the-world tour in 1909. Since the first vessels would not be able to pass through the Panama Canal

The Halekō structures were badly damaged by Hurricane ʻIniki on September 11, 1992. Almost a decade passed before their reconstruction began.

In 1964 the horse trough was relocated from the northwest side of the main Līhuʻe intersection—the Mokihana Club also maintained a rose garden there—across the street to its current location in front of the Halekō duplexes.
Kauaʻi Historical Society

for another four years, it was crated up and shipped around the Horn of South America, arriving on Kaua'i the next year.[36] The Isenbergs installed the fountain by the intersection of Halekō Road and Rice Street, a little below the Lihue store.[37] They also paid to pipe running water to the fountain; it flowed through the lions' mouths into the trough below.

The equine drinking fountain remained in place long after horses had disappeared as standard conveyances on Līhu'e streets, whether seeking water in antique Italian marble fountains or not. In 1951 the *Honolulu Star-Bulletin* reported that the plantation had donated the fountain to the Kauai Humane Society, which was conducting a capital funds drive to build a facility in Hanapēpē.[38] That building was completed, but the fountain was never transferred. Whatever happened to change those plans, the trough remained on the north side of Rice Street until the great Līhu'e redesign of the 1960s, when it was moved across the street to its present site in front of the duplexes.

BANK OF HAWAII

The Bank of Hawaii, Ltd., was incorporated in December 1897, less than eight months before the United States annexed the islands. It was organized by prominent Honolulu men of affairs Peter Cushman Jones and Charles Montague Cooke. The latter had ties

The first branch bank in Hawai'i was opened in the Lihue Store building in 1903. The bank sign is to the right of the larger store sign. Ray Jerome Baker, Kaua'i Historical Society

to Lihue Plantation through his wife, Anna Charlotte Rice. She had moved to Kaua'i in her infancy when her father, William Harrison Rice, became manager of the nascent plantation at Līhu'e. The family lived at Koamalu, above the mill and millpond, and Anna later inherited a financial interest in the plantation. In 1903, when Bank of Hawaii directors decided to open a branch office, they chose the commercial center of Līhu'e as the location for the new enterprise.[39] It was the first bank branch to be maintained in the islands. For nine years the Bank of Hawaii conducted its business from a space at the Lihue Store that had formerly been used as a coffee shop. Frank Crawford, who arrived from Indiana in 1901 to serve as the U.S. postmaster on Kaua'i, became the bank's cashier.

28 BANKING LICENSE.

Know All Men, that

In conformity with the provisions of Act 64, of the Session Laws of 1896, entitled an Act "To Amend, Add to and Consolidate the Laws relating to certain Licenses, etc., approved June 12, 1896,

The Bank of Hawaii Ltd

is hereby Licensed upon the terms and conditions as set forth in said Act, and in accordance with the requirements of, and subject to the Statute Laws of the Territory of Hawaii, to Carry on a Banking Business, at Lihue

District of Lihue Island of Kauai

for the term of ONE YEAR from Jany 2. 1905

The term "Banking" shall mean the engaging in buying or selling drafts or bills of Exchange on banks or persons in other countries, or the receiving of deposits and paying of checks thereon.

This License is not Transferable.

Given Under My Hand, and the Seal of the Treasurer's Office, at Honolulu, this 23 day of Mch 1905

A. J. Campbell
Treasurer,
Registrar of Public Accounts.

Amount paid $

The Territory of Hawai'i licensed the Bank of Hawaii to operate a branch in Līhu'e. Bank of Hawaii

On April 12, 1912, Hans Isenberg wrote in his diary: "Saw Clarence Cooke re land for new bank in Lihue business block."[40] The land was a half-acre lot the plantation sold to the Bank of Hawaii while planning its new town core and shortly after deeding five acres down the street to the government for a grand county building. The reinforced concrete building was designed with solid, symmetrical lines and classical columns to convey a sense of security, permanence, and stability in its affairs. The style was reminiscent of banks then being constructed in small towns across America. Until 1921 Bank of Hawaii business utilized only one side of the building. Post office operations were conducted on the other, with patrons' boxes located on the exterior, Isenberg memorial side of the building. Communications technology was improving the ability for this isolated island to receive news, and in 1923 the branch announced installation of a "radio set" that would provide customers with "stock quotations, crop and weather reports, as well as the shipping news."[41]

Despite the plantation's grand design for a dignified town center, however, Līhu'e was still very much a village. The *Garden Island* ran a page-one story in 1924 poking fun at the bank's staff, whose "after-luncheon nap" was rudely disturbed when "Lihue plantation steers being driven down the street entered the bank and paid the bankers a call."[42] Two of the bankers "showed great presence of mind by diving under the counters," the story chuckled, while the third "remembered that he had not been to lunch, so left via the rear entrance. The cowboys driving the steers were finally able to shoo the steers out of the lobby and the bankers hung up the business sign as usual and went back to sleep."

As town and commerce grew, so too did the Bank of Hawaii's business. In 1938, about

The Bank of Hawaii and the post office shared space in the new building. Patrons' boxes are visible along the exterior wall by the driveway. Bank of Hawaii

the time the post office next door was under construction, the building was enlarged and modernized by Honolulu architect Guy Rothwell. He transformed the original Classical Revival design by adding a steep, double-pitched tile roof that was in vogue at the time. A 20- by 60-foot extension was added at the rear; asphalt tile flooring, with leg-relieving rubber tile in the tellers' cages, was installed; and the vault was enlarged another seven feet.[43]

Bank of Hawaii employee Katsutaro Yamasaki (1878–1952) was among Hawaiʻi immigrants who experienced the dark side of America's participation in World War II: internment. Born in Hiroshima, he spent time in California as a cook in a mining camp in the 1890s before returning to Japan to marry. The couple immigrated to Hawaiʻi in the early 1900s, and he began work at the bank some time after 1916. As assistant manager

John Frederick Janssen Jr. later remembered, "old man Crawford hired him because he spoke English so well. He used to make out yen drafts and help people send money back to Japan." On December 8, 1941, the morning after the Pearl Harbor attack,

> two gentlemen came in with "coat and tie." . . . they came over to me and said "Mr. Janssen, you have a Mr. Yamasaki working here" . . . called Yama over. They explained the problem to me and said "We are going to have to take him along with us because he is the Consular's agent (Japanese)." Now, I'm telling you—I could have wept. He happened to be on the Consular's list because he was helpful to the people but I don't think he did any reporting back to Japan or anything like that. He just helped them send money home.[44]

Yamasaki had also been providing assistance as a go-between for many Japanese-style marriages, confirming birth records for the Japanese government on behalf of those

In the late 1930s architect Guy Rothwell designed the roof of the Shell station on Kūhiō Highway to resemble traditional Hawaiian thatching. He also added the tall, double-pitched roof to the Classical Revival bank building in an early remodel. Throughout later structural updates and expansions, the Rothwell roof profile has remained.

with dual citizenship, and assisting his compatriots with general letter writing and communications.[45] After the war ended he returned to the Bank of Hawaii, where he worked until his retirement.

The Bank of Hawaii participated in central Līhuʻe's makeover in the mid-sixties with another remodel. The original reinforced concrete walls were covered with a lava rock façade; a patterned concrete block "curtain" was built in front of the entry doors; and a drive-through window was added on the *mauka* side of the building, where post office boxes had served a different generation.

In 2003, during the branch's centennial, both exterior and interior were altered once again. That most recent renovation coincided with work going on in the civic center across the street, in this case the Piʻikoi Building, which was remodeled for departmental space after standing vacant for many years.

U.S. POST OFFICE BUILDING

The charming Mission Revival–style post office stands as proof that public pressure can occasionally become the irresistible force that shifts a seemingly immovable government bureaucracy.

The original building design was a government issue, Depression-era plan for a mini-fortress completely discordant with Hawaiʻi's climate or the adapted Mediterranean style currently in fashion. Such a structure "would have fitted nicely into a farming community in the Middle West," groused the *Garden Island,* but "the monstrosity" was out of place on Kauaʻi.[46] Public complaints, however, were refused consideration in Washington, D.C., until after the plans had been approved, construction bids opened, and lot clearing begun. It was then that postal engineer Floyd Williams visited Kauaʻi, recognized the inappropriateness of the design, and successfully interrupted the process. Williams gathered input from Chamber of Commerce members and other residents, then convinced authorities to draw up new plans sensitive to a tropical setting. The Mediterranean-via-California–style building, dedicated in May 1939, was the result of his efforts.

A century previous to the building's construction, island mail was an informal affair. Letters in those early days were given to ship captains, who delivered them to an American post office once they reached port on the Atlantic coast. The first post office on Kauaʻi was actually located at Nāwiliwili, but Līhuʻe had become the distributional hub for mail by the 1860s.[47] Forty years later, post offices were operating at Keālia (which had replaced the

Lihue Plantation utilized the lot adjacent to the Bank of Hawaii as management housing before selling the parcel to the U.S. Post Office in the 1930s. Bank of Hawaii

A sketch of the proposed post office design that was published in the *Garden Island* in June 1937 brought howls of protest from the community. *Garden Island* archives

Kapaʻa location in 1893), Kekaha, Kilauea, Makaweli, Mānā, Moloaʻa, Nāwiliwili, Wahiawa, Waimea, and Waiʻoli in addition to Līhuʻe.

For several years around the turn of the century, the Līhuʻe post office was housed in what had once been a tailor's shop next to Lihue Store. It moved into the *mauka* portion

of the new Bank of Hawaii building in 1913, then relocated in 1924 to leased rooms at the Tip Top previously occupied by a plumbing store, a vegetable shop, and a tailor. The call for proposals made public in 1923 had specified a need for at least 2,000 square feet of rental space that included "heat, light, water, toilet facilities, safe or vault, and all necessary furniture and equipment," with important considerations given to "good daylight and a reasonably central location."[48]

In 1927, territorial senator Charles Rice introduced a resolution asking the U.S. Congress to provide funds for a new post office, a request that took a decade to become reality. After an initial proposal to place the post office on the county building lawn, the federal government paid $4,500 for the lot the plantation offered on the Nāwiliwili side of the Bank of Hawaii. It did so after rejecting an offer by Rice's company, William Hyde Rice, Ltd., to sell the government the former 30,000-square-foot *Garden Island* newspaper parcel on lower Rice Street for what was then an astronomical $15,000.

The dedication of the new post office on May 6, 1939, recognized many of those who had negotiated the bureaucratic maze leading to its construction. *Garden Island* publisher Charlie Fern, who acted as master of ceremonies for the Chamber of Commerce–

Post office dedication ceremony, May 6, 1939. Tom Fujii, Kauaʻi Historical Society sponsored event, recounted the community's battle and its success in obtaining a well-designed, stand-alone post office for Kauai.[49] Postal engineer Floyd Williams, who had successfully changed the government's plans for the original design, was named guest of honor. The community postponed the dedication from April 18 to May 6 so that Williams could attend, though in a twist of fate he was absent that day too, having missed his connecting flight from the mainland. Judge Wood, the U.S. postal inspector for Hawai'i, read his address. Among others who spoke, Dora Isenberg reminisced about the 1870s, when her father Paul Isenberg was postmaster and she would "climb a tree to look for the sailing vessels as they came to bring the mail to Kauai, an event for which all the town turned out."[50] Boy Scout Troop 94 raised the flag on the pole in front of the building for the first time, and the Kauai Community Orchestra provided the musical interludes.

Post offices across America were beautified during the Depression thanks to the federal government's Works Progress Administration programs. The sculpture of a *pū 'olē 'olē* blower created by Marguerite Blasingame was designed for placement between the patrons' rental boxes in the Līhu'e post office. Tom Kunichika, Kaua'i Historical Society

Inevitably, changes to the building, which was added to the National Register of Historic Places in 1989, have occurred over time. The back was extended in the 1970s, and the metal-framed glass panels and doorway were added to the lobby entryway to protect postal employees and patrons from occasional damp, chilly weather. Until recently, a fine wooden sculpture of two hands gripping an adze hung above the doorway to the left of the service windows inside the post office. The artwork is attributed to Marguerite Blasingame (1902–1947), a Honolulu-born artist who received an M.A. from Stanford University. Her work has been placed in both public and private domains, including the Ala Moana Park in Honolulu, the Honolulu Museum of Art, and the Volcano House on the island of Hawai'i. A second Blasingame sculpture, around the corner of the lobby between mailbox bays, portrayed a man gripping a *pū 'olē'olē,* a conch shell "trumpet." Unfortunately, the piece was vandalized in 2002 and the lower portion is now missing.

Both of the sculptures on site have been removed from view, although post office officials report that both remain stored on site in an administrative office. Their future, however, is imperiled by the U.S. Postal Service's skyrocketing deficits and the shortage of viable solutions to reverse the ever higher debt. The future of the Rice Street building itself is in question: the post office plans to relocate the Līhu'e operations to its sorting facility by the airport, rendering this historic building but a shadow of the past.

FIRST HAWAIIAN BANK AND LIHUE PLANTATION BUILDINGS

If Lihue Shopping Center served as hub of the urban renewal wheel that rolled through town in the 1960s, the new First National Bank (now First Hawaiian) and Lihue Plantation administration buildings were two of the spokes that radiated from the commercial center through the town core. The two rectilinear structures with their copper crowns were constructed after their former buildings were scheduled for demolition to make way for the shopping center. Conceived as a pair by architect Edwin Bauer, bank and administration buildings share at least one design element of the era with their neighbor across the street, the coral rock wall facings.

But these were not the first buildings to occupy this land. A social hall was built on the site in 1903 that served for two decades as the community's entertainment nexus. Although no pictures of the building are known to exist, the social hall was described as a long, two-story frame structure with surrounding lanai and entrances on each side.[51] Prominent Līhu'e citizens contributed most of the money for the hall's construction costs through the purchase of shares. Funds to clear the balance of the debt were raised at a fair organized by Dora Isenberg, with dozens of women—and the occasional gent—grouped in committees to devise games and gather clothing, toys, potted plants, and other items for thirteen enticing booths. "The man who started down that avenue with full pockets, found himself 'dead broke' and richly freighted with things more or less sweet, dainty, artistic, valuable or useless long before he reached the ice cream soda at the end," the *Garden Island* bantered in its report of the event's success.[52] The fundraiser, held on June 17, 1905, was seen as such a triumph that the newspaper's report promised it would remain "a red letter day long to be remembered in the annals of Lihue."

Indeed, the fair was so enjoyed that it prompted participants to coalesce into the Mokihana Club, which would play an important role in social welfare, community beautification, and cultural expression on Kaua'i for many decades. The hall was well used for theatrical events, dances, and other gatherings until its demolition in the 1920s, when it was replaced by homes for Lihue Plantation supervisors.

Forty years later, when plans were drawn up for the plantation office, bank, and adjacent service station, those homes were not destroyed. Rather, in the time-honored local tradition of conserving limited resources, they continued their old residential function in a new location on Ho'omana Road. They were lifted off their foundations and trucked down Halekō Road, where one narrow trailer and its top-heavy load tipped over, causing

In 1960 the First National Bank was located near the top left of the picture, adjacent to the Lihue Store's light-colored roof extension. The Lihue Plantation administration building, bottom right, faced Rice Street opposite the post office. Behind it and to the right of the bank was the Lihue Store warehouse. The store is at the intersection. A few concrete duplexes were still located across the street from the bank. Alan Fayé Jr., Pacific Skyways

Several houses were moved from their Rice Street origins to make way for the construction of the bank and Lihue Plantation buildings. Kaua'i Historical Society

several moments of heart-racing anxiety but no damage to the house. The route circled around the mill and up the far side of the valley to Kaumuali'i Highway. From there it turned right across from the old Lihue Plantation manager's home, Koamalu, onto a haul cane road that wound down into the gulch on the Lihue Lutheran Church side of German Hill (a still-used phrase hearkening back to the days when Germans dominated the plantation's supervisory positions), then back up the hill, where it joined Ho'omana Road above Molokoa, the old Hans and Dora Isenberg home. During the process the electric company cut overhanging tree branches, moved three utility poles, and lifted other power and telephone lines clear of the rolling houses-in-transit. More excitement ensued near the entrance to Molokoa, reported the *Garden Island,* when "the right wheels of the big flatbed trailer [came] dangerously near a sharp drop, and a third of the house [hung] over thin air."[53] All ended happily: the structures were set down *mauka* of the Lutheran church, where they remain in use as private residences today.

When the bank moved to its current site, it was known as the First National Bank

Known as Bishop National Bank when the building was constructed, the name had been changed to First National Bank of Hawaii when it was demolished to make way for the Lihue Shopping Center. Senda, Kaua'i Museum

of Hawaii. That was but one of the name changes in its 150-year history: Bishop and Co., 1858; Bank of Bishop and Company, Ltd., 1919; Bishop First National Bank of Honolulu, 1929; Bishop National Bank of Hawaii at Honolulu, 1933; Bishop National Bank of Hawaii, 1956; and First National Bank of Hawaii, 1960. The name it has kept since 1969 is First Hawaiian Bank, though it is now a subsidiary of BancWest Corporation, itself a subsidiary of BNP Paribas, a French global banking group.

The two-story, 20,000-square-foot Lihue Plantation office building constructed behind the bank at the edge of the valley was the third building to house the company administration. It replaced the two-story structure built across Rice street in 1901, in what is now the front of the civic center parking lot immediately *mauka* of the Kaua'i Museum. That in turn replaced an office constructed in the 1870s elsewhere on the bluff overlooking Nāwiliwili Valley.[54]

Unlike most places in town, the Lihue Plantation building was designed to accommodate the automobile age by including a lower parking level for tenants (the State Office

Lihue Plantation administration building, December 1964. Kaua'i Historical Society

The First National Bank, now First Hawaiian, ca. 1965. Tom Fujii, Kaua'i Historical Society

Building and Kauai Community Federal Credit Union on Hardy Street being other exceptions). In 2003 its front façade was interrupted by the construction of an elevator shaft next to the entry, added to comply with the Americans with Disabilities Act. Sold twice since the plantation closed, the building now houses an architectural firm, law offices, a secretarial service, and other professional enterprises. An office for the remnant Amfac operations is staffed part time by a lone employee there.

KAUA'I'S FIRST PUBLIC LIBRARY

By the end of World War I, the village of Līhu'e had become a bustling center of activity that extended beyond plantation and government operations. The 1920 U.S. census reported a population of 6,223 in the Līhu'e District, a 340 percent increase in forty years. Plantation employment accounted for a lot of that growth, but banking, insurance, health services, and other businesses run by professionals who were living in homes on Rice Street and elsewhere in the district contributed to the population increase as well. Whereas single men had once characterized the plantation workforce, families were becoming commonplace at the turn of the century. Opinions about education for children of alien workers varied. Some argued that to educate them would mean to lose them as future field hands; others championed the extension of literacy to this population, with access to books in a well-stocked, open library.

The Līhue bandstand stood between the plantation's administration building and the county building on land that eventually became part of the Kaua'i Museum. Kaua'i Historical Society

But education of immigrant laborers' children was not the sole motivation for a library: many among the town's privileged classes sought increased availability of books and ideas for their own intellectual recreation. An informal system of literature distribution had been part of the life of English-speaking residents for decades. "The foreign population of Kauai is emphatically given to reading good books, and the best periodicals of the age," enthused an 1860 issue of *The Friend*.[55] It reported that a club existed whose members bought American and European publications to "circulate from family to family, as regularly as the weekly mail around the island. Such associations," the newspaper concluded, "bespeak intelligence, taste, and elements of genuine refinement." That club was similar to reading rooms that had begun as early as the 1830s in Honolulu and Lahaina when missionaries attempted to provide sailors with alternatives to drunkenness and other miscreant behavior.[56]

A full Honolulu Library and Reading Room opened in 1879 with entry fees and monthly dues, and before the turn of the century on Kaua'i Rev. J. M. Lydgate and his wife Helen had created a subscription library along similar lines. They used their own substantial book collection and housed it in the Sunday school of the Lihue Union Church. Mokihana Club members contributed additional volumes, and the Honolulu library sent others. Many civic-minded individuals donated still more books and periodicals. Library revenues derived from patrons' annual membership fees, with a yearly fair raising additional funds. The collection gradually outgrew its allotted space at the church, and in December 1920 it was moved to the centrally located Līhu'e social hall.

The next year, when the Territory passed the County Library Law to support free public libraries on all of the islands, several committed citizens quickly organized the private, not-for-profit Kauai Public Library Association, Ltd. It received its charter of incorporation in January 1922. The group then set about creating a building to reflect its lofty mission. Lihue Plantation donated land across the street from the social hall; the Territorial Legislature budgeted $25,000 for salaries, books, and operating expenses in the first biennium; Emma Kauikeolani Wilcox gifted the library association with $75,000 (the equivalent of more than a million 2013 dollars) for a building to be constructed as a memorial to her late husband, Albert Spencer Wilcox.

The Library Association voted on June 13, 1922, to retain Honolulu architect Hart Wood to design the library. His much-praised Lihue Union Parish Hall, a short distance beyond the mill, had been dedicated the previous month, and "this fact alone assures the perfected success of the library project," the *Garden Island* commented. A follow-up article in November reported that the library would be of native lava rock. "The entrance lanai however, will be built of concrete and will be finished off to resemble cut stone. The roof of the building will be red tile."[57] (The tile specifications changed to a glazed Mediterranean blue before installation, because Wood happened upon stock in that color readily available in Honolulu.)[58] The tile cascades down to an almost touchable height in the rear of the building. There, the edgeline of the roof is interrupted by an enclosed lanai that originally served as a reading space and periodical room. A concrete-block, jalousied staff room was added to the rear of the building in 1957, woefully compromising the poetry of that side of the structure.

School children and their teachers enjoy a field trip to the Lihue Library during Book Week, 1928. Lihue Public Library

But no one would mistake the back for the front of this building. The entry's wide brick stairway rises to a trio of double-columned arches, with a pair of two-tiered, domed niches sculpted between them and a classical pediment set above the central arch at the roofline. The architect clearly intended his elaborate front façade to establish an elegant and beautiful entryway along Rice Street, the main road of the county seat at the heart of Kaua'i. Wood's sensitive touch is felt in other aspects of the library's design. The interior, barrel-vaulted ceiling and the high Palladian windows on each side of the building hint at a reverence for a house of learning and its contents. Below those windows and repeated at the rear of the building, steel-framed multipane awning windows complement similarly constructed entry doors at the front lanai.

While Wood was working on the library building, his First Church of Christ Scientist in Honolulu, generally considered a masterpiece of design in Hawai'i, was also in progress. A cohesiveness of style is apparent in the two buildings' steeply pitched roofs and unusual detail of layering the lava rock walls between horizontal bands of concrete. Hart D. Wood, the architect's son, paid tribute to his father's work when he wrote that the Līhu'e library building is "a particularly fine example of what I like to think is a truly indigenous style of architecture, completely original to Hawaii, with no counterpart anywhere else." Many others, including architect Robert Fox, consider it "the finest example of architecture in the downtown Lihue area."[59]

KAUA'I MUSEUM AND ANNEX

The dream of expanding the library site beyond a collection of books and related services into Līhu'e's literary and cultural center began shortly after the A. S. Wilcox Memorial Library opened in 1924. The manifestation of that dream, a companion museum building to showcase the arts and history of the island would wait another thirty-five years.

Library interior, 1930.
Lihue Public Library

In 1925, Honolulu insurance executive and maritime artist Alfred R. Gurrey Sr., who had retired on Kaua'i, saw the potential for art in the new library but was denied permission to exhibit his paintings there because of lack of space. Five years later Emma Wilcox, at the request of the Kauai Library Association, donated a portrait of herself. She accompanied it, according to association minutes of August 11, 1930, with a $10,000 check (equivalent to about $140,000 in 2013) to be "used as the nucleus for a fund for building an addition to library for museum purposes." The next year the association paid Lihue Plantation a token sum for 5,053 square feet of adjacent land that could accommodate such a structure. Forward motion then stalled until 1949, when Dora Isenberg, William Harrison Rice's granddaughter, left a bequest of stocks, the interest from which, with Wilcox's earlier donation, provided over half of the total funds necessary to construct a museum building.[60]

In 1954 a museum committee of the library association formed to raise the remaining funds needed to make the long-held dream a reality. Juliet Rice Wichman, a great-granddaughter of William Harrison Rice, led the effort and was able to obtain "substantial funds" from the Rice estate to reach the capital campaign's goal.[61] Museum committee members at the building's opening included Harold Milnes, chair; Alice Anderson; Mrs. E. J. Dworzack; Helen Rice Ellis (another great-granddaughter of W. H. Rice); Priscilla Leong; Beatrice Lovell; Richard Sloggett; Henry Wedemeyer; and Samuel Wilcox. A third W. H. Rice great-granddaughter, Dora Jane Isenberg Cole, who had been much involved with the institution's development, became the museum's first "custodian," or manager, with Wichman its director.[62]

The planners contracted architect Kenneth Roehrig, a partner at Merrill, Simms and Roehrig (successor firm to Hawai'i architectural icon C.W. Dickey), to design the museum, and they awarded construction to Līhu'e contractor M. Morishige. The building featured a lava rock façade on reinforced concrete walls and horizontal banding to harmonize with its next-door neighbor and philosophical companion. Primary exhibition space, office, dressing rooms, and some storage were housed on the first floor; a group work area plus additional display and storage were on the second floor.[63]

The building was conceived as the second of an eventual three-unit plan. "That, in case you are wondering," explained an early fundraising flier, "is why the present building is set so far forward on the lot."[64] The plans called for each of the buildings to be separated by a central court with a raised platform for performances. Ten years later another fundraising brochure included the architect's site plan with a plea to "Ha'awi me ka loko

Juliet Rice Wichman poses next to an immense Hawaiian calabash at the opening of the Kaua'i Museum, 1960. Kaua'i Museum

Museum manager Dora Jane Isenberg Cole in the museum gift shop with a young visitor. Nancy Bannick, Hawai'i State Archives

maikai—give generously!" in order to complete the Story of Kauai permanent exhibit and the third building, described as a "redwood structure . . . [which] will be a studio home for the active and growing Kauai Art Group."[65]

The museum opened in December 1960 with a gala attended by many of Hawai'i's social elite and featured in newspaper society pages around the state. Hawaiian heritage was the theme of the inaugural exhibit. A collection of Hawaiian artifacts bequeathed to the museum in the 1930s by Alexander McBryde provided the exhibit's highlight. Paintings

The Kauaʻi Museum was not initially connected to the library. Its entrance opened directly onto Rice Street. George Senda, Kauaʻi Museum

and other objects loaned by Kauaʻi *kamaʻāina,* primarily descendants of Lihue and Grove Farm plantation pioneers, supplemented the McBryde collection.

After the library and its contents moved to Hardy Street in 1969, the two buildings became, jointly, the Kauaʻi Museum. Architect Geoffrey Fairfax created a second-floor walkway, with display cases along its expanse, to connect the two balconies that Wood, Weed and Kubala had designed in 1958 to provide increased book space on either side of the original library building. The Rice Street entrance originally on the face of the newer building was walled off, and Hart Wood's gracious library entry became the point of welcome for the entire museum complex. A covered walkway in the back courtyard connected the two structures. Today, the 1960 William Hyde Rice Building houses a permanent installation, the "Story of Kauai," and the A. S. Wilcox Building features cultural and historical exhibits in the main gallery downstairs, with rotating local artists' work in one of the second-floor balconies. The original performance platform was removed in 2012, however, to provide additional patio space for activities in the courtyard, but the proposed third building has not yet been built.

The touch of A. R. Gurrey is still felt at the Kauaʻi Museum. In 1996 the artist's children donated thirty of his paintings to the institution. That collection was unveiled as a major

Interior of the Kaua'i Museum before merging with the library. Harvey Tam, Kaua'i Historical Society

exhibition in 1998, seventy-three years after the artist's request to display his work in the building. A second exhibit of his paintings opened in the fall of 2008, and several of his pieces have been displayed since then.

THE HISTORIC COUNTY BUILDING

The preeminent land sale in early twentieth-century Līhu'e, and the jewel in the crown of Lihue Plantation's town development efforts, was the five acres of sugarcane fields along the main street that the company sold to the County of Kaua'i in 1912. The *Garden Island* was exuberant about the purchase, "probably the most important transaction which has

FOLLOWING PAGE
County building, 1918. William J. Senda, Kaua'i Historical Society

Lihue.

ever taken place in Lihue since the creation of County government" in 1905.[66] The process had begun at least a year earlier, when the newspaper wrote an open message to Charles A. Rice, a member of Hawai'i's Territorial House of Representatives, that suggested he redirect 30 percent of $100,000 earmarked for public works on O'ahu. With such funds, the paper advised, Kaua'i could construct a badly needed county building. The timing was good, it continued, because architect Clinton Ripley was already engaged on Kaua'i to design a school at Hanapēpē. He could be drafted to do a "little work on that County building." (Ripley would shortly design the Lihue Store and Tip Top too.)

There is a misconception that until this building was constructed the Board of Supervisors (predecessor to the current government structure of mayor and County Council) regularly met some distance from town at the old courthouse above Nāwiliwili Harbor, the present site of Kaua'i High School. In fact, by 1912 the supervisors were already housed in a borrowed space within Līhu'e Town itself, "the old language school" on Board of Supervisors chair H. D. Wishard's property, nearly across the main street from the present Kaua'i Museum. The county auditor, clerk, and attorney were also housed there.[67]

Architect Clinton Briggs Ripley (1849–1922) was responsible for much of Līhu'e's transformation in the early territorial period. He designed the Lihue Store and Tip Top in addition to the county building. Hawai'i State Archives

Creating a substantial structure on a five-acre parcel in the heart of the village would not only consolidate government affairs but also provide a majestic setting appropriate to the stature of government business and the effort to instill civic pride through all segments of the population. As the newspaper had suggested, the County retained the Honolulu firm of Ripley, Reynolds and Davis—though Arthur Reynolds soon left the partnership—to design the monumental two-story, neoclassical, fireproof building. ("Even the laths inside of the plastering will be of steel, so that there will be little about it that could burn.")[68]

The plantation harvested its final sugarcane crop from the land in the spring of 1912. That summer architectural plans were unveiled, and requests for construction bids were advertised. Lord-Young Engineering Co., another Honolulu firm, won that contract and would later win the bid to provide fixtures and furnishings too. By the following spring a driveway encircling the building site was finished and preparations to lay the foundation were complete. Materials for the project were shipped to Ahukini landing (Nāwiliwili would not be completed as a deepwater harbor for almost two decades) and then hauled by Lihue Plantation trains right up to the job site on temporarily laid portable tracks in much the same way cane was transported from outlying fields to the mill. Electricity, Līhu'e's new amenity, was installed to light the work buildings and to power necessary machinery such as a concrete mixer. By January 1914 the exterior concrete work was complete, scaffolding had been removed, and the finishing plaster was being applied. Painting and interior work continued for the next three months. In April 1914 the Board of Supervisors accepted the job as virtually complete, withholding only a small final payment until the conclusion of inevitable cleanup details.[69]

On May 9, 1914, circuit court judge Lyle A. Dickey dedicated the building with a grand ball. He "summoned" a thousand people to attend the event, and very few declined the honor. One who was "obliged to miss the evening and its pleasures" was Hawai'i governor L. E. Pinkham. Instead, he sent a congratulatory message with the counsel that "the spirit of the people must be of their own breeding, conscience and enterprise, and let us hope will always be that of unselfishness and justice. Long may Kauai retain its designation as The Garden Island."[70]

The almost completed county building, 1914. Kaua'i Historical Society

Motorcylists make their way up the central drive to the county building during an annual Kamehameha Day parade. Harvey Tam, Kauaʻi Historical Society

As the locus of representative government, and with the added benefits of an expansive lawn and adjoining ballpark, the county building provided a backdrop for celebrations and seminal moments in the life of the island. Parades ended at its steps and celebrations continued in the lawn and around the building. Shortly after Japan's World War II capitulation in August 1945, a jubilant crowd crammed the grounds to sing, dance, and ignite celebratory fireworks. In March 1959, after Congress had finally voted to admit Hawaiʻi into the union, veteran political powerhouse Charlie Rice stood in the building portico, framed by its tall columns, and shared with another large gathering his pleasure that statehood had arrived.

OPPOSITE PAGE
The front lawn of the county building was typically the destination for parades and celebrations of major events. On March 13, 1959, the Venerable Norman Alter, of All Saints' Episcopal Church, Kapaʻa, gave a prayer of thanksgiving during Hawaiʻi statehood festivities that concluded at the steps of the county building. Grove Farm Homestead Museum

If the site acted as the center of festive occasions, the building's existence as a metaphor for the government it housed also made it vulnerable. On the night of January 31, 1981, someone exploded a bomb against the southwest corner of the first floor, where the mayor's office was located. The next year a package of explosives and metal pellets encased in plastic was lodged against a window outside the mayor's office; about nine o'clock that quiet Sunday night in September the second bomb exploded. There was little damage, and no one was ever charged with the crimes, but many suspected them to be the

HAWAII 50 STATE

work of Save Nukolii activists intent on stopping resort development at the old Nukoli'i dairy north of Hanamā'ulu, where the Kaua'i Beach Resort is currently located. Mayor Edwardo Malapit openly blamed the anti-development activists, though the Save Nukoli'i committee termed his accusations "irresponsible" and insisted in a public statement that it "had nothing to do with either of the bombings and doesn't approve of them in any way."[71] Despite Save Nukoli'i's denial, the mayor cited the committee's actions as a reason for his decision not to seek reelection.

By that contentious era, government business had long outgrown the dimensions of the county building; it had spilled beyond the next-door annex as well. In 1975 the County leased the original Hale Kauai building a couple of blocks down Rice Street for its planning department, personnel office, and liquor commission. It found separate accommodations for other departments, such the office of elderly affairs, which was relocated to a rented house on 'Akahi Street. Those were temporary fixes, however, and the County deemed more space, in the form of a new county building, essential. Consultants and a community

The cornice and dentils that once provided a formal decorative band around the top portion of the building had been removed before this photo was taken in 1941. They were replicated and replaced during the extensive building restoration in 2010. Hawai'i State Archives

advisory committee suggested building on a section of the county lawn or purchasing land either near Kaua'i Community College at Puhi or by Vidinha stadium in the Līhu'e industrial district. An unexpected solution presented itself when Harry Weinberg offered his Lihue Shopping Center property for sale. After the requisite public discussions, disputes, and debate, the County purchased the property in 1987.

Today the 1914 structure is often referred to as the Historic County Building, and in 2010 it closed for a sixteen-month restoration (the Kaua'i Historical Society alone, housed in the former mayor's offices on the ground floor, remained in place during the process). Many of the changes—new wiring and plumbing—were invisible improvements. Others, such as the removal of window air conditioners and replacement of jalousies with reproductions of the original casement windows, reconstruction of the cornice and dentils that had been removed about 1940, restoration of the concrete floors to suggest marble

Kaua'i Historical Society annual meeting, 2007, in the foyer of the Historic County Building. Front row seated: Pat Griffin, Liberta Hussey-Albao, Frederick B. Wichman, Peter Dease, Randy Wichman, Joe Stoddard, Robert Schleck; second row standing: Frances Frazier, Sharon Cloud; seated Bette Layton, Gini Stoddard, David P. Scott, Victoria Wichman, Mal Dorhman; Third row: Jack Layton, Andy Bushnell, Marylou Bradley; Fourth row: Bob Stevens, Big John Kaua, Mary Requilman Kay Koike, Marie Fifield; Top row: Toya Carlson, Dave Carlson, Randy Rask. Kaua'i Historical Society surfaces, and painting of both interior and exterior walls, gave the building a renewed spirit of the historic place. Leaks in the skylight above the central entryway, which had bedeviled maintenance staff for decades, were finally fixed as well. During the restoration, Kauai County Council operations relocated to the former Hale Kauai building (now the Kauai Athletic Club) at Nāwiliwili Harbor. They returned on September 21, 2011, with a formal blessing and celebration.

Today the historic building, the oldest continuously used county building in Hawai'i, is headquarters for the seven-member County Council and its support services. The Kaua'i Historical Society, an organization founded in 1914, the same year that the building was completed, retains its lease on the ground-floor space and archives some of the county's old records. According to its 1995 by-laws, the society's purpose is to

> bring together those people interested in history, and especially in the history of Kaua'i and Ni'ihau, who will endeavor to: collect, study and preserve any material which may help to establish or illustrate its history; compile catalogues and indexes of the same; secure and preserve material and documents pertaining to its genealogies and biographies; investigate and recommend for permanent marking and preservation sites and objects significant to its history and culture; collect and preserve stories and traditions relating to the same; and generally, to cultivate an interest in and knowledge of its history folklore and custom; encourage historical research and inquiry, and disseminate historical information.

COUNTY ANNEX

In contrast to the hoopla surrounding the creation of the Historic County Building next door and later the courthouse behind it, the Kaua'i County Annex received so little attention when it was built as the Territorial Office Building that references to it now sometimes misdate its completion as 1934 rather than 1930. Even today, more than three-quarters of a century afterward, many on Kaua'i are only vaguely aware of its existence in the civic center.

When the 1929 legislature voted to provide funds for a headquarters in Līhu'e, it seemed unlikely that Governor Judd would actually release the money. Unexpectedly, after he withdrew a large appropriation for the Kapalama Basin in Honolulu, Judd did allot $35,000 late in the year for the Līhu'e project.

The Territorial Office Building, right, designed by Hart Wood, 1930. After the State Office Building was completed in 1969, ownership of this structure was transferred to the County, and it became known as the annex. Kaua'i Historical Society

Construction began in June, 1930, and the building opened late that November. After its completion the two-level building, with a ground floor and full lower level, housed the territorial land agent, tax assessor, fish and game warden, forester, and Board of Health personnel. Once the tax offices were completed in the building, the island's tax assessment and collection were centralized here, and other tax offices in the districts of Līhu'e, Kawaihau, Waimea, and Hanalei were shut down. In 1949 the island's first federal Social Security Administration office opened in the building's lower level.[72] When Hawai'i became America's fiftieth state ten years later, the building became known as the State Tax and Land Office.

The building's Mission Revival style, with its stucco walls, red-tiled roof, and decorative concrete grillwork, expresses an aesthetic distinctively different from the county building's neoclassical lines. It was designed by Hart Wood, familiar to Kauaians today as the designer of the nearby museum building. Many also know him as a charter member of

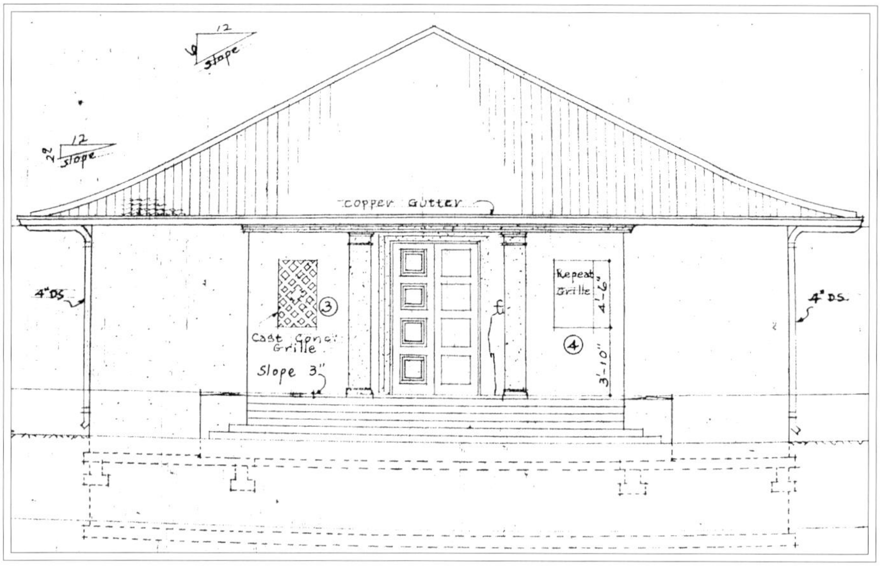

Hart Wood's Territorial Office Building elevation shows design details such as the concrete grilles and wooden double doors.
Kaua'i Historical Society

the Hawai'i chapter of the American Institute of Architects. He designed with C. W. Dickey the exquisite Alexander and Baldwin Building in downtown Honolulu, and he was one of the team of renowned architects who created Honolulu Hale (city hall) in the related Spanish Colonial Revival style. Mission Revival, which embraces a mix of spanish, Italian, and French elements, often with local adaptations such as a double-pitched roof, was clearly a dominant island fashion for public architecture of the period. The style redefined the landscape of the Honolulu's Capitol District during the 1920s; it defined the very concept of "Hawaiian-style" architecture. It is expressed in Honolulu's 1922 U.S. Post Office and Custom House, the 1927 YWCA and the Hawaiian Electric buildings, the 1928 Hawai'i State Art Museum (originally the Armed Forces YMCA), and the 1929 Honolulu Hale.

Mission Revival became so popular that in 1937, after the Territorial Office Building was complete and the courthouse behind it was in progress, the Kaua'i Board of Supervisors decided to change the old-fashioned lines of the county building by adding a steep, sloping tile roof to it so that it would "harmonize" with its new neighbors.[73] Preservationists who worked on a restoration of the historic building in the 1980s could be comforted that such an "improvement" never came to pass.

After the State completed its new headquarters at 'Eiwa and Hardy streets in 1969, it transferred ownership of this building to the County, which subsequently used it as an annex to its main county building next door. Several county departments have made their home in the building since then, the last before restoration being the Kaua'i Police Department Investigative Services Bureau. It vacated the premises when the new police station opened near the airport in October 2002.

The building remained unoccupied for six years, vacant except for the front porch, which sheltered groups of the homeless for a time. In 2008 the County began restoration of the building in consultation with Mason Architects, Inc., a firm that specializes in historic building preservation and restoration. (The same firm was contracted as restoration consultant for the Historic County Building.) Completed in 2009, the County Annex now serves as headquarters for the Kaua'i Elections Division.

The original front doors, which had been replaced by aluminum and glass doors, were reproduced and installed during the building's restoration.

LĪHU'E COURTHOUSE

The Līhu'e courthouse is a third 1930s-era example, with the post office and County Annex, of Hawaiianized Mission Revival architecture in central Līhu'e. The building was designed by Territorial Department of Public Works architect Harry Stewart, who also created the plans for the larger but similarly styled Hale 'Auhau (Department of the Hawai'i attorney general) on Queen Street in Honolulu. Funds for the courthouse were made available in September 1936 by the U.S. Public Works Administration, one of President Franklin Roosevelt's New Deal programs intended to put people to work and distribute enough money through the country to kick-start the economy—and maybe also to dampen a perceived threat of a proletarian uprising that more than a few citizens feared during the Depression.

The courthouse provides an opportunity to step back from the building—indeed, step away from the decision makers themselves—and try to "see through the glass darkly" at struggles of laborers during the long, difficult years of the Great Depression, because it was significant labor unrest that caused the construction delay of this house of justice. An oft-stated platitude maintains that Hawai'i didn't suffer during the Depression as did most of the states. Perhaps not. Certainly many of the sugar companies managed well enough during the 1930s, and extravagant new homes were constructed for Lihue Plantation manager Caleb Burns (Iliahi) and Grove Farm president Gaylord Wilcox (Kilohana). On the

'Umi Street, the Līhu'e Circuit Court, and the armory, 1941. Hawai'i State Archives

A child at work. Kaua'i Historical Society

other hand, a record number of businesses in the territory declared bankruptcy in 1932.[74] For labor, as late as 1937 there was no minimum wage law in the territory and brutally long hours for unskilled and semiskilled workers. Little protection existed for children, either. When American Factors sent a letter about the summer employment of school children on its plantations, Burns responded that about half of the 650 children working for the plantation were younger than fourteen years old.[75] He argued that the children "accomplish a great deal of work" over the summer vacation. And he added that the benefit was not to the plantation alone: "We might get some severe criticism from the children's parents if they are not permitted to work for us"—an unwitting hint at the level of plantation wages.

Newspaper editor Sanford Zalburg referred to the era as the "sweatshop days in Hawaii. Restaurant workers labored an average of sixty-four hours a week for thirteen cents an hour and no days off. Maids earned as little as five dollars a week. And there were men, desperate for work, who were willing to do hard labor for fifty cents a day." A National Labor Relations Board regional director who spent nine months investigating working conditions in Hawai'i labeled island workers in 1937 as "more slaves than free."[76] Unionization efforts had declined in the late 1920s and early 1930s, but they picked up later in the Depression decade after Congress passed the Wagner Act, which legalized workers' rights to join unions.

Hawai'i was also vulnerable to labor unrest beyond its shores. The West Coast maritime strike in the fall and winter of 1936–37 effectively delayed shipment of materials for construction of the Līhu'e courthouse long enough that Honolulu contractor John Hansen considered importing Japanese cement to use in the building.[77] In response to that strike and continuing efforts of Hawai'i longshoremen to unionize, Paul Townsley, president of the Kauai Chamber of Commerce, wrote a letter to Chamber members in September 1937 inviting them to a meeting to discuss the threat and devise preventive tactics:

> The present labor unrest on Kauai, is becoming increasingly serious due to the actions of a professional mainland labor agitator. His actions have really interfered with the normal movement of ships in our harbors and if continued, may result in a general strike. . . . These conditions [affect] every business organization and individual on the Island. . . . the time has come for the community to take some action toward ending these conditions.[78]

A dock workers strike began in Hilo the next February. It turned violent that August when police opened fire on protesters. No one died, but fifty or more people were shot, including four women and children. Two years later Lihue Plantation dock workers struck at Ahukini landing and terminal, precipitating the longest strike in Hawaiian history, 298 days. When the plantation attempted to divert cargo to Port Allen, longshoremen there initiated a sympathy strike. Since the majority of Port Allen longshoremen were Japanese and those at Ahukini were primarily Filipinos, the multiethnic strike signaled a sea change of labor solidarity in Hawai'i.[79]

By March 1937, after the West Coast strike was resolved, officials anticipated courthouse completion within five or six months.[80] The prediction was accurate for the unemployment office; that October, appropriately for the Depression years, it became the first department to open in the building. The circuit court quarters themselves weren't ready for occupancy until six months later. When completed, the stuccoed building, with its decorative under-gable tile vents, rounded rafters, and foliate concrete screening, received enthusiastic reviews. "As fine a building as the territory has," declared Robert

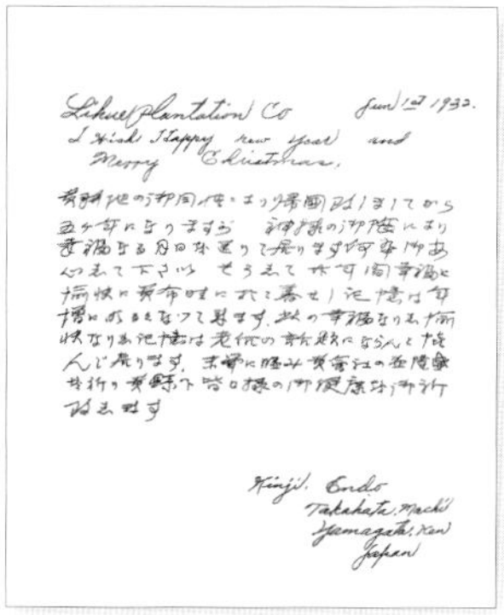
Lihue Plantation Co Jan 1st 1932.
I Wish Happy new year and Merry Christmas.

Kinji. Endo
Takahata Machi
Yamagata Ken
Japan

"Gentlemen. Five years have passed since my return to the land of my birth. I thank God for my health and the peaceful, pleasant days I am spending here. As the years go by—I recall the many years I have spent in Hawaii—many pleasant memories of the past come to me. They cheer me up as I spend my remaining days quietly and contently at home. I offer my prayers for your company's prosperity, and that health and happiness be bestowed upon everyone under your care. Sincerely yours, Kinji Endo Takahata Machi Yamagata Ken Japan." Periodic strife characterized management-labor relations, but hostility was not universal, as this Kinji Endo letter testifies. Hawaiian Sugar Planters' Association archives

The West Coast maritime strike that had delayed construction of the Līhu'e courthouse was followed by a bitter dock strike in Hilo in 1938, pictured here. Two years later Lihue Plantation workers at Ahukini Landing walked off the job in an attempt to gain wage parity with their West Coast colleagues; they were joined in a remarkable show of solidarity by workers at Port Allen. Hawai'i State Archives

Kuhns, territorial inspector of public works.[81] From the projecting entry lanai, Nāwiliwili could be seen beyond the canefields and the homes stretching down Rice Street. Inside, the law library occupied the space to the left of the entry, with room for 25,000 volumes. Court clerks worked in the office to the right. The entry hall led into a central octagonal rotunda, from which corridors radiated, leading to the Fifth Circuit Court courtrooms and offices for judges, the county attorney, court reporter, probation officers, and bailiff.

Eventually the Līhu'e District Court chambers and personnel were relocated to this building from elsewhere in the civic center, the library was removed to the basement, and space was made for newer services and judicial subdivisions. The original, massive, period-lighting fixture that once brightened the rotunda is rumored to have disappeared at auction after being replaced by 1970s-era frosted white globes, a harsh contrast to the warm wood ceiling with its great, intersecting beams that complement the fortress-like doors.

The boot scrape on each side of the courthouse entry steps served as more than a useful decorative detail when the building was constructed.

The courthouse in 2004, before the judiciary complex opened near the airport.

The building's life as a courthouse ended when the massive state judiciary complex near the airport opened in 2005. Between 2007 and 2009 the building was used for transitional housing, with portable showers for the boarders constructed on the lawn. It has remained vacant since that project ended. The long-term plan is to utilize the building as office space for other state government personnel.[82]

HOUSING THE KEEPERS OF THE PEACE

The shell of a building that now languishes across ʻUmi Street from the courthouse was once among the most appealing headquarters inhabited by a police force on a tropical island anywhere in the world. Designed by Honolulu architect Guy Rothwell, the floor plan featured a fountain at the center of an open-air courtyard, around which were positioned offices, evidence room, armory, photographic dark room, radio room, meeting space, and other areas necessary to fulfill law enforcement duties on Kauaʻi. The opening of the facility in 1953 not only enabled the police to move out of their noisy, overcrowded space on the second floor of the county building, it centralized the seventy-person force, eliminating (at

In 2013 the former Līhu'e police station, now owned by the State, has been shuttered for more than a decade.

least for a few years) district stations around the island, with the exception of a substation at Waimea.

The sheriff in 1953 was chosen locally, a protocol established during the formation of county governments in 1905. Historically, the Hawaiian monarch had appointed both a marshal, or high sheriff, for the kingdom and a governor for each of the kingdom's divisions (one of which was Kaua'i and Ni'ihau). The marshal, "with the approval" of the governor, appointed the island sheriff.[83] After the Bayonet Constitution, in which King Kalakaua lost much of his power, an Act to Abolish the Office of Governor on each island passed in 1888 without the approval of the king, and the marshal then appointed the sheriffs with the approval of the kingdom's attorney general.[84] Once responsibility was transferred to the county in the early twentieth century, the high sheriff of Kaua'i became an elective position. William Henry Rice easily won the top spot in 1905, a victory he would repeat seventeen times over the next thirty-six years. Many of the deputy sheriffs of the five districts (Waimea, Kōloa, Līhu'e, Kawaihau, and Hanalei) held their positions long-

Kaua'i policemen at Nāwiliwili, late nineteenth century. Kaua'i Historical Society

term as well. Several—Crowell in Waimea, Blake in Kōloa, and Sheldon in Kawaihau—are names recognized multigenerationally in police, government, and legal circles.

As with most aspects of life during World War II, law enforcement dramatically changed after the bombing of Pearl Harbor in 1941. The military moved quickly to institute martial law. Attorney Philip Rice was named to fill in as sheriff for his ailing brother while a new system was formed, a gubernatorially appointed police commission whose responsibilities included choosing the sheriff. Before war's end, however, power to appoint members of the Kaua'i police commission had shifted back to the county, first to county supervisors, currently to the mayor. The seven-person police commission continues to hold responsibility for hiring and firing the sheriff, now called the chief of police.

Crime on Kaua'i includes the usual mix of the mundane and tragic, the vicious and the comical. History records the typical array of thefts, "estray" cows, fights (and the occasional murder), labor unrest, and periodic political corruption. In 1923 a raid on a

Sheriff William Henry Rice sits with two unidentified employees in his office on the second floor of the county building. The hanging light fixture, top left, remains in the historic building, but the spittoon at Rice's feet is long gone. Kauaʻi Museum

gambling party in Keālia exposed the latter issue when participants claimed that they were supposed to be "immune" from arrest that day, protected by a promised 10 percent earnings payoff to police. A deputy sheriff was charged with accepting bribes and four officers with assault in connection with the shooting of a bystander. All were ultimately cleared—insufficient evidence—but not before accusations that "politics," specifically an attempt to smear High Sheriff Rice prior to upcoming elections, had been bandied about through the community.[85]

Even as the Keālia events unfolded, another gambling raid took place in Līhuʻe on July 11, 1923. According to the following week's issue of the *Garden Island:*

> Wednesday, last week was payday in Lihue and money was plentiful in the camps. A large game was in progress, but was left undisturbed until after the movies were out, when the ful[l] police force with one full swoop made

Aloha, law enforcement Kaua'i style: the police department's Hawaiian Troupe performed with a dancer to serenade visitors at the Līhu'e airport in the 1950s. Mike Ashman, Kaua'i Historical Society

> a descent on the unsuspecting wooers of Dame Fortune, with the surprising result that 24 gamesters were landed at points of guns. Each and every mother's son was made to pony up $10 as bail and were allowed to depart hence.[86]

The same newspaper issue bantered during the dry years of the 1920s, after the Eighteenth Amendment of the U.S. Constitution made alcohol illegal: "One celestial bearing the cognomen of Ah Wai, fell into the clutches of J. F. Bettencourt Jr., the prohibition sleuth, and was found to have five gallons of delectable oke in the house. The ante was raised and bail furnished in the tidy sum of $150."

Neither gambling parties nor journalistic playfulness ended in the 1920s. Longtime *Garden Island* reporter Georgia Mossman, who covered the police department news for over twenty years, added more than a little humor to many entries from the department's blotter. In 2000, Mossman published a collection of her work in *Police Blotter Kaua'i*

Style. In it she remembers the late 1970s effort to break up gambling around the island. One Sunday police raided the old Kealia Camp, "where about 200 people had gathered. They had set up two food booths, and were getting the chickens ready to fight and the cards shuffled so the monte game could begin. Police broke up the game and suggested everyone just go home peacefully and watch the basketball game on TV." The game dutifully ended, but that afternoon, in another raid near Anahola, police discovered many of the same gamblers patronizing the same food booths they'd dispersed at Keālia that morning. Fred DeBusca, the Lihue Plantation mill's chief engineer, recalls a similar raid in the Isenberg tract in Līhu'e, when he and Kauai Stores manager Pat Cannon had to hightail it through chicken coops and underbrush to slip down into the valley and escape embarrassing detection by Kaua'i's finest. Attention eventually turned to public officials, who had seemingly held immunity from illicit betting laws: in December, 1978, during the annual Christmas party in the Kaua'i County Council offices, police raided the gambling game in progress there, reportedly a common sport up to that time.[87]

The island's increasing population in the late 1960s and 1970s, combined with additional layers of bureautic paperwork, added personnel duties, and new technology, cramped quarters enough in the police station to prompt a redesign. In 1973 the beautiful courtyard and fountain succumbed to the need for office space. That fix didn't last long, though. Department divisions were gradually scattered around town. The Investigative Services Bureau was relocated to the county annex; Civil Defense moved to the basement of the county building; prosecuting attorneys were housed in portables behind the Kaua'i War Memorial Convention Hall.

Eventually, the County's attention turned to constructing a new facility. A 65,000-square-foot building was constructed on eight-and-a-half acres of former cane land at the fringe of town near the airport. The $17 million-plus building was designed by Architects Hawaii, Ltd., and built by Shioi Construction. Groundbreaking for Ka Hale Maka'i o Kaua'i, "the House of the Kaua'i Protectors," took place in 2001. The facility was dedicated in October 2002, and the Kaua'i Police Department, Civil Defense, and the prosecuting attorney moved in. Only automobile licensing, once part of the old police station, has remained in the heart of Līhu'e at the civic center, where Woolworth's once housed its fabric department.

Today the old police station is owned by the State of Hawai'i. According to former Department of Accounting and General Services district manager Stanley Doi, the County sold the building in a complex land transfer to raise funds for the purchase of the Lihue

The massive new police station opened in 2002 near the Līhu'e airport.

Shopping Center.[88] Since the police department's move to new quarters, the building has remained vacant, but the State is considering the feasibility of future use of the lot as a multistory parking structure for state workers.

LIHUE HEALTH CENTER

In 1920 life expectancy at birth averaged forty-five years in Hawai'i; by 1950, a mere generation later, it had catapulted above sixty-eight years.[89] Both in the islands and on the mainland, that most phenomenal lifespan gain in perhaps all recorded history was primarily accomplished not by exceptional leaps in medical or surgical innovation but through concentrated efforts in the field of public health to improve standards of hygiene and nutrition. The resulting drop in maternal, neonatal, and childhood mortality would have been unimaginable a few years earlier.

Today it is routine, a "commonsense" practice, for doctors to avoid the spread of infection by washing their hands between, for instance, handling a corpse and delivering a baby. Such was not always the case, however, and the consequence was untold misery and death from puerperal fever, tetanus, and other bacterially transmitted diseases. Not until the late nineteenth century did a key weapon—recognition of the germ theory of disease—

Mothers with their children at a well-baby clinic, ca. 1925. Grove Farm Homestead Museum

emerge in the battle to combat those and many other killer illnesses. Unfortunately, the discovery came too late to save much of the Hawaiian population.

In the century after the arrival of Westerners in 1778, Hawaiʻi provided a tragic showcase for the effects of contagion. Despite the best efforts of both traditional and Western healing practices, epidemics of newly introduced diseases decimated the indigenous people. Venereal disease, smallpox, cholera, diphtheria, measles, whooping cough, typhoid fever, and flu created calamity. On Kauaʻi the population plummeted from an estimated 54,000 when Capt. James Cook and his crew arrived to less than 5,000 in 1872.[90]

The Hawaiian monarchs did not stand idly by as their people perished. They made numerous efforts to reverse the combination of high disease and low birth rates. In 1850, King Kamehameha III and his Privy Council established the kingdom's first board of health in an attempt to combat epidemics and increase sanitary measures (the latter mainly through developing reliable sources of potable water). Three years later, a smallpox epidemic killed 30 percent of the population of O'ahu. James Marshall wrote to his father from his home at Koamalu that on O'ahu, "the accounts of the ravages of the small pox & the neglect & sufferings of some of the victims have been shocking."[91] He noted that Kaua'i had been "largely spared" the epidemic, with a total of only nine deaths, they being "confined to those who brot it from Oahu." In the letter Marshall credited the "superior climate" of Kaua'i as well as "the efficient measures adopted by us (Bond, Smith & myself, commissioners with almost absolute powers)." He might also have attributed the low incidence of the disease to Kaua'i's relative remoteness compared to the other islands in the chain and the frequent travel among them. After the epidemic the government quickly instituted a kingdom-wide program of mandatory vaccination to deter future outbreaks.[92]

Kauikeaouli, King Kamehameha III, established the first board of health in Hawai'i, 1850. A. T. Agate, *Narrative of the United States Exploring Expedition*

Other devastating scourges were on the way. A case of Hansen's disease, then known as leprosy, was reported in Kōloa in 1835, and it grew into an epidemic by 1863. At the end of the century bubonic plague visited every major port in the island chain. And the continuing lack of rudimentary sanitation as well as basic nutritional needs sustained Hawai'i's appalling infant mortality rate, nearly a quarter of all births in 1920.[93]

In the 1910s, however, a champion emerged in the Līhu'e District whose influence would alter the shape of twentieth-century health care on Kaua'i. Mabel Wilcox (1882–1978) was the youngest of six children born to Sam and Emma Wilcox. At an early age she resolved to become a nurse, and in 1911 she graduated from the Johns Hopkins Hospital Nursing School with specialized training in both clinical nursing and public health. Two years later she was appointed territorial tuberculosis nurse in the visiting nurses service, the first such position on Kaua'i. After World War I, she became the first field supervisor for public health nurses under the Territorial Board of Health.

Tuberculosis, or consumption as it was also known, was a dread disease in both Asia and Europe during the nineteenth and early twentieth centuries. Though TB was especially prevalent in overcrowded, urban slums, the mortality rate in Hawai'i during the early years of the last century was even higher than on much of the mainland.[94] To identify both active cases and carriers of the disease, "Mabel crisscrossed the island, making home visits to search out the unusually tenacious disease and talking with infected, highly contagious persons. In so doing, she mapped a largely uncharted public health terrain and acquainted herself well with the residents of Kauai."[95] In her efforts to stem the spread of the disease—and the death rate from it—Mabel successfully convinced her aunt and uncle,

Mabel I. Wilcox at her desk in the cottage she used as her public health office on the grounds of Grove Farm. Grove Farm Homestead Museum

Emma and Albert Wilcox, to donate funds for Mahelona, the TB hospital in Kapaʻa, and she became its first general manager. In the 1930s, with her brother Gaylord, sister Elsie, and others, she would also be instrumental in founding the island's first private, nonprofit general hospital, the G. N. Wilcox Memorial Hospital.

She also utilized her membership in the Mokihana Club to expand public health efforts, especially in the arena of maternal and infant care. The club's Public Health Committee was established in 1916 with Wilcox as chair, and it quickly acted to hire a district nurse, who was invited to work within the public schools. After the discovery of widespread tooth decay in children, the Mokihana Club contracted a dentist on a part-time basis. The club was pleased to report in April 1918 that, in addition to considerable dental work, 4,236 children had received physical examinations. Treatment was given for 504 skin problems, 123 eye cases, and 1923 emergencies such as "broken arms, tubercular pneumonia, grippe, measles, cuts," as well as a variety of other nursing ministrations.[96] Mabel Wilcox's efforts at both the Board of Health and the Mokihana Club, combined with

ABOVE
A Kauaʻi public health nurse in the field. Grove Farm Homestead Museum

Mabel Wilcox is standing in the third row, far right, among the island's midwives and territorial public health nurses. Takasawa, Grove Farm Homestead Museum

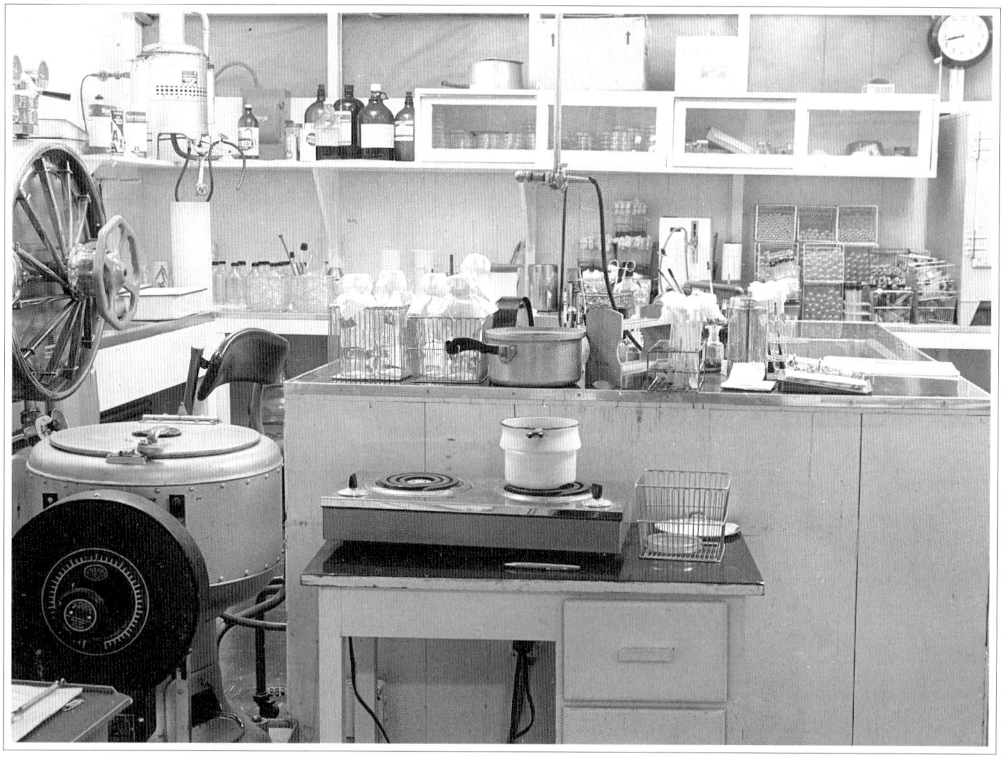

The Department of Health laboratory before the current complex was built.
Hawaiʻi State Archives

initiatives of the Hawaiian Sugar Planters Association, raised health standards considerably; by 1927, Kauaʻi led the way with the lowest infant mortality rate in Hawaiʻi.[97]

For the first dozen years, public health nurses met in Wilcox's cottage office at Grove Farm. In 1930, when the Territorial Office Building was completed, the public health offices were housed in the two rooms in the northeast corner of the building. Over the years, as Department of Health duties expanded, so too did its need for space. Hawaiʻi's shift from territory to state in 1959 necessitated an entire building dedicated to the now highly centralized public health department. Architects Bradley and Wong, Inc., designed the one-story Lihue Health Center perpendicular to ʻUmi Street on land adjacent to the police station. The mansard-roofed, concrete-masonry-unit building was constructed by Kauai Builders, Ltd., and dedicated in April 1966. Bradley Wong Sjoberg and Associates teamed with Kauai Builders again in 1972 to complete the adjoining two-story annex in the same style as the original building, creating an L-shaped configuration with parking in front.

After World War II, core public health activities addressing tuberculosis, neonatal

The first increment of the Lihue Health Center was constructed perpendicular to ʻUmi Street, with parking in front. The new convention hall can be seen in the background at right. Hawaiʻi State Archives

care, and student care continued. The nurses also performed outreach tasks on both Kauaʻi and Niʻihau that are little remembered today. Nellie Hiyane, a Hawaiʻi Island native who was attending school in Texas when World War II erupted, arrived on Kauaʻi late in 1945 to work as a public health nurse; she remained a Department of Health employee for almost thirty years. Hiyane vividly remembered one difficult assignment shortly after she arrived. When a tidal wave inundated the north shore of Kauaʻi on April 1, 1946, she and two other public health nurses received orders to visit the wrecked communities of Hāʻena, Wainiha, and Kalihiwai. There they performed the heart-wrenching duty of gathering and preparing the bodies of at least fourteen people who had perished in the tsunami, including several children. Another of her "back-in-the-old-days" career activities was to accompany the sheriff on inspections of houses of prostitution to assure their cleanliness and compliance with the rules and regulations of the times. Nearer the end of her career, Hiyane accompanied the sanitation department to perform similar inspections of Taylor Camp, the makeshift hippie utopian community that bloomed at Hāʻena for several years in the late 1960s and '70s.[98]

By the 1970s, traditional public health department activities had expanded. Sanitation (including clean water, clean air, sewage control, restaurant, and related industries),

A duty of public health nurses in the 1960s and '70s was site inspections of Taylor Camp. Alpin Hamilton, standing above the "wipe your feet" notice on the house door, was only three when her family settled in the free-wheeling hippie community. John Wehrheim

vector control (especially rats and mosquitoes, carriers of diseases such as typhus and dengue fever), nutrition, and communicable diseases remained important aspects of public health activities. In addition, mental health and developmental disabilities programs became part of departmental duties. After the introduction of the vaccines to prevent polio, measles, mumps, and whooping cough, mandatory immunization for school children became law in Hawai'i. The State Department of Health hired epidemiology specialists in each county to assure that every student was vaccinated against those diseases.

Retired Kaua'i epidemiology specialist Sally Jo Manea remembers that in the 1970s Hawai'i also pioneered the investigation, recording, and partner notification of sexually transmitted diseases such as gonorrhea and syphilis.[99] The department's systematic approach to combating those STDs greatly assisted its efforts against HIV/AIDS that began in the mid-1980s, and the island has remained "ahead of the rest of the country in integrating

The second increment of the Lihue Health Center, pictured here in 2013, was completed in 1972.

infectious-disease testing and prevention," according to a senior U.S. Centers for Disease Control and Prevention official.[100] "Kaua'i has continued to lead the way in prevention efforts against HIV/AIDS, hepatitis and STDs," the official reported in December 2009, a success achieved in part through a unique partnership between the health department and community-based service organizations Mālama Pono, the Kaua'i YWCA, and Kaua'i Hospice.

The population's major health problems in the early part of the twenty-first century have evolved from infant mortality, infectious disease, and acute illness to lifestyle-related chronic diseases and degenerative illness. The public health department has responded by increasing its focus on needs of the elderly as well as on issues such as smoking, diabetes, and obesity.[101] After the 2001 attacks that destroyed the World Trade Center in New York, another set of tasks began: the Kauai District Health Office, through the State Department of Health, in coordination with the federal government, instituted its Bioterrorism Preparedness Program to plan for a potential enemy attack with biological or chemical weapons such as smallpox, anthrax, or ricin.

THE COUNTY LAWN

The county lawn—with the county building, annex, and courthouse—was placed on the National Register of Historic Places in 1981 as the Lihue Civic Center Historic District. The lawn, a park technically owned by the County Council but maintained by the administration-controlled parks department, contains almost as much history as the

The *Garden Island* reported in July 1914 that two rows of palms had been planted from Rice Street to and around the ends of the county building. By 1930 the graceful palms provided an elegant frame for the entryway to the building. Kaua'i Museum

structures that surround it. Alternately treasured as a stately village green and coveted as vacant real estate, the area has managed to remain relatively unencumbered for a century. From the beginning it provided a context for, lent dignity to, and highlighted the importance of the county building. Shortly after the building was completed, an alley of royal palms was planted through the center of the lawn from the street to the building's entry, providing a framed view of and grand passageway to the seat of government.

Actually, when the County purchased the five acres from Lihue Plantation in 1912 to create a government building, a roughly 96- by 65-square-foot rectangle of land in the southwest corner of the plot was excluded from the sale. It was owned by William Hyde Rice, and on it were two businesses. A harness and uphostery shop owned by J. P. Alohikea, who worked for Rice for many years, occupied one portion of the lot.[102] Born on Maui, he had learned his trade at Schumann Carriage Co. in Honolulu, then moved to Kaua'i at the turn of the century. In 1914, when Rice renovated the corner plot, Alohikea moved the entire building to what is now Kalena Street and went into business for himself.

The second building housed a butcher shop run by Rice's third son Arthur, who also

served as county treasurer until he left for Honolulu in 1912 to pursue a career in business. (Archaeology students, unaware of the building's first use, were surprised to unearth bones when they excavated there in the 1990s.) Two years later the modest frame structure, with a front lanai spanning the building, was remodeled and converted into offices for attorney S. E. Hannestad.[103] Within a year Hannestad had departed the islands for Pennsylvania, and the structure assumed the identity it would retain for the next three decades: the law offices of Rice's youngest son, Philip.

In 1938, when the County badly wanted the 6,238-square-foot plot (one seventh of an acre) to complete its civic center plan, Wm. Hyde Rice, Ltd., offered to sell it for the princely sum of $8,500, or $1.36 per square foot (as compared with $0.18 per square foot for the post office property across the street that Lihue Plantation had sold to the federal government two years earlier). The deal was finalized in January 1945, and the Līhu'e District Court immediately moved into the premises. The former district courtroom, on the second floor of the county building where the Kaua'i County Council now meets, was placed in service as the police department's radio equipment room.[104]

On July 4, 1917, Mrs. Charles Rice, who headed the Red Cross auxiliary on Kaua'i, utilized the W. H. Rice-owned building at the corner of the county lawn to hold a membership drive to aid in the World War I relief effort. For most of its existence this building was used as the law office of her brother-in-law, Philip Rice. Kaua'i Museum

Prior to the Rice law office's demolition in 1946, the old wooden building at the corner of the county lawn served briefly as the district court. Kaua'i Historical Society

That attempts have been made over the years to build on the greenspace are hardly surprising. Nature abhors a vacuum, and for some a couple of acres of grass and a few palm trees in a tight real estate environment constitute emptiness awaiting fulfillment. In 1936 the territorial superintendent of public works, Louis Cain, proposed that half of the lawn be used for the circuit courthouse, with the post office erected on the other half. The community outcry was overwhelming.[105] In response, the Kaua'i Chamber of Commerce Public Improvements Committee developed an ultimately successful civic center plan that retained the lawn by locating the post office across the street and the courthouse behind the Territorial Office Building.[106] As recently as the 1980s, the grounds in front of and around the Historic County Building were suggested as a possibility for county facilities expansion before the Lihue Shopping Center site became available.

Since statehood, several monuments have found homes on the county lawn. The first, a five-storied stone pagoda and companion stone lantern, arrived in May 1961 as a goodwill gift from Japan. The two pieces are reproductions of originals in the Gotokuji Zen Temple at Hikone City, Shiga Prefecture. The gift marked the seventy-fifth anniversary of the 1886

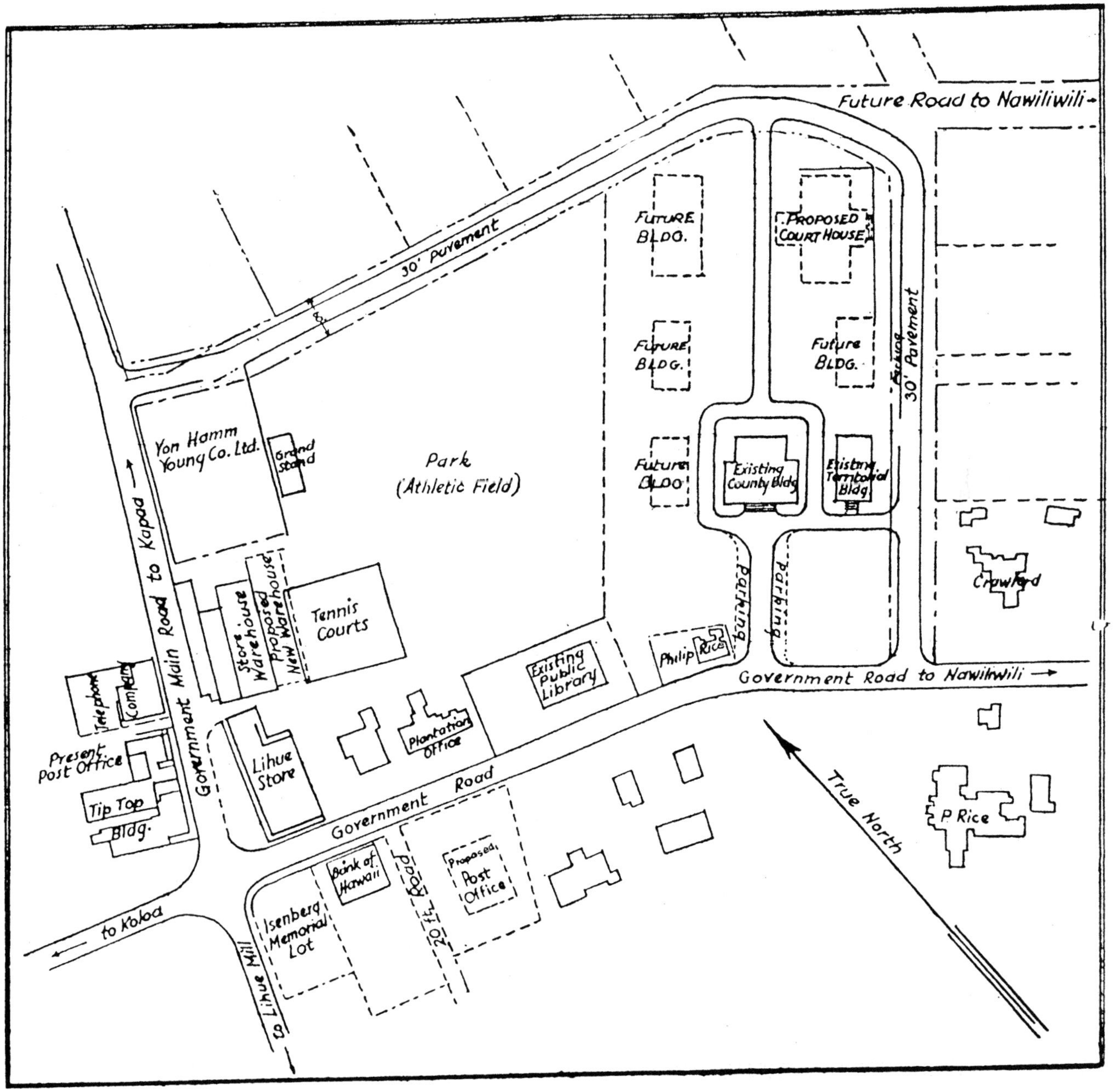

The Chamber of Commerce reacted strongly against a plan to construct the post office and courthouse on either side of the county lawn. The organization instead proposed the locations ultimately chosen for the two buildings, along with possibilities for future additions as county activities expanded. Their descriptive map, published in the *Garden Island,* shows the layout of the town core as it existed in October 1936. *Garden Island* archives

immigration agreement between Japan and the Kingdom of Hawai'i that resulted in the importation of 200,000 Japanese laborers by 1924. The pagoda and lantern were shipped aboard the Japan Nautical College training steamer *Ginga Maru* and formally presented to the people of Kaua'i by the vessel's captain, Hiroshi Orihara.[107]

Although the 1886 agreement provided the impetus for Hawai'i's massive period of Japanese migration, it was not the first attempt to import contract laborers from the Land of the Rising Sun. In 1868 the British ship *Scioto* brought 141 men, six women, and two boys to test their desirability as agricultural workers in Hawai'i. The Japanese government's unhappiness with that first, experimental transaction led to the eighteen-year delay in the two countries' conclusion of a formal agreement. To commemorate the centennial of the first exchange, celebrations across Hawai'i took place in 1968. On Kaua'i the Emperor Hirohito's younger son, Prince Hitachi, and his wife Hanako spent eight days in June participating in various commemorative events. The princess herself unveiled the memorial clock tower on the county lawn, which had been paid for and donated to the Kaua'i community by the island's Centennial Committee.

At the southeast corner of the lawn stands a statue of Philippines liberation hero José Protacio Rizal Mercado y Alonso Realonda. A bust of Rizal, made of bronze-covered, reinforced cement, had been installed there and dedicated on June 19, 1979, the anniversary of the martyred freedom fighter's birth, but it was destroyed by vandals the following April, shortly before a scheduled visit to Kaua'i by Philippine president Ferdinand Marcos. First lady Imelda Marcos, who had been instrumental in donating the first sculpture, also donated the second, a full-length statue. According to Alfredo Villanueva, who was Kauai Filipino Community Council president when the statue was relocated to the lawn, that happened because educator and community leader Rosalina Arzadon had visited the Philippines and met Mrs. Marcos. After the first statue was destroyed, Mrs. Marcos sent the second. It was housed in the lobby of the county building for awhile before being moved to the lawn in 1984.[108]

An additional memorial to the many Kaua'i citizens whose ancestors hail from the Philippines was installed during the 1979 celebrations. It is the rarely noticed narra *(Pterocarpus indicus),* the national tree of the Philippines, which is prized for its fine, furniture-quality hardwood. The narra grows directly in front of the county

OPPOSITE PAGE
The 250 officers and men of the Japanese navy destroyer *Harusame* provided an escort during the week-long celebration of the 1968 centennial of the first Japanese importation of plantation workers to Hawai'i. Harvey Tam, Kaua'i Historical Society

Prince Hitachi and his wife Hanako took part in the dedication ceremony of the Japanese immigration memorial monument, 1968. Harvey Tam, Kaua'i Historical Society

Pā'ū riders. Harvey Tam, Kaua'i Historical Society

annex doorway between two later-planted monkeypods.

Finally, a century of Puerto Rican immigration to Hawai'i was marked in 2000. A granite plaque on a concrete and moss rock-veneer column near the Japanese monuments commemorates that event.

The lawn is a quieter place than it once was, when it served as the terminus for so many of the victory commemorations, annual Kamehameha Day parades, and other celebrations. The Brown Bags to Stardom lunchtime performances held there in the 1980s are long gone as well. But the lawn still fills with people on the first Friday of each December, who come to enjoy the exuberant Lights on Rice Parade as it wends its way from the Vidinha Stadium parking lot to the county building grounds. Demonstrators also occasionally gather there to protest or defend a particularly controversial issue. And the lawn continues to give space and a pride of place to the century-old seat of the Kaua'i county government.

The full-length statue of martyred Philippine liberation hero José Rizal was moved from the interior of the county building to its present location on the lawn in 1984. Harvey Tam, Kaua'i Historical Society

FOUR

BEYOND THE CIVIC CENTER

Everything is in a state of flux,
including the status quo.

—**Robert Byrne,** writer, billiard player, amateur stage magician

Commercial enterprises now line both sides of Rice Street *makai* of the civic center, but for a significant portion of the past century much of the area was residential and pastoral.

William Hyde Rice with Kolohaiole at the doorway of the thatched house on the grounds of Rice's home, Hale Nani. William J. Senda, Mary Moragne Cooke

Before Liliuokalani was deposed in 1893, the Hawaiian kingdom's monarch appointed governors for the separate islands. The last governor of Kaua'i and Ni'ihau served for a year, from February 8, 1892, to February 28, 1893, during the queen's short reign. His name was William Hyde Rice (1846–1924), and he lived with his wife Mary Waterhouse and their eight children on an estate across the road from the county building and its lawn. It was called Hale Nani, "Beautiful Home."

HALE NANI BUSINESS TRACT

William Hyde Rice as a young man. Grove Farm Homestead Museum

Willie, as he was known to friends, Wile Laiki to Hawaiians, and "The Grand Old Man of Kauai" to distant admirers, was the only son of missionary William Harrison Rice, who had moved to Kaua'i in 1854 to manage the budding Lihue Plantation. The younger Rice entertained an early passion for the saddle. Fifty years after Civil War veteran Zephaniah S. Spalding's 1867 visit to Kaua'i, he would still recount his memory of the twenty-one-year-old Rice as a remarkable horseman who (like many Hawaiians described in that era by intrepid adventurer Isabella Bird) "could pick up a coin while riding at full speed [and who] gave me my first experience at 'cattle driving.'"[1] Even at the age of seventy-one, Rice would describe his favorite recreation as "wild cattle hunting."[2] Rice's love of livestock developed into a lifelong business breeding, importing, and exporting cattle and horses. Between 1867 and 1869 he had worked for Lihue Plantation's ranch, and he later owned stock in and was for some years director of the plantation. In 1872 he married Mary Waterhouse, and he bought the Kīpū lands from Princess Ruth Keelikolani. There, he started his own company, the Lihue Ranch, and eventually became the largest livestock dealer on Kaua'i.[3]

Two other passions occupied William Hyde Rice: politics and the Hawaiian language. In 1870 he became the youngest member of the Hawai'i House of Representatives and served for several sessions before his appointment to the governorship of Kaua'i in 1892.[4] He then became a senator of the Republic of Hawai'i during the 1895–1898 sessions. Of the intricate Hawaiian language, William Hyde Rice was an adept speaker and a scholar. For over half a century he collected Hawaiian *mo'olelo*, sometimes with the advice and learning of Paul Kanoa (ca. 1802–1885), who served as governor of Kaua'i between 1846 and 1877 and whose home was at Niumalu.[5] During the last ten years of his life, Rice translated those manuscripts into a book, *Hawaiian Legends,* which was originally published by Bishop Museum in 1923.

When Hawai'i became a U.S. territory in 1900, Rice handed his sons the political

OPPOSITE PAGE

Rice was a noted horseman and breeder of horses and cattle. Alfred Mitchell, Kaua'i Museum

W. H. Rice and his family ca. 1897. Front: Charles, Anna Charlotte (whom everyone knew as Daisy), Philip. Middle: wife Mary Waterhouse, Emily, William Hyde, Mary. Back: Arthur (inset), William Henry and his wife Mary Girvin, Harold. Hobey Goodale

torch and retired from public life. They accepted it eagerly. "For the Rice family, politics was not an obligation," *Hawaii Pono* author Lawrence Fuchs observed, "it was joy."[6] William Henry Rice (1874–1945) became deputy sheriff of Kaua'i in 1900, was subsequently elected sheriff when the county system was established in 1905, and retained the county's top law enforcement post for the nearly forty years. Charles Atwood Rice (1876–1964) won election to the Territorial House of Representatives in 1905, where he served until 1913, then became a territorial senator, a position he held until 1938. Arthur Hyde Rice (1878–1955) was elected county treasurer in 1905 but left Kaua'i a few years later to establish himself as a Honolulu businessman. He did not seek further elective office, although he accepted appointments to the Territorial Board of Agriculture and Forestry and the Public Utilities Commission. Harold Waterhouse Rice (1883–1962) moved to Maui in 1906 and served as a territorial senator from 1918 to 1934, then spent three years on the Maui County Board of Supervisors. Philip LaVergne Rice (1886–1974) dipped his toe into the political pond, but after being trounced by his opponent in a 1924 bid to become the Hawai'i delegate to Congress he settled into a law career in Līhu'e. In 1943 he donned judicial robes for the Fifth Circuit Court on Kaua'i and was later appointed to the Territorial Supreme Court.

An early view of Hale Nani and the Rice family. A. A. Montano, Kaua'i Museum

He is distinguished as the last chief justice of the Territory, 1956–1959. William Hyde and Mary Waterhouse also had three daughters: Mary (1880–1923), who married W. H. Scott; Anna Charlotte (1882–1948), who married Ralph Wilcox; and Emily (1889–1975), who married Lloyd Sexton.

The Rices originally settled in a simple cottage at what was then the edge of the hamlet of Līhu'e. They later built Hale Nani, which the *Pacific Coast Commercial Record* applauded in 1892 as

> the most elegant residence on Kauai. It is superbly situated on the side of the Nawiliwili Valley, and commands a most delightful view of the valley beneath, and the mountains in the distance. The house is approached through a magnificent avenue of Royal Palms, and is embowered in beautiful shade trees and other tropical foliage. A stately banyan spreads its branches over the front yard, and furnishes ample shade for two dozen people. Most of the trees in the yard were set out by Mrs. Rice's own hands, and are with her a matter of especial pride.[7]

Granddaughter Edith Rice Plews recalled the home as a sprawling, one-story, wood-framed building that was sand-painted in a local technique almost lost today. A porte cochere led to a large lanai furnished with *lauhala* mats and rocking chairs and decorated with baskets of Boston fern. The interior was described in a 1972 *Honolulu* magazine feature based on her memories: "There was a large living room with ohia floors covered with Persian carpets and furnished in mahogany and oak, a spacious dining and music room, two kitchens, pantries and six bedrooms."[8] In addition to the main house, there was a grass house that was a favorite of the Rice grandchildren and two guest cottages, one of which had been William Hyde and Mary Rice's first home. Ethel Damon wrote in *Koamalu* that there was no public hall in Līhu'e until the Rices erected a small YMCA building in 1890 "on the grounds of their Hale Nani home, a little makai of the house."[9] A 1934 map also indicates a tennis court, milk shed, and office on the property.

Hospitality at Hale Nani was renowned. Victorian traveler Isabella Bird stayed there in the 1870s, as did Queen Liliuokalani—along with several members of her royal party—during her grand tour of the islands after her accession to the Hawaiian throne in 1891. Granddaughter Juliet Rice Wichman remembered that there were "always guests—often family and friends, sometimes strangers off the weekly interisland boats. Friends from Waimea or Hanalei on occasion left their horses with Grandpa while they were away and on their return to Kauai, set off homeward after an early, but lavish breakfast."[10]

Upon William Hyde Rice's death, ownership of Hale Nani passed to one of his daughters, Anna Rice Wilcox, although his youngest son Philip continued to live there and walk across the street to his law offices in front of the county building until World War II. After the bombing of Pearl Harbor, the military set up radar stations around the islands; Philip and his wife Flora moved out of Hale Nani and lent the estate to the military effort. Between July 1942 and January 1944, Hale Nani became the base of operations for the Women's Air Raid Defense radar plotting station on Kaua'i. Supervised and recruited by Flora at the request of Brig. Gen. Howard C. Davidson, Army Air Defense commander, about fifty young island women, ages seventeen to thirty-four, were recruited as WARDs. These "shuffleboard pilots," as they were called, spent two months in intense training at Lihue Grammar School to learn "plotting, filtering and how to vector Barking Sands airfield's Curtiss fighters." To protect the grounds and the personnel, the estate was surrounded by barbed wire, "and now an armed sentry stood at the gate once guarded by Hawaiian *pohaku kupua* (sacred stones)." Everyone entering or leaving was checked, and "night and day, jeeps, reconnaissance cars and two and a half ton trucks thundered through the gate."

THE ICE CREAM CONE—INVENTED ON KAUA'I?

Juliet Wichman wrote in *Early Kauai Hospitality* that one ingenious Hale Nani treat became a worldwide custom. After innumerable spoons disappeared when Sunday school children were served ice cream there on special occasions, Mary Rice instructed her baker to make Japanese-style *senbei* tea cookies, which she rolled into self-contained ice cream "cornucopias." The result, according to her granddaughter, was the "invention I saw credited to her years ago in Ripley's 'Believe It or Not'"—the ice cream cone![11] Not everyone agrees with that claim. Some argue that a patent for the ice cream cone was first granted in 1903 to Italo Marchiony, an Italian immigrant to New York. Others, including the International Association of Ice Cream Manufacturers, credit Syrian immigrant Ernest Hamwi with rolling up his Zalabia pastry for ice cream vendor Arnold Fomachou, who popularized the ice cream cone at the St. Louis World's Fair in 1904. At least one Rice descendant dismisses such contradicting claims with the assertion that it all began on Rice Street and a traveling salesman spread news of the treat from here to there.

The older women were quartered in the house itself, and the high school girls slept in a seven-bed, converted fertilizer shed dubbed Hale Brats. Another modified building on the estate, sandbagged and enclosed by barbed wire, served as the restricted Work Center, the radar-plotting room.[12]

The Rice family's Hale Nani life in what had become central Līhu'e formally ended in October 1946 when Anna Wilcox sold the property to a *hui* of local businessmen, with

Tip Top owner Mitchell Ota on record as trustee.[13] The group divided the four and a half acres into the Hale Nani Business Tract, with paved roadways into and through the interior of the area and shared ownership parking for seventy-eight cars in the center of the tract. Around its perimeter they situated twenty-seven discrete commercial lots, including the street-front shops along Rice Street. The plan was almost precisely the reverse of the shopping center concept that would emerge a few years later: a commercial island of shops surrounded by an ocean of parking.

One of the first businesses to open in the tract was Daniel Lee's Drive-in on the corner of Rice and ʻUmi streets. It was advertised as "YOUR FIRST DRIVE INN" on Kauaʻi and promised "motor hopper's service right to your car." Indoor tables and lunch counter seating were also available. Daniel Lee's was open for lunch and dinner, and old-timers remember it as a postwar "hot spot" in Līhuʻe, open until 2:00 A.M. on Saturdays. After Daniel Lee retired, the rounded-corner building with the glass block wall was converted to accommodate the Kauai Savings and Loan building, and Tony's Charcoal Broiler occupied the space behind. Today, Prosser Realty and Kiibo's Restaurant inhabit the properties.

The *mauka* end of the block houses the Lihue Missionary Church, an evangelical Christian denomination. For many years it was home to Sharon Sue's dress shop. A

On May 11, 1907, forty-eight members of the U.S. Congress and their families enjoyed a luau on the grounds of Hale Nani during a one-day tour of Kauaʻi. They had arrived at Hanalei Bay that morning from Honolulu, where they were entertained with a breakfast fête at the summer home of A. S. Wilcox. Their busy day next took them west by water around the island to the McBryde plantation at ʻEleʻele, then via train to Kekaha, and finally by carriage to Līhuʻe, where they enjoyed the Rice hospitality. After that event the group boarded a ship and continued on to Maui during their whirlwind, twenty-three-day tour of the islands. Grove Farm Homestead Museum

During World War II, Women's Air Raid Defense sites were established on the four largest Hawaiian islands. A Kaua'i center was housed at Hale Nani to track planes in the area via radar. The WARDs used rods that looked like small shuffleboard sticks to post and move markers representing the planes' positions on boards similar to this one on O'ahu. History Services, USS *Arizona* Memorial, National Park Service

The members of the Kaua'i WARDs, shift 2, pose on the steps of Hale Nani: Laurie Song, Chin Soon Chun, Frances Wong, Kee Soon Kim, Iwalani Luke, Kuulei Akana, Harriet Lara, Dorothea Schimmelfennig, Florence Ching, Elizabeth McCoy, Annie Kure, Lillian West, Mary Samson. Pauline Mahikoa Hadama collection, Kaua'i Museum

Dancers perform in a Kamehameha Day parade near Sharon Sue's before moving up the palm drive to the county building. Harvey Tam, Kaua'i Historical Society

distinctive Art Moderne sign that projected above the roof embellished the shop and proclaimed its owners' names in a contemporary script dominated by a pair of sweeping S's. Between Daniel Lee's and Sharon Sue's were other tenants, including the U.S. Social Security Administration, Gony's House of Beauty, Hawaii Thrift and Loan, and Sears, which retailed there until moving to the Lihue Shopping Center in 1967.

Hale Nani Studio was located in the next block. Owner Tsutomu Fujii (1907–1995) was born in the Kilipaki camp across from the Lihue Plantation mill on Halekō Road.[14] Tom Fujii was a self-trained photographer who opened his first studio in Kapaia Valley on the Hanamā'ulu side of Līhu'e in 1929. When the Hale Nani tract lots became available, he relocated there, naming the studio to match the new neighborhood. In his highly visible location on Rice Street, Fujii offered portrait services and provided Kodak supplies to both the wholesale and retail markets. He also worked on location to photograph graduations, weddings, communions, funerals, and other events, in addition to being employed as a photographer for the *Garden Island*. For many years he also snapped the police department mug shots, not always a pleasant experience, he said, because he occasionally had to take pictures of friends. When the Fujiis retired in 1972, they sold the business to Mike Miyake. The building has since housed several other tenants.

The far end of the block contains one of the two masonry, two-story buildings in the Hale Nani Business Tract that were constructed in 1964. It is an L-shaped structure at the corner of Rice and ‘Ewalu streets. Most of the building is occupied by dentists, accountants, and other professionals; the ground floor facing the street is occupied by longtime tenant City Liquor.

Immediately behind the Toyota dealership across ‘Ewalu is the second of the 1964-built, two-story structures, this one highlighted by a triple row of vivid blue windows that replaced the original jalousies after Hurricane ‘Iniki in 1992. It is also the second religious center in the tract and a place that remains a mystery even to some lifelong Līhu‘e residents. The name Tensho-Kotai-Jingu-Kyo (Religion of the Shrine of the Heavenly Goddess) proudly declares its identity in bold letters mounted above the building.

Tom and Fusayo Fujii in Hale Nani Studio, 1956. Kaua‘i Historical Society

The Tensho-Kotai-Jingu-Kyo building in the Hale Nani tract.

The Shinto-based, syncretic religion was founded by Sayo Kitamura (1900–1967), a peasant woman in Tabuse, Yamaguchi Prefecture, Japan, who became known to her followers as Ogamisama (Great Goddess). In the 1940s Kitamura experienced divine revelation and began preaching at her home shortly before Japan's crushing defeat in World War II. Her personal charisma, reported faith healings, and open criticism of the trappings of wealth, power and status—which extended to her excoriation of Japan's emperor—garnered considerable attention and more than a little scorn from the media. Because of Ogamisama's ecstatic religious dance and that of her worshipful followers, the sect is often referred to as the Dancing Religion, though some consider the title demeaning.[15]

In 1952, Ogamisama made the first of five proselytizing trips to Hawai'i, where she reportedly met Governor Oren Long, University of Hawai'i president Gregg Sinclair, and Honolulu mayor John H. Wilson. The latter sent her a letter after her visit calling the stay "too brief" and describing her as "veritably an angel of everlasting peace and understanding."[16] Ogamisama remained in Hawai'i for six months on that first visit, followed in 1958 by an eighteen-month trip and shorter stays in 1961, 1963, and 1965. She was widely welcomed into the islands initially, but strife developed in some locations between her followers and others in the Japanese community after she decried ancestor worship and insisted that her believers forsake all other religious practices and destroy their Buddhist and Shinto symbols.[17] Nevertheless, her teachings and the force of her personality gained many disciples. Converts on Kauaʻi initially met in a Hanapēpē home, in accordance with their leader's teaching: "Ogamisama prohibits the building of special halls for these meetings, and so they are held at the homes of followers."[18] After that stricture changed, the group purchased land and built the Līhuʻe headquarters, the first permanent Tensho-Kotai-Jingu-Kyo center in Hawaiʻi. The founder visited there and lectured for two days in July 1965 on her last visit to Hawaiʻi, part of a thirty-two-country evangelical journey that took her to the United States, Asia, Europe, Africa, and South America.[19]

When Ogamisama died in 1967, Kiyokazu Kitamura, the granddaughter she chose at birth to succeed her, became the sect's religious leader as Himegamisama (Princess Goddess). In 1973 the religious movement was considered Japan's third-largest "new religion" (the label given to Japanese theologies founded since the mid-nineteenth century).[20] It continues to have a few hundred thousand adherents around the globe, and it maintains a magnificent, architectural award–winning headquarters in Tabuse, where devotees visit and sometimes spend months or years.[21] As the first generation of members has grown old and begun to die, those who experienced the magnetism of Ogamisama's presence firsthand, the Kauaʻi congregation has dwindled. Tensho-Kotai-Jingu-Kyo currently has

Kauai Sales Company, ca. 1960. Later, Jack Wada Electronics was housed in this building. Among its most popular products were rental movies in the VHS and Beta videotape formats of the day. Currently it is the home of Aloha Furniture. Tom Fujii, Kauaʻi Historical Society

about a dozen members on Kaua'i who gather one evening a week for services, which are conducted in Japanese.

The mix of owners and tenants in the Hale Nani tract has changed since the era when a multitude of grocers, fish markets, and other small shops serviced the public along Rice Street and in the buildings behind it. Today, although retail enterprises still occupy spaces in the area, professional, financial, and human services mingle abundantly with such shops. One of the many examples of that evolution is the building two doors *mauka* of City Liquor, the one with an adjacent parking alleyway. For many years it housed Duarte Sales and Service, a tire recap center. After the closure of that business, James Licke, Esq., bought the property, installed his law offices there and, in 1990, added a second-floor living quarters to the wood frame building. Other properties, such as Aloha Furniture (behind Prosser and Kiibo's), have changed hands over time but continue to provide goods on offer to the public. Though the types of businesses have evolved in the Hale Nani tract over the decades, the area continues to cater primarily to island residents.

THE RICE STREET BUSINESS BLOCK

Across the street from Rice's Hale Nani estate, Lihue Plantation carved a row of fourteen lots out of the canefields immediately *makai* of the county lawn in 1912. Positioned along the main street (it would be named the William Hyde Rice Street in the 1930s), it was not the first residential neighborhood in Līhu'e; various laborers' camps already dotted the landscape. Whereas the camps were owned and controlled by the plantation, however, Lihue Town-Site lots were offered for fee-simple sale to the public.

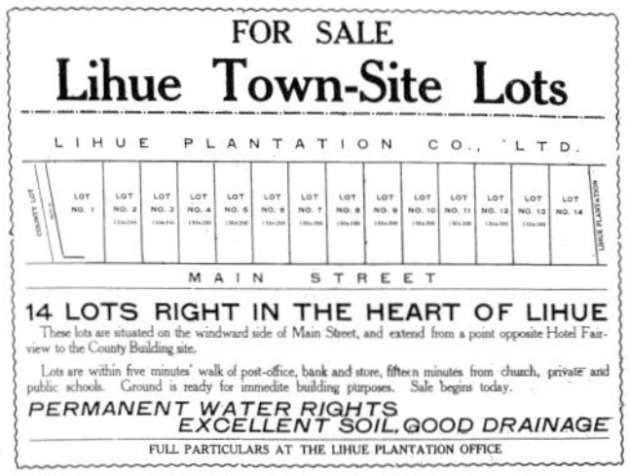

Advertisement promoting Lihue Town-Site lots, 1912. *Garden Island* archives

The availability of house lots convenient to work and social activities assured the continuing expansion of the town. A genteel neighborhood emerged over the next decade, one soon dubbed "Elite Street." The lots were large—150 by 200 feet—and the houses too were spacious. On the grounds were built garages, servants' quarters (often inhabited by "country girls" who attended school during the day and worked for the family before and after class), and other structures such as wash houses, tool sheds, and chicken or duck pens.

If Līhu'e's main street nurtured prominent island residents, it also contained the jumbled assortment of human DNA found in any flourishing Our Town. There was the smart guy who sank into alcoholism and ended up a Honolulu street drunk, the tragic suicide, the convicted embezzler. Talk of others' personal failings usually stay within the realm of bridge table gossip and sidewalk whispers, but embezzlement finds its way into

The Lydgate children, Margie, Joan, and Lois, in the yard of their family home on Rice Street. Margaret Rinker

print. The arrest and conviction of Christopher G. Kuhlmann, cashier at the Bank of Hawaii, was trumpeted in *Garden Island* headlines in August 1938, the day after his twenty-fifth anniversary at the bank. Kuhlmann confessed to embezzling money and forging someone else's signature. He was sentenced to twenty years in O'ahu prison. Prior to his fall, Kuhlmann had been an active community member and had lived on Rice Street in a "commodious cottage, comfortable and artistic," provided by the Bank of Hawaii.

On the whole, folks who grew up there in the 1920s and 1930s remember the neighborhood fondly. They recount stories of spending their allowance at Kress, the five-and-dime, and of watching cowboy movies at Lihue Theater's Saturday matinee, which they followed with "two sushis" at Ota's Sweet Shop next door on Kūhiō Highway. They wax nostalgic about meeting the interisland steamers *Hualalai* and *Waialeale,* seeing animals of the E. K. Fernandez show unloaded, and later sitting on the stone pillars at the entry to their driveways to watch the parade of elephants, "Czechoslovakian midgets," and other circus wonders of the era. They remember yanking off their shoes as soon as they were "out of mother's sight" and enjoying a barefoot walk down the road past the mill to Lihue Grammar School.[22]

Bank of Hawaii manager and one-time postmaster Frank Crawford was in the thick of

In 1915, after a dozen years in the photo supply and movie business, Edwin Kane Fernandez debuted a new entertainment in Hawai'i, the E. K. Fernandez circus, which performed on all the islands. In the fall of 1933, the Līhu'e ballpark in the center of town was converted into an E. K. Fernandez circus midway. private collection business activities when the home sites became available, and he quickly bought the first two lots nearest the county building. Crawford had had a bit of banking experience before moving from his native Indiana to Kaua'i in 1901 to become the Līhu'e postmaster. When the Bank of Hawaii opened its Līhu'e branch two years later, he became cashier there in addition to continuing his postal duties, and he oversaw the construction of the bank/post office building in 1912. In 1917 he married his Indiana sweetheart, Mary Wilson, and the couple settled into life on Rice Street. By the time the Crawfords died in the 1960s, their property contained several structures. The main house was a 3,700-square-foot, two-story, tongue-and-groove building with pine floors and a wood shingle roof. An auxiliary building included a maid's quarters, garage, and wash house. The lawn included two fern houses, a fashionable property enhancement before World War II.

The Crawfords' residential structures are long gone; today, the two-story Lihue Plaza Building is located on the property. On the ground floor is Central Pacific Bank, begun, according to its own description, "by a small group of World War II veterans in 1954 to help immigrant families build a life away from the plantations."[23] The building also houses a travel agency, an insurance company, and other businesses.

Lihue Plantation retained ownership of the next three lots. The first to be developed, the one adjacent to the Crawfords, housed a succession of local dentists, the first of whom

The Crawford property (center) was adjacent to the county building and lawn, 1918. The vegetation at the edge of the lawn obscures the Rice law office. William J. Senda, Kaua'i Historical Society

was Dr. A. J. Derby. Typically, the property accommodated servants' quarters and a garage at the back of the lot. The primary residence was constructed nearly in the middle of the lot, slightly left of center. In front of the home grew a banyan, a *Ficus benjamina*. On the *makai* side of the house near the road, the *Garden Island* reported in 1915, Derby built his "dental parlors as completely and elegantly fitted up as any to be found in the city, being equipped with the latest, approved appliances." But Dr. Derby did not remain in Līhu'e long; after he left the following year, Lihue Plantation hired young Dr. F. M. Branch, who had been working in Honolulu for the doctors Wall. In time he too left Līhu'e, and Dr. Justin Smith moved in. All the while the banyan grew in front of the house.[24]

In the early 1970s this property—or more particularly the exceptional old banyan tree on the property—became the focus of an impassioned environmental battle. It began after the County Planning Commission rezoned the property to allow American Savings and Loan Association to demolish the home and construct an office building on the site. The women of the venerable Mokihana Club led the fight. Since 1916 the club's efforts had included a Garden Committee, also known variously as the Village Improvement Committee, Beautification Committee, and Outdoor Committee. Over the years the women of the committee distributed seeds and plants to island schools and worked to landscape and beautify roadsides, parks, and public buildings. They viewed the defense and retention of imperiled trees as one component of their commitment to the environmental aesthetics of the Garden Island. By the time of the Battle of the Banyan, they'd had practice.

In the 1950s the group had protested the removal of a false *kamani* tree that grew in the main intersection of town between the Tip Top and Lihue Store. It argued in a letter to the Board of Supervisors that "this tree adds to the beauty of our island and is a landmark of significance."[25] Its location was deemed unsafe for the increasing vehicular traffic, however, and the Mokihana Club was ultimately forced to compromise. The tree was removed to the grounds of Wilcox Hospital. Unhappily, the old *kamani* could not withstand the shock and died within a year. In the mid-1960s the group rallied to defend a second massive false *kamani* tree. This one fronted the former Lihue Plantation physician's home on Ahukini Road near its intersection with Kūhiō Highway, now occupied by Sleeping Giant Sotheby's International Realty and a few professional offices. After responding to a *Garden Island* article that the tree was in danger of the axe, Mokihana Club women again protested, this time with more success.

The group's efforts to save the two *kamani* trees armed it for its 1974 Battle of the Rice Street Banyan, an effort that would lead to seminal protective tree legislation in Hawai'i.

When the community learned that a bank building would replace the dilapidated house and its tree, "such a wave of public reaction arose that Mokihana Club with its 125 members was led to organize a drive to preserve it." Many discussions ensued with the mayor, County Council, planning director, and bank officials. Thousands of citizens signed petitions and participated in a letter-writing campaign. The effort achieved victory when real estate agent and developer Bernice Midkiff, who owned the lot next door, stepped forward with an offer to exchange properties, thereby enabling American Savings to construct its building on an unobstructed lot. On December 9, 1974, Mokihana president Lee Hoxie wrote a letter to the *Garden Island* congratulating all who participated to save the tree. "The Rice Street banyan," she concluded, "will continue to be a landmark and a monument to the fact that progress CAN go hand in hand with concern for the unique environmental character and beauty of Kauai."[26]

The *kamani* tree that had figured prominently at the main Līhu'e corner for many decades did not survive the radical pruning and relocation to the grounds of the G. N. Wilcox Memorial Hospital in 1959. Kaua'i Historical Society

But the group had not finished. "Encouraged by this success and fired with enthusiasm

A banyan on Rice Street, pictured in February 1975, precipitated the Hawai'i exceptional tree law. Ironically, it was never included as an Exceptional Tree of Kaua'i. Nancy Bannick, Hawai'i State Archives

to extend their efforts to preserve other exceptional trees," recounted club historian Alice Wedemeyer, the Mokihana women lobbied for passage of a tree ordinance "as a major step in preserving the beauty of the Island by which Kauai can come one step closer to being the true Hawaii."[27] Martha Remitio and Sally Netzer led the charge, and their timing was excellent. By the mid-1970s enough boom years had spurred development around the island to cause alarm about the long-term implications of such fast change. U. S. Senator Hiram Fong, Representatives Patsy Mink and Spark Matsunaga, Governor George Ariyoshi, and State Representative Tony Kunimura were among many officials who lined up at a public hearing to testify in support of legislation to protect special island trees. The Kaua'i County Council passed the ordinance on December 27, 1974. It established an Arborist Committee, whose responsibility is to find and recommend exceptional trees for listing and protection "on the basis of age, rarity, location, size, aesthetic quality, endemic status, or historic and cultural significance." On May 17, 1975, the Hawaii State Legislature followed Kaua'i's lead. Act 105 (Chapter 58, Hawaii Revised Statutes) mandates each county to establish arborist advisory committees and enact appropriate legislation to protect exceptional trees worthy of preservation.

The members of the Mokihana Club had effected great change on both county and state levels, but they also understood that ongoing efforts dedicated to preservation and beautification of the landscape were vital for long-term success. They reached out to the Outdoor Circle, which had branches on other islands but not on Kaua'i. The Outdoor Circle had been active in Hawai'i since 1912, when it organized to abolish the visual blight of billboards on island roadways. As a result of Mokihana's interactions with the Honolulu group, the Kauai Outdoor Circle was formed on October 22, 1975.[28] For a couple of years the two clubs shared projects with the County Task Force for Beautification. Then member Adelaide Ward suggested that the Mokihana Club drop its decades-old Beautification Committee because "the Outdoor Circle is doing such a thorough job in this area that it does not seem needed in Mokihana."[29] The Kauai Outdoor Circle acknowledged its Mokihana Club roots by dedicating its 1979 cookbook to its founding members, Sally Netzer and Martha Remitio, the leaders of Mokihana's exceptional tree movement.

Herb's Tree Trimmers cut back the banyan before construction of the Watumull Building began. Kaua'i Historical Society

The Rice Street banyan remained undisturbed until 1981, when a plan for another bank and office building was designed for the site. Specialists were called in to prune the old tree to a point where branches and building could safely coexist. So it remains today. The banyan still lives in its original site but only hints at the grandeur of its former self. Meanwhile the bank vacated quarters in the Watumull Building years ago. In its place the Kaua'i Visitors Bureau staff now works to promote the desirability of this Garden Island to the outside world.

As of 2013, 259 exceptional trees were listed around the state, but Kaua'i, known as the Garden Island for its stunning natural beauty, has not kept pace with entries of other counties; only nineteen of the state's total number of exceptional trees reside on Kaua'i, as compared with 156 on O'ahu.[30]

The Battle of the Banyan took place at a time when this section of Līhu'e was changing quickly. In the late 1960s and early '70s, Lihue Plantation divested itself of its eight residential properties along this stretch to various, mostly local investors. The transition had begun at the end of World War II. The first of the Elite Street residential properties demolished to make way for commercial use was the one directly across Rice Street from the current Lee's Furniture. In February 1945, Samuel Wilcox, through his wife Edith, together with William Moragne and Wayne Ellis bought the Lydgate home and double lot to establish Hale Kauai. Daughter Lois Lydgate Coleman, one of many children who had been sent to the mainland for their safety during World War II, recalls the strangeness of returning "home" to find nothing remaining of the house she'd grown up in but the front steps.

At the time, Sam Wilcox was Līhu'e branch manager of the Bishop National Bank—now First Hawaiian—and secretary of the Grove Farm board of directors. Bill Moragne had been trained as an engineer and was working as Grove Farm's assistant manager (he became manager of the company in 1953). Both men were Hawai'i *kama'āina,* but their partner, Wayne Ellis, was a Missouri native and a newcomer to the islands. He had arrived on Kaua'i in 1938, via college in California, to teach industrial arts at Kauai High School. Two years later he married Helen Rice, one of sheriff and hotelier William Henry Rice's five children. In 1942, Ellis took over the management of Lihue Hotel for his ailing father-in-law. After the latter's death in 1945, the family sold the hotel and Wayne Ellis became

The Lydgate home shortly after it was built. In 1946 it was demolished and replaced by Hale Kauai.
Margaret Rinker

the managing partner of Hale Kauai. When it incorporated in 1950, he became its majority stockholder.

The Hale Kauai building was designed in much the same style as the Grove Farm office in Puhi. Both feature stuccoed walls, steep, double-pitched roof, recessed doorway, and bathroom window ornamented by concrete screens, sugarcane and pineapple at Grove Farm, and heliconia at Hale Kauai (still in place on the Nāwiliwili side of the building, though now opaquely backed in concrete rather than screened). Later, Hale Kauai would be best known as a building supplies and construction firm with a ready-mix and concrete block manufacturing plant, but it opened primarily as a machine and appliance store. Hale Kauai carried an eclectic mix of equipment tailored to both home and business markets. Its inventory included Hotpoint appliances, RCA and Emerson radios, Wilson sporting goods, Carrier air conditioners, Evinrude outboard motors, Hobart kitchen and restaurant equipment, National cash registers, Monroe adding machines, De Walt contractors' supplies, Boice cranes, Duro shop tools, and Fuller paints.[31] The new electronics

Fuller Paints and *lauhala* mats were among the products offered at Hale Kauai. Hale Kauai

appealed to a population with wallets fattened by war savings and wearied by long years of rationing and shortages.

The date of Hale Kauai's grand opening, November 18, 1946, coincided with another event that changed life in Hawai'i forever. The next day, November 19, marked the official end to the seventy-nine-day sugar strike that successfully unionized plantation workers throughout the territory. Sam Wilcox's aunt, former territorial senator Elsie Wilcox, had recognized the implications of the strike. She wrote in a September 1946 letter to a friend that finally, with the war's end, she and her friends were able to vacation and travel again, but "now comes the sugar strike with its ominous threat to our basic living!"[32] After unionization, "basic living" changed for workers and management both. The old paternalistic system of plantation-provided perquisites—housing, medical care, fuel, and water—was dissolved in a contract that granted higher wages for workers along with their assumption of responsibility for those necessities.

The ability to own their own homes created in plantation workers a spirit of independence that was matched in confidence by returning GIs. A long-term building boom began as one indication of an incipient middle class on Kaua'i. Responding to the demand, Hale Kauai moved confidently into the building trades. For a time it acted both as a retailer, supplying other contractors with building materials, and as a developer itself. The company capitalized on its ties with Grove Farm by securing acreage for a lumberyard at Nāwiliwili that had once been the site of G. N. Wilcox's beach house, and also by developing the Pua Loke subdivision on Grove Farm land along Nāwiliwili Road south of the mill. Eventually, though, the company left the construction side of the business to avoid competing directly with some of its best customers.

Both the postwar construction boom and a shifting political landscape led the County to enact building regulations in the 1950s. As early as 1917 the need to establish codes had been suggested. An editorial in the *Garden Island* that year called for a building ordinance, because villages and towns on Kaua'i were "growing up, it is to be feared, very much hit or miss according to the barbaric taste of the builder."[33] The consequences, the newspaper observed, were "an unsavory collection of slums that are noisome, and rookeries that are fire-traps; a menace to themselves and to their neighbors." But the wheels of change grind slowly in government; nearly four decades would pass before a committee of the Kaua'i Board of Supervisors drafted a building code. Representatives of both sugar and pineapple industries opposed the code, arguing that it was too elaborate for Kaua'i and a burdensome expense to the public. Bill Moragne testified: "It is our contention that a

The Hale Kauai building's steep double-pitched roof and large glass display windows provided an attractive addition to the expanding commercial neighborhood on Rice Street. Hale Kauai

simple building code applying to the construction and alteration of public buildings would be ample and that costs of such code could be absorbed by the County engineer's department."[34] Sinclair Robinson, manager of Gay and Robinson, complained that the proposed code was neither suitable nor desirable. McBryde Sugar Company manager John Sandison advised minimal government intervention: "Greater severity of requirements should not be imposed than are justified."

Despite such testimony, the building code became law in 1956. It was followed by electrical and plumbing codes later in the decade. The new safety standards, with their accompanying review processes, benefited both residential and commercial structures. One casualty of the laws, however, was the ability of a builder to complete a commercial structure in less than two months, as had been accomplished in the 1930s with the Kawakami store, now Lee's Furniture, across the street.

In 1973, Hale Kauai moved out of the Rice Street location after expanding its Nāwiliwili facilities to become a one-stop building supply center that included paint, hardware, and lumber as well as some household products. The company later opened stores at Kōloa and Kapaʻa, but by the end of the century competition from other building supply businesses had eroded Hale Kauai's market share. With the opening of the 125,000-square-foot Home Depot in 2003, Hale Kauai sold its Nāwiliwili operations to Honsador Lumber Corporation and began plans to refocus its Kōloa and Kapa'a locations. Ultimately the transition was unsuccessful, and Hale Kauai owners, descendants of its founders, converted the company to a real estate investment and development firm.[35]

The Rice Street buildings remained unoccupied between 1973 and 1984, when the County of Kaua'i entered a ten-year lease to house its planning, building, drivers' licensing, and a few other departments there. Vacant again for several years, the back building was reconstructed and the front one refurbished before the U.S. Transportation Security Administration took occupancy in 2003. The building is now identified only as 4280 Rice Street.

THE TRANSFORMATION OF RICE DAIRY

On the south side of the street, Rice Shopping Center parking lot was once an exercise pasture for cows. Rice Dairy, which stretched from the family's Hale Nani estate to the end of the block at Kalena, had been a fixture on this road to Nāwiliwili as long as anyone could remember. In the mid-1920s about two dozen cows were milked there, producing a total of slightly more than twenty-five gallons a day.[36] The product was used by the family itself as well as by guests at sheriff Willie Rice's nearby Lihue Hotel a short way down the road to Nāwiliwili. Local customers could go to the dairy to purchase milk, which was bottled and placed for pickup in boxes in the milk room. The dairy also supplied milk to workers at the ranch and sugar operations at Kīpū, with the cost deducted from their pay.

By the time the battle to save the banyan was waged, the dairy was a generation and more gone, and this end of town had long since lost both its residential and its pastoral character. The transition to commercial use began in 1937 when William Hyde Rice, Ltd., headed by Charles Atwood Rice, sold the dairy lands to entrepreneurs, mostly Līhu'e outsiders. The motive for the sale was revenge.

Lawrence Fuchs characterized Charlie Rice as having assembled in the first half of the twentieth century what was probably "the most efficient political machine in the territory." Rice's rise to political power was sparked by Prince Jonah Kuhio Kalanianaole, Hawai'i's delegate to Congress, who successfully fought to establish county governments in 1905, partly as a way to dilute the sugar interests' oligarchical power in Honolulu and to increase the leverage of Hawaiians in the political system. Charlie Rice quickly recognized

Before S. H. Kress and Co. bought the property, the Rice's dairy gave the neighborhood a pastoral setting. September 1937. William J. Senda, Kiyoto Okimoto

in the Home Rule Act, which created Hawai'i's five counties, the opportunity to build his own power base on Kaua'i. He ran successfully for a seat in the Hawai'i Territorial House of Representatives that year, as did his brother, William Henry Rice, for the position of Kaua'i's high sheriff. The two of them then capitalized on the rewards of political patronage by creating an islandwide police force of loyal followers. In time the Rice machine commanded such influence that it dictated gubernatorial appointees to seats on boards, commissions, and other important nonelective positions at both county and territorial levels. The brothers reportedly could redraw electoral district lines on Kaua'i as they saw fit.[37]

During the early twentieth century, sugar interests and men in tangential industries such as transportation and banking—Republicans all—largely controlled both the economic and the government affairs of the territory. Democrats provided but a whisper in the affairs of state. Although he too was a Republican, Charlie Rice was not a diehard "party man"; he would ultimately place personal power over party preference. Neither did he subscribe to the ethnic and class-based allegiances of the era. Rice encouraged and supported many aspiring candidates, whether Japanese, Portuguese, or Chinese, working men or shopkeepers, as long as he could count on their unqualified loyalty to him.

As Fuchs observed, "Rice generously used the carrot at least as much as he employed the stick." He wielded his power in the legislature to channel funds for public works projects that benefited all of Kaua'i. He was also known to help members of his constituency with everything from the pension problems of widows to cash handouts for the needy. When one Filipino business couple encountered blatant racism while trying to borrow money to buy a house in Kūpolō, off lower Rice Street, Charlie Rice intervened with the bank, threatening to buy the house and sell it to the couple himself if the financiers did not reverse their decision.[38]

If Rice rewarded loyalty, he also carried a big stick. He supported Henry Aki for the Senate in 1925, then endorsed Elsie Wilcox to oppose him in 1932 after Aki voted against Rice on several issues. He did the same to Wilcox eight years later, backing her opponent, Clem Gomes, when she proved an independent voice in the legislature.[39] A letter from the wife of a Kapa'a shop owner in 1931 implied fear of Rice's power of retribution. Desperate that rumor had reached Rice about her husband holding opposition meetings at their place, she blamed "dirty dogs that accuse others innocent [sic]. Mr. Rice this was the most quiet election around our store this year."[40] She accused a competitor of having held meetings at his place instead. "I've always thought so much of you and also through the help you have given us, and we

Sheriff William Henry Rice, with his brother Senator Charles A. Rice, marshaled a political machine on Kaua'i that reportedly could dictate gubernatorial appointees and redraw electoral lines at will. Kaua'i Museum still need your help at all times," her letter pleaded. "We don't have any ill feeling toward your people and hope to God, that if you have any towards us, please forget, I hate to see you feel bad against John when he is not to blame for anything."

Senator Charles A. Rice, 1915, early in his political career. Hawai'i State Archives

Charlie Rice and his family had long owned stock in Lihue Plantation, but American Factors (it was still Hackfeld and Co. before World War I) held controlling interest. The company named Rice managing director of all their Kaua'i plantations in 1914 when he was a freshman senator. In that capacity too, Charlie Rice capitalized on gaining loyalty through patronage; his hand gripped the lever of the hiring engines for most supervisory positions. The Rice family's clout elicited strong reactions, as a 1920 letter from A. H. Waterhouse recommending someone for a political appointment noted: "The Anti-Rice people cannot object to her as it is well known that her husband is Anti-Rice. On the other hand, Chas. Rice favors her appointment."[41]

Perhaps Kaua'i was simply not big enough for two powerful entities to share political dominion. Possibly conflicting principles drove Rice and American Factors leaders down their different paths. Undoubtedly, a complexity of circumstances increased the animosity that simmered between the two. Whatever the reasons, during the political campaign of 1932 Rice openly worked to defeat two legislative candidates backed by American Factors, while the "Interests," as he called them, bitterly opposed the reelection of Sheriff William Henry Rice. Edith Plews, Charlie Rice's daughter, captured the vehemence of political hostilities swirling around the family in a letter to her Uncle Tom Foster recounting events of primary election night:

> We have *all* felt very keenly indeed because of Jack Moir's horrible, dastardly, and venomous attack in which he said, "Rice blood is bad blood. Anyone who has a drop of Rice blood is dirty. And I don't mean maybe. Anything I have said against Charlie Rice or Willie Rice goes for the whole family." . . . when Philip [Rice] got up to answer him there was hooting and jeering led by men I *saw* and *heard* myself. Jack Moir yelled, "Don't be yellow, Don't talk Hawaiian. You're a coward. Speak English!"
>
> Then Philip said, "I am speaking to my Hawaiian friends, now, and then I'll talk English, and I have plenty to say." . . . [Philip's wife] Flora said, "Hector Moir, there will be no fight! I thought you said you stood for law and order!" She was quick enough to see that a riot was wanted by the "group of young men who want good government" to discredit the police. . . .

> Uncle Tom, during all this speech by Jack Moir I saw Broadbent jeering, leading the applause, and Scott Pratt, Phyllis Horner, Ray and Frances Allen as bad, jeering too and gloating and Albert Horner clapping too, but looking a bit more sober and less jubilant than the others I have mentioned. There were others too. Is there a bite so sharp as "friend remembered not" a sting so nigh as "benefits forgot"? If there is, I pray I shall be spared it.[42]

The 1932 election took place in the depth of the Great Depression, and the Rice faction unequivocally carried the day. Most of the candidates who defended a conservative status quo and were endorsed by big sugar interests went down in defeat. But the heat of that election boiled antagonisms right over the edge of the pot: Charlie Rice was fired as managing director of the island's American Factors plantations. Frederick Wichman, Rice's son-in-law and protégé, apprehensively confided in his journal entry of November 20, 1932, that Rice's termination was "the first political flare back and from now on they will try and break us. They can if they want to, for they are Special Privilege and have the money."[43] Charlie Rice was not, however, a man to be easily dismissed. In 1933 he resigned his position on the Republican Central Committee, a seat he'd held for thirty years. He then proceeded to introduce bills in the legislature that were guaranteed to rankle Hawai'i's business interests, bills such as the proposal to institute a universal 1 percent income tax to generate unemployment funds.

The next year, when Charlie's brother Harold left the Hawai'i Senate, Henry Alexander

Senators Charles Rice, Harold Rice, and Robert Hind, Hawai'i Territorial Senate, 1933. Hawai'i State Archives

Baldwin ran successfully for his Maui seat. The one-time U.S. congressional delegate from the Territory and then member of the Hawai‘i House of Representatives wrote a friend, Lihue Plantation manager Caleb Burns, that he thought it also "would be a good thing if Charlie Rice did not run this year, but apparently he is going to."[44] Antagonism on both sides flowed deep and personal, as a 1935 letter from attorney Arthur Smith to Burns revealed. Smith, a principal in the firm of Smith, Wild, Beebe and Cades, sarcastically confided, "Your good friend Charles Rice, the man without a party," introduced a concurrent Senate and House resolution requesting the commissioner of public lands to acquire more than four acres of Lihue Plantation land in the center of Līhu‘e for public use. According to Smith:

> It was obviously introduced for the purpose of annoying your company and your good friend Charles slipped it through the Senate at a time when no one was expecting it. He caught Senator Wilcox unprepared, much to her disgust. I did not dare to do much talking about it with the different senators for fear he might find out about it.[45]

The resolution ultimately failed, he reported, and "was finally buried without military honors at approx. 3 a.m. Thursday morning by the House."

In 1936, Rice publicly challenged the monopoly that American Factors' Kekaha plantation had long enjoyed in its lease of government lands for sugarcane, arguing that small-farmer homesteading would provide better and fairer use of those lands.[46] When the "Interests" responded by blocking Rice's bid to become chairman of the Senate Ways and Means Committee, Charlie Rice departed the Republican Party altogether. Then, in a gesture of retribution beyond the control of political enemies, one meant to assault both Lihue Plantation's wallet and its authority, Rice made the move that upended that company's control of how Līhu‘e would develop and who would participate in its growth. Rice retaliated by subdividing his family's dairy land into the Fairview Business Tract lots. In so doing he opened the town to people who had long been denied access to business ownership in the county seat, and several merchants from the then lively communities of Nāwiliwili and Kapaia seized their opportunity. Particularly injurious to the hegemony of the plantation-owned Lihue Store was the sale of prime spots along Rice Street to the national five-and-dime-store chain S. H. Kress and Co., and to up-and-coming Waimea merchant Harvey Saburo Kawakami.

The two new Līhu‘e retailers made an undeniable impact. Certainly they increased the

Eighteenth Legislature, Territorial Senate, 1935. Seated: William Hill, Henry Freitas, Elsie Wilcox, George P. Cooke, Joseph Silva, David Trask. Standing: Lester Petrie, William H. Heen, Harry H. Holt, Charles H. Silva, Charles A. Rice, Harry A. Baldwin, James Campsie, Joseph R. Farrington, William J. Kimi. Hawai'i State Archives

availability of moderately priced goods. They also presented a challenge not only to Lihue Store but also to the island's retailing status quo, striking fear in many "mom 'n pop" shops of the day. In words reminiscent of end-of-the-twentieth-century trepidation about the influx of "big box" stores, a *Garden Island* editorial in June 1937 spoke of "A Threat to Meet":

> The start of the construction of the new Kawakami Store in Lihue and the announcement by S. H. Kress & Co. that they desire to train employees for their new store in Lihue, is the first step in the expansion of the new business district in Lihue. The establishment of a bus service to both sides of the island by the Nawiliwili Transportation Co. will complete the picture.
>
> The bus service will provide cheap transportation to Lihue from the outer communities and with the attraction of the chain store there is certain to be a swing of traffic and trade to Lihue. Many local merchants will find it necessary to change their merchandising plans to meet the competition that Kress and bus service will bring to them.
>
> The smaller merchants over the island will feel the pinch most if the experience on Maui is any criterion. Merchants who are aggressive in their merchandising and who are willing to meet changed conditions have very little to fear.[47]

The Central Service Station originated as a destination for Nawiliwili Transportation buses and a gas pump for automobiles. Standard Oil leased it from 1946 to 1963. During the Līhu'e redesign it was transformed into shops, offices, and eateries. William J. Senda, Kaua'i Museum

The Nawiliwili Transportation Company, one of Lihue Plantation's subsidiaries, inaugurated its bus service between Līhuʻe and Keālia on Saturday, June 26, and to Hanapēpē two days later. To accommodate the buses Lihue Plantation erected the Central Service Station at the main Līhuʻe intersection, much to the dismay of Von Hamm-Young, who had leased space from the plantation and built an automobile sales and service facility plus a stand-alone gasoline station a block up the road. Von Hamm-Young vice-president E. E. Bodge had written plantation manager Caleb Burns the previous February to ask about the "rumor" that a station was being erected on the corner. He protested that there had been a noncompete understanding between the two companies before Von Hamm-Young "put such a large investment in Lihue." Burns would have none of it. He confirmed that Nawiliwili Transportation would probably put up a gas station on that corner with "a bus or two to transport school children and others," but he insisted that it was the plantation's right

Hawaii Statehood Commission and Legislative Holdover Committee, July 1947. From left: Gavien Bush, Eric Beecroft, Judge Delbert E. Metzger, Charlie Rice, A. T. Longley, Sam King. Hawaiʻi State Archives

to do so. In a masterful show of the era's alpha-male power politics, Burns stated: "While we naturally would not permit you to compete with us, we certainly did not and would not be willing to forfeit our right to lease our land to any one else because they might compete with your Company." With a backslap at Charlie Rice, he reminded Bodge that Rice's Garden Island Motors had unsuccessfully tried such competition. Burns then demonstrated the full force of the plantation's land ownership by letting Bodge know that it had also leased property on the other side of Von Hamm-Young, on what is now Ahukini Road, to Kauai Motors Company, Limited.[48]

Although Charlie Rice retired from elective office in 1938, his title as Kaua'i's elder statesman remained secure. He never withdrew completely from government activities; he was a delegate to both constitutional and statehood conventions in the 1950s and served on county police and liquor commissions as well. He also continued to manage William Hyde Rice, Ltd., which operated Lihue Ranch among other business interests, and he served as president of both Garden Island Motors, Ltd., the local Ford and Goodyear franchise, and Atwood Distributing Co., the island's Shell Oil distributorship.

THE S. H. KRESS FIVE-AND-DIME

Samuel Henry Kress opened his first five-and-ten-cent store in 1896 in Memphis, Tennessee, and quickly expanded through the American South and into the West. By 1937, S. H. Kress and Company was a presence in Hawai'i, too, with profitable five-and-dimes open in Honolulu, Wailuku, and Hilo. In seeking to establish a Kaua'i location, Kress officials explored land at Hanapēpē and in Kapaia Valley after a Līhu'e location seemed unavailable.[49] When Charlie Rice offered property in the Fairview Tract, Kress officials jumped at the chance to set up shop in the island's major town. The benefit was mutual: Kress provided a compelling anchor for the new commercial district.

The national success of the Kress retail model was propelled by efficient distribution of high-quality goods sold at the lowest possible prices in well-designed and constructed "environments."[50] Its corporate philosophy included creating a distinctive visual presence within a community. To do so, Kress formed an in-house architectural department in 1905 with responsibility to design and build its own stores rather than leasing existing buildings, the standard practice of the time. In 1931 the company announced that it intended to utilize a new architectural style, one that would modernize central commercial districts in cities and towns across America: Kress brought Art Deco to Main Street USA.[51] Kress

The Kress store under construction. William J. Senda, Kiyoto Okimoto

hired architect Edward F. Sibbert and assembled a hundred-person design team to create its new stores. Their façades would complement the scale of each local area while retaining a consistent corporate identity based on welcoming surroundings with bright interiors, neatly maintained and product-laden cases, easy customer access to merchandise, clearly marked prices, and a helpful staff.

Translating these concepts to Kaua'i, the store was built of reinforced concrete in an open, one-story structure that occupied 22,000 square feet of the 30,000-square-foot lot.

The reinforced concrete building takes shape.
William J. Senda, Kiyoto Okimoto

It featured sizable display windows on the street front, with curved glass "corners" leading to two entryways on Rice Street. Along the 300-foot length of the Kress Street side of the structure, a wooden awning covered parking stalls to keep shoppers' cars shaded during extended visits. Inside, mirrors lined several walls, and fourteen counters—more than a thousand linear feet—displayed jewelry, hosiery, toilet goods, notions, stationery, toys, hardware, and more. Kress prided itself on its sanitary candy department, which contained patented display units that the *Garden Island* described as being "entirely enclosed and rat proof . . . made to retain every degree of freshness."[52]

For many years Kress was open daily, 7:30 A.M. to 5:30 P.M., and on Friday until 9:00 P.M. That was when plantation folks congregated in central Līhuʻe for family outings, shopping, and convivial companionship. Unlike other stores of the era, which extended customer credit and delivered purchases, Kress policy was strictly cash and carry.

Former Kress manager Kiyoto Okimoto (1918–2010) began at Kress in 1938

Kress on opening night. William J. Senda, Kiyoto Okimoto

Inside Kress on opening night, a full house and great excitement. William J. Senda, Kiyoto Okimoto

The Kress restaurant counter after the store's remodeling by Genesco. William J. Senda, Kiyoto Okimoto

immediately after graduating from Kauai High School. A native of Nāwiliwili, Okimoto was sent to the Honolulu Kress store for six months of training before starting at the Kaua'i store, initially as a stock boy. To help get the Līhu'e location up and running, he even pounded in some of the nails during the building's construction. Although Okimoto served capably as assistant manager for many years and helped train five or six managers who were brought in from elsewhere, Kress resisted elevating him to the top Kaua'i position. They finally capitulated in 1962 and appointed Okimoto store manager, a promotion he believed made him the first minority in the chain to be named to a store's top position.[53]

The national decline of Kress paralleled the abandonment of downtowns as the focus of retail activities in favor of suburban shopping centers. In 1964 the twenty-eight-state, four-hundred-store S.H. Kress and Co. chain was bought by Genesco Corporation. The new ownership remodeled both building and merchandise mix at the Kaua'i store and added a restaurant. But the changes

Kiyoto Okimoto, 1958. William J. Senda, Kiyoto Okimoto

here and elsewhere proved inadequate to meet shifting societal tastes, and the company shut down Kress's remaining five-and-dimes, including the Līhu'e store, in 1980.

Though more than a quarter of a century has passed since Kress's demise, many people who grew up in this community fondly recall its restaurant, where Sunday breakfasts—"the best pancakes and best waffles on the island," according to Okimoto—were a family tradition. Others reminisce about the aromatic blend of candy, uniquely flavored popcorn (according to Okimoto: sugared, always popular but with difficult-to-clean equipment), new fabric, and who-knows-what-else that melded into the essence that distinguished Kress from all its competitors.

After Kress closed, the building was used by a furniture store and warehouse before being purchased by the Salvation Army in 2003 for its thrift store. The Army has reportedly sold the property, but new owners have made no changes as of late 2013.

WAIMEA ENTREPRENEURS CHANGE LĪHU'E

Across the side street from Kress is the current Lee's Furniture. It was built in 1937 as the Kawakami Store, the first of several Kawakami enterprises in Līhu'e. Harvey Saburo Kawakami had emigrated from Japan as a youth, brought to Hawai'i with the help of his brother Fukutaro, the first family member to reach Hawai'i. Through hard work and audacity Kawakami made a success of his first store, an 18- by 22-foot operation he established on the Waimea waterfront in 1926.

As a Japanese alien Kawakami was denied the right to vote. (The U.S. Naturalization Act of 1790 guaranteed citizenship rights to "free, white persons." Congress extended suffrage to people of African descent in 1870, and to American Indians in 1924. First-generation immigrant Asians, the issei, would not gain citizenship rights until 1952.) Although he couldn't vote, Kawakami enjoyed politics. He remembered, "Whenever Charlie [Rice] and his group came around I had a little party for them. It was just a little food and drink to be friendly, and every campaign we got a little better acquainted."[54]

When Rice opened the Fairview Business Tract on the family's old dairy lands, H. S. Kawakami bought the property at the corner of Rice and Kress streets to establish a combination dry goods and furniture store that could, according to his autobiography, "catch the spillover from [Kress's] tremendous drawing power." Kawakami hired Taro Iwasa, a young Waimea-born contractor, to build the concrete-fronted building with sand-painted wood sides for a tenth the cost of its larger neighbor, Kress. Iwasa completed construction in an

FOLLOWING PAGE
H. S. Kawakami and his wife Tomo stand together (center) at the opening of Kawakami Store on Rice Street. William J. Senda, Kawakami family archives

KAWAKAM

STORE
T.H. Davies & Co.
40-448

astonishing fifty-one days. A *Garden Island* article that announced the Kawakami Store's opening described the interior as "most modern. The display tables are of terraced masonite in the latest backgrounds to lend color and distinctiveness to the goods displayed."[55]

Kawakami approached attorney Philip Rice to incorporate his stores in 1940. He also placed Rice on a monthly retainer, an astute investment that would pay off many times over the years as he dealt with various business issues as well as the occasional ethnically based harassment inflicted by a cocky cop or bigoted bureaucrat. He remained friendly with Charlie Rice as well, and, though his own leanings were Republican, he contributed to Rice's fundraising efforts for Franklin Delano Roosevelt after Rice became a Democrat.[56]

In true entrepreneurial spirit, Kawakami took advantage of the huge influx of military personnel during World War II by opening stores near the U.S. Army encampment at Kōloa and the Marine Corps camp at Wailua. To overcome the wartime shortage of building materials, he cut off the back portion of his Waimea store and the walkways leading between it and his home, then used the wood to construct the eastside store. In 1944,

Rice Street, 1941. The Kawakami Store was located across the side street from Kress. The Royal Theater opened on the Nāwiliwili side of the store; Waimea Garage was next to it. The canopy above the gas pumps at Garden Island Service is barely visible at the end of the block. William J. Senda, Kauaʻi Museum

Kawakami enlisted in the army. His son George was already fighting as a member of the 442nd Regimental Combat Team; they became the only father-and-son army pair from Kaua'i. As a war veteran Kawakami was able to obtain American citizenship, which enabled him to run for office and receive public appointments. In 1950 he was elected to the territorial constitutional convention. Its job was to draft a plan for Hawai'i's statehood. Kawakami served there with seventy-four-year-old Charlie Rice, who had come out of political retirement to be part of the delegation.

The 1937 Līhu'e furniture and dry goods store was one of many steps Kawakami would take in a career so successful that the *Garden Island* crowned him the Merchant Prince of Kauai. (Tom Coffman, Kawakami's autobiography collaborator, wrote in the book's introduction that he had "the good sense to laugh at that.")[57] In the 1950s, Kawakami and his older brother Fukutaro merged their independent businesses. With Kapa'a businessman Minoru Furugen, they created an umbrella organization called Big Save, Inc. The Kawakamis, Furugen, and a fourth investor, one-time mayor Antone Vidinha, bought state land at auction and established a Big Save and a gas station at Kapa'a in 1961. Other Big Saves followed at Kalāheo, Kōloa, 'Ele'ele, and Hanalei, in addition to the Waimea store, which was labeled a Big Save market as well. In the early 1970s the Kawakamis negotiated a long-term lease with William Hyde Rice, Ltd., for what had once been the cow pasture on Rice Street. There they created the Rice Shopping Center, named, Kawakami wrote, "after our old friends," and opened a Big Save market in the anchor space.[58] The Big Save later moved to the former Foodland location in the civic center, and a bowling alley was opened in the old space. After QSI, Inc., a subsidiary of PAQ, Inc., and parent company of the Times Supermarket chain, bought the Big Save markets in 2011, the Līhu'e store closed.[59] A Kawakami company, Commercial Properties, Ltd., still owns the original property across from Kress, which is leased to Lee's Furniture.

Commercial Properties also owns the Royal Theater building next door. It was constructed in 1940 in the Art Deco–related style known as Moderne. Though it never gained premier movie house status—Lihue Theater, a Consolidated Amusement licensee, held that distinction—it was well attended. For many years the Royal ran Japanese-language films on Tuesday and Thursday nights and family fare the rest of the week. Events such as high school graduations were held there as well.[60]

Changing times eventually brought new programming, and by the 1970s the Royal (renamed Kauai Theater) had become the primary X-rated movie venue on the island. In addition to the films, other porn media were sold there. Above the otherwise empty

The former Royal Theater in 2005.

concession stand in its lobby, a menu read: "Now on sale—For adults only—Porno films—Magazines—Super & reg 8MM films in color—Illustrated magazines—Ask cashier or concessionist."

The building currently accommodates several businesses. "I Buy Gold" was the biggest sign in front of the building in 2013, but a realtor also utilizes space there. Lee's Furniture warehouses inventory in the back. The pocket-sized Kawamoto Barber Shop on the *makai* side of the theater entry was founded by Kōloa barber Tadao Kawamoto, who began cutting hair in Kōloa in 1932 with equipment purchased from "a less favored barber in Lihue."[61] According to Old Koloa Town historical records, Kawamoto taught his brother the trade so that the latter could run the Līhu'e operation. It remains a family business today.

Noboru Miyake bought the third lot on the Rice Street block. He would seem to have had a lot in common with H. S. Kawakami. They were both Waimea residents of Japanese ancestry, both dynamic entrepreneurs, and both politically minded Republicans. It would be easy to assume that the two were good friends and associates, but such was not the case. According to Kawakami's autobiography, "bad feelings" between the two men erupted after a falling out over an enterprise they had once begun together. Their rancor spilled over into electoral politics when they opposed each other for a seat on the 1950 constitutional convention.[62] Whatever their personal antipathy, both were men of energy and vision, not unwilling to be commercial neighbors in order to seize the promise of a street-front location on Rice Street, in the heart of Līhu'e.

Miyake's father, Yasusaburo Katsuhei, had arrived in Hawai'i in 1890 during the great wave of Japanese immigration during the two decades around the turn of the century. He was sent to work at Kekaha Sugar Company. His wife, Tama, joined him a year later, leaving their eldest son, Tokuichi, with her parents. (Tokuichi never emigrated from Japan; he died in the atomic bombing of Hiroshima, 1945.)[63] The Miyakes remained at Kekaha for a few years before striking out on their own to cultivate rice in Waimea Valley. Noboru, the couple's fourth child, was born there in 1896.

At fifteen he began work for the Kekaha plantation in ditch construction and later as a surveyor's assistant during the installation of a hydroelectric plant in Waimea Canyon. In 1913 he became a mechanic at William Olin Crowell's Waimea Garage and Electric Company. In 1921, Miyake and two partners formed a corporation and bought Waimea Garage and Electric from Crowell. With that purchase they acquired the Westside Chrysler dealership, reportedly the first American automobile franchise owned by Americans of Japanese ancestry; the grant of the electric franchise from the government in 1927 made them the first to own a U.S. public utility as well. In those pioneering days, electrical power was neither constant nor centralized. Miyake's 25 horsepower generator supplied electricity to subscribers in one section of Waimea Town, 6 P.M. to midnight. By the time Kauai Electric bought the utility in 1953, he had upgraded to four synchronized diesel generators with a 2,400-volt capacity.[64]

Noboru Miyake was a man of "firsts." During World War I he joined the National Guard, and some have credited him as the first American of Japanese ancestry to serve in the U.S. military. During the 1920s and '30s an increasing number of second-generation Japanese Americans, the nisei, were coming of age and entering the political arena, including Noboru Miyake. His election to the Kaua'i County Board of Supervisors in 1930 may be the pioneering role for which he is best known today. By winning the election—he received enough votes in the primary to gain an outright victory—Miyake become the first Japanese American elected to public office in Hawai'i. His victory preceded that of two other nisei in the general election, Tasaku Oka (island of Hawai'i) and Masayoshi Yamashiro (Honolulu), who won seats in the Hawai'i Territorial House of Representatives. Miyake was defeated for reelection in 1932 but regained his seat in 1934. He continued to serve, sometimes as top vote getter, until 1942, when he withdrew from the general election in the face

Noboru Miyake, front row center, was first elected to the Kaua'i Board of Supervisors in 1930. Shortly after this photo was taken in 1941, Miyake withdrew his reelection bid in the face of widespread anti-Japanese publicity across the country. The other men pictured in front of the county building are, front row: William Ellis, Kaua'i Board of Supervisors chair, and supervisors David K Luke, Yutaka Hamamoto, George Watase. Back row are county officials: James Burgess Jr., clerk; K. C. Ahana, treasurer; W. H. Rice, sheriff; K. M. Ahana, auditor; A. G. Kaulukou, attorney; Henry Matsuki, engineer. Kaua'i Historical Society of widespread anti-Japanese sentiment across America during the early days of World War II. Too old to serve in the military, he participated instead with the Federal Office of Price Administration, which established price controls and administered rationing of scarce materials.

In 1948, Miyake resumed his political career. He was elected to two terms in the Territorial House of Representatives, then to fourteen years in the territorial and state senates; from the 1959 special session to 1962 he served as the powerful chair of the Senate Ways and Means Committee. The *Honolulu Advertiser* rated him one of the state's top ten legislators in 1961, describing him as "a gentleman . . . truly a statesman."[65] Miyake retired from politics after the 1966 election. Reapportionment had cut Kaua'i's representation from three senators to one, and he was defeated by eastside incumbent heavyweight William E. "Billy" Fernandes, who surfed Hawai'i's tidal wave of Democratic victories in once solidly Republican Hawai'i.

Miyake's impact on Kaua'i included several civic improvements. As a supervisor he followed up on his early ditch and hydroelectric work experiences by spearheading the creation of Kaua'i's Bureau of Water Works. Through his efforts at the war's conclusion, the army fire stations and equipment were transferred to the County—the beginning of the Kaua'i Fire Department. The sale of his Waimea utility to Kaua'i Electric in 1953 was a

Garden Island Service, Waimea Garage, and Royal Theater. Kaua'i Historical Society

step toward unification of electrical power into a single islandwide system. Mayor Francis Ching would recognize those contributions in a 1973 testimonial dinner to honor Miyake. He joked that, except for Miyake, "I don't know of anyone other than God who has ever had powers over water, fire, and electricity!"[66]

Miyake established Waimea Garage on Rice Street shortly before World War II. Leonora Albayalde, at the *Filipino News* next door, remembered it initially operating as an auto repair and glass shop. By 1961, however, the height of Miyake's political career, it had long functioned as a souvenir and general merchandise store.[67] In 1971, Bulatao Enterprises, Ltd., purchased the property to establish the Guadalupe Garment Factory, and Waimea Garage built a new plant in the Lihue Industrial Park in 1974 to sell and service Chrysler, Plymouth, and Dodge vehicles. A dozen years later the property was leased for use as a furniture store and drapery and carpet sales. Sculptor and former Kauaʻi Community College shop instructor Ralph Kouchi bought the lot in 1997, then sold it in 2003 to Iguana Properties, Ltd., owned by Kapaʻa entrepreneur Kevin Hurst. The Guerber family now owns the building and has opened a micro-brewery, the Kauai Beer Company, on the premises.

FILIPINO NEWS

The Fairview lot adjacent to Waimea Garage was purchased from William Hyde Rice, Ltd., to house the *Filipino News*.[68] Astute *Garden Island* editor Charlie Fern had begun publishing the *Kauai Filipino News* in 1931 as a way to tap an island market not being served by the English-language media. Abraham Albayalde became its editor in 1933. It was he who led the way to purchase the paper in 1942 and run an independent operation. At his right hand was associate editor Leonora Curammeng, who would later become Mrs. Albayalde. Nora, as she was known, had been hired as a reporter for the *Garden Island*—supplied with a Dodge automobile to get around the island and do her work—after she graduated from Waimea High.

Albayalde and Curammeng also worked for Fern at local radio station KTOH, he as a program director, she as an announcer and news editor. They were on the air afternoons and evenings in Ilocano to disseminate news and events from the world, the Philippines, and around the island. Nora remembered Abe as "very innovative, brilliant, in Filipino media." Their programs were not solely studio produced: they also broadcast via remote control from Kekaha, Moloaʻa, and elsewhere, airing on-the-scene interviews with people in the area.

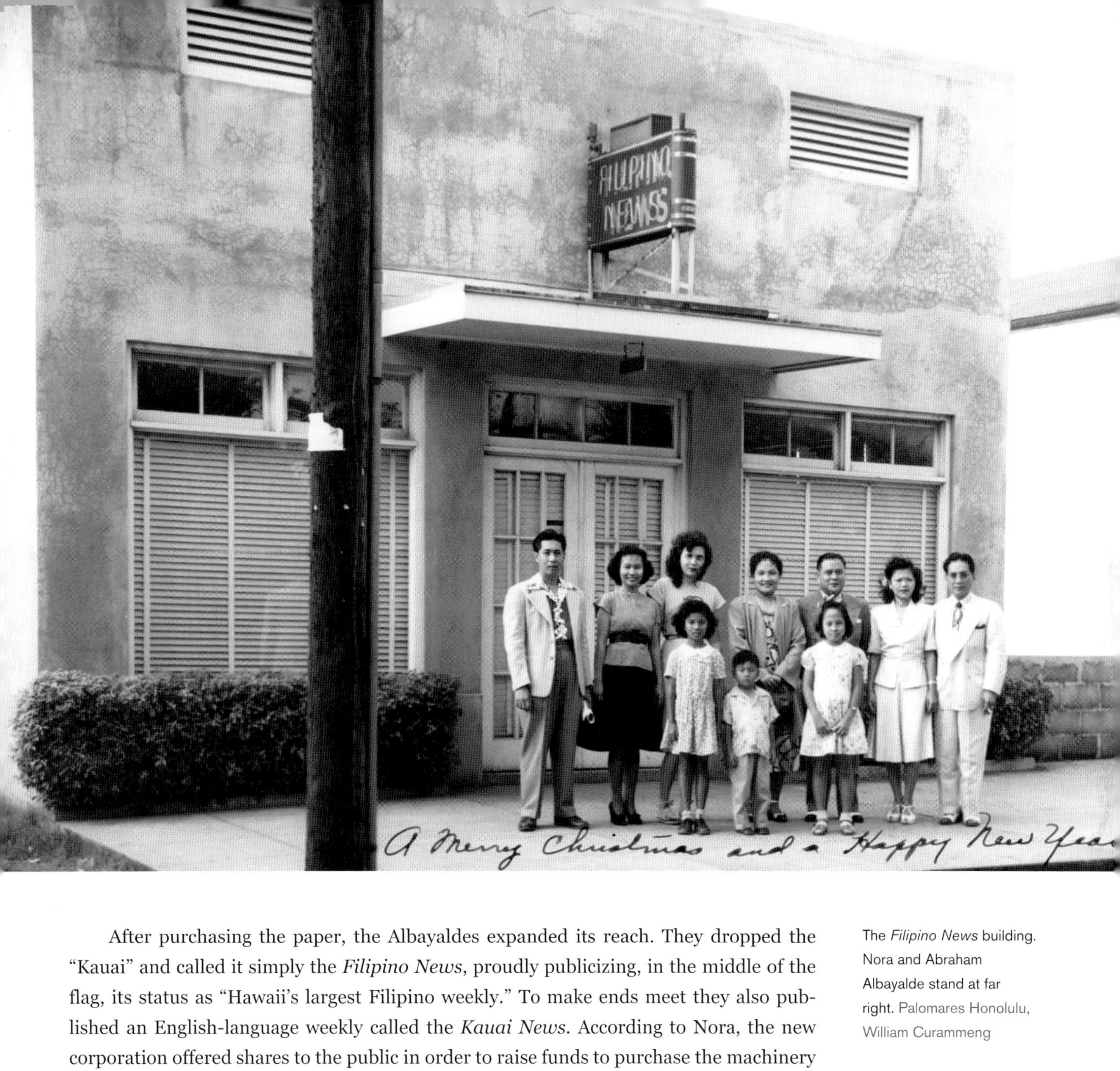

The *Filipino News* building. Nora and Abraham Albayalde stand at far right. Palomares Honolulu, William Curammeng

After purchasing the paper, the Albayaldes expanded its reach. They dropped the "Kauai" and called it simply the *Filipino News*, proudly publicizing, in the middle of the flag, its status as "Hawaii's largest Filipino weekly." To make ends meet they also published an English-language weekly called the *Kauai News*. According to Nora, the new corporation offered shares to the public in order to raise funds to purchase the machinery and construct the building as well as, literally, to encourage "buy-in" and participation from the Filipino community:

> We told them "we're not buying this property—we're not building this place—to make money. We're going to have to spend a lot of money to put up a place

like this. If you want to join us, invest your money (we started with ten dollars) . . . because we have to make the *Filipino News* and this building what we want it to be." And that's what we did.

The military, cognizant of the publication's value for dissemination of wartime regulations and information to monolingual Filipinos, encouraged its publication.[69] It also allowed the *Filipino News* to build the facility for its operations despite the materials rationing and other restrictions on civilian construction. Contractor Itsuzo Maeda was hired to erect the straightforward, flat-fronted building with two decorative vents at the top (the current red tile overhang, arched entry, faux-hacienda look was a later remodel). The front portion of the interior housed the reception area and editorial and advertising staff; typesetting—they used Intertype, the old hot-metal, slug-casting typesetters—and printing machines were in back. Storage for newsprint and archived editions was accommodated behind the work areas. Although the space between the *Filipino News* building and the Waimea Garage was filled in by a later owner, it was originally open for automobile parking, pickups, and deliveries.

The paper was published primarily in Ilocano (the majority of Filipinos in Hawai'i have roots in the Ilocos provinces, traditionally a farming region), with small sections also written in Tagalog and Visayan, two other languages of the Philippines. It reported local and world events but particularly featured news of the Philippines. Births, deaths, marriages, beauty contests, sports, and other items of personal and community interest were also included and always popular. Published every Friday, the *Filipino News* was delivered to homes across the island by women paid to pick it up and take it to subscribers along their routes. Papers were also air-shipped bulk to the other islands for distribution.

Editorial philosophy was nonpartisan. Plantations and others who wished to communicate with the Filipino community—sometimes even local folks wanting to showcase personal items such as family photos—paid to have their messages translated and printed in the paper. That policy occasionally led to problems. During the unionization struggle in 1946 the paper was picketed, accused of being a mouthpiece for sugar plantation management. Leonora Albayalde seized the opportunity to confront labor leader Harry Bridges about the paper's treatment when the two sat next to each other on a plane one day. She assured him that the *Filipino News* was simply doing its job as translators. "Give me your copy, pay me too, because the plantations are paying me. I'll translate your information too," she said. Bridges called off the picketers.

Leonora Curammeng Albayalde (1920–2013), on the grounds of ʻIolani Palace between Governor Ben Cayetano and his wife Vicky. William Curammeng

The Albayaldes dedicated themselves to the *Filipino News*. They ate in its office, they often slept there, they tackled whatever was necessary to make the paper a success. "I'm the manager, I'm the janitor, everything," Abe Albayalde used to say. He also believed in apprenticing youth, not only to handle menial tasks such as hand folding the papers but also to learn typesetting and other aspects of newspaper publishing. At least one of Abe's protégés, Rick Rasay, would never forget the experience he gained at the paper. He later bought Kauai Printers and operated it for several years on Halenani Street behind the *Filipino News* building.

Abe eventually returned to the Philippines, exhausted by years of overwork. Nora continued in the news industry and worked in Honolulu for the ILWU weekly paper and the Hawaii Newspaper Agency. Long active in public affairs and the advancement of Filipinos in Hawaiʻi, she was honored as a Kauai Filipino Centennial awardee during the hundredth anniversary of migration celebrations in 2006.

The *Filipino News* building started a new life in the hands of Guadalupe Ledesma Bulatao (1918–1994). If H. S. Kawakami held the title of Merchant Prince of Kauaʻi, Bulatao was its First Lady of Fashion.[70] The woman who bought the *Filipino News* property

The much altered *Filipino News* building, 2007.

was born in Pasuquin, Ilocos Norte, Philippines. She came to Kaua‘i as a young girl to visit her mother's brother, the Reverend Catalino Cortezan, who was pastor of Koloa Union Church. The Great Depression delayed her return home to the Philippines; falling in love with a young policeman, Jose Bulatao, and marrying him in 1934, scripted a new life for her on Kaua‘i. The couple lived in Kōloa until 1937, when he was offered a job at Kekaha Sugar Company, initially in industrial relations but later as the company's housing supervisor.

From her earliest days fabricating dresses for her dolls, Guadalupe Bulatao had been interested in fashion design. After the Bulatao family, which then included three children with a fourth on the way, was established on the west side of Kaua‘i, Guadalupe opened the Rendezvous Dress Shoppe in Waimea. She complemented her own clothing line with outside suppliers' ensemble items such as handbags and jewelry. The store was a hit, not only with the local population but with servicemen during the war who could ship the "look" of Hawai‘i home to mothers, wives, sweethearts. A disastrous 1949 flood in Waimea washed away the Rendezvous and its inventory, but other Bulatao establishments eventually replaced it.

OPPOSITE PAGE
Fashion designer Guadalupe Bulatao in a hat of her own creation. Pete Asao, Millicent Wellington

HAWAI'I FASHION WOWS THE WORLD

An early fashion industry leader in Hawai'i, Alfred Shaheen, utilized his Lebanese family's generations-long expertise in the garment business to build a factory and make his own fabrics for the aloha shirts and "bombshell dresses" that can still, one reporter asserted in a 2013 review of Bishop Museum's Shaheen retrospective, "make women swoon for their impeccable tailoring and sheer sexiness." When Hawai'i became the fiftieth state in 1959, Shaheen's clothes were being sold across the United States, produced by four hundred employees in Honolulu. Other local designers emerged and were showcased. The bold splashes of color and geometric forms that characterized 1960s pop art and the London modernists—the Mods—translated well into the brilliant new floral patterns of Hawaiian fashions, whether any given piece redefined the traditional full muu-muu as a sleek A-line maxi-dress or followed the mini-skirted style of British fashion icon Mary Quant. The flamboyant prints even spiced up much-mocked bell bottoms with Hawaiian flavors. By the end of the '60s, media across the continent were saluting the stars of Hawai'i fashion designers.[71]

Lifting the silkscreen for an iconic Alfred Shaheen fabric. Camille Shaheen-Tunberg

Guadalupe Bulatao was very much present when Hawai'i fashion splashed onto the international scene. Professionally undaunted after her husband's death in a 1959 automobile crash, she opened a modest shop in front of her Kekaha home. She also bought the property that had housed the *Filipino News* and opened a retail outlet in Līhu'e called Jose-Lu. Celebrities stopped by to explore her designs: Elizabeth Taylor, Shirley Temple Black, and the wives of John Wayne, Rory Calhoun, and astronaut Neil Armstrong were among those known to have patronized her work. Bing Crosby and his wife arranged a showing of eighteen Bulatao garments at a Pebble Beach golf tournament in California—it completely sold out. Leading retailers of the day, including Liberty House and McInerny's, carried her fashions, as did Kauai Stores. Bulatao's creativity, augmented by a flair for marketing, also led to experiments well beyond traditional fashion bounds. In the mid-1960s she introduced the "kanemuu," a novelty, below-the-knee, pocketed and belted aloha *skirt* for men's party-going and leisure wear; the first to purchase a kanemuu was reportedly not an islander but "an oil-rich Texan."[72] When the Kauai Sheraton Hotel opened in Po'ipū in 1969, Bulatao became the first local designer in Hawai'i commissioned to coordinate employee attire for the property of an international hotel chain.

A splashy Originals by Guadalupe advertising photo promoted the company's fashions at Kauai Stores, 1972. Bulatao family collection

Formal wear and bridal gowns were always her specialty, and Bulatao was a popular wedding consultant for brides. Her services included designing the dress, decorating the church, arranging the floral bouquets and generally doing what it took to create an entire memory-of-a-lifetime *event*. The affection her patrons felt for Bulatao and her work was evident in her being chosen as *ninang*, or matron of honor, for scores of weddings over the years. Success spurred the need to expand production. Bulatao negotiated to purchase the Waimea Garage building next to her Līhu'e shop and, with great fanfare, the Guadalupe Garment Factory was dedicated on November 25, 1972. Mayor Antone Vidinha and H. T. Cagampan, the Philippine consul in Honolulu, untied the ceremonial ribbons. During the celebration Cesar Portugal, president of the Kauai Filipino Community Council, recognized the achievement she had made, saying, "For Kauai, it is another milestone of economic development—for the Filipino community, a source of great pride." Son Jose Bulatao Jr., a drama instructor at Kaua'i Community College and

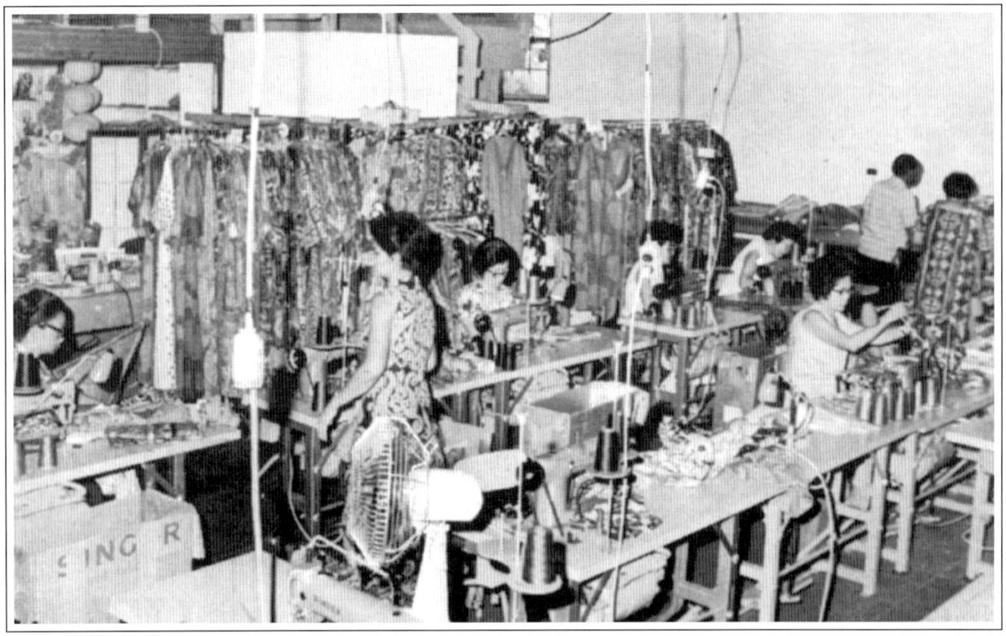

The Guadalupe Bulatao factory on Rice Street, 1972. Bulatao family collection

director of the Bailes de Jose Troupe, performed folk dances from the Philippines with his group.[73]

The Rice Street factory contained parallel rows of sewing tables in the middle of the room. Each table supported a Singer powered by an electrical outlet suspended over the machine by a cord from the ceiling. Work tables and an electrically powered, revolving dress rack were positioned along the walls. Bulatao's daughter, Millicent Wellington, recalled several of the company's seamstresses in Kekaha following her mother to the new Līhu'e factory to continue working for her.[74]

Wellington credits a measure of her mother's success to her talent for cutting fabric freehand, without the need to use a pattern. It enabled her to mold a dress to a customer's less-than-perfect body without the garment developing sags or puckers in unsightly places. The fabrics, too, were carefully chosen, colorful-to-explosive designs emblematic of their era. "She was always one step ahead of the crowd," remembered Wellington, with a ruffle here, an innovative cut to a sleeve there, or a redefined neckline that adapted the classic muumuu to a fresh new interpretation for its time. A few Guadalupe Originals can still be found in closets around the islands, and they pop up occasionally at vintage shops and online auctions.

YONEJI BUILDING

The present site of Yoneji's at the corner of Rice and Kalena streets once housed a gas station owned by Garden Island Motors.[75] (The Garden Island Service Station's paint shop was located at what is now a parking lot at Kress and Halenani streets.) Mitsuo Yoneji was among the merchants who moved his store up from Nāwiliwili when the opportunity arose in 1949. His sister Setsuko Isoda and son Owen, who managed Yoneji's together until the latter's death in 2008, remember their early life in the valley and childhood routines such as climbing the shortcut up "Pake Mountain" to Nāwiliwili Road on their way to Lihue Grammar School near the mill. Employees in those days made deliveries on horseback to customers in Nāwiliwili, Līhu'e, Grove Farm, Puhi, and Kīpū.

The Yonejis sold dry goods and groceries, including beef from Lihue Ranch and staples such as rice, which was bought in 100-pound sacks, then divided into smaller weight bags for sale to the public. For many years another of the Yoneji family members operated a soda fountain on the *mauka* side of Rice Street (currently the site of Don's Camera and

Yoneji's, 2013.

Fine Jewelry Center), where hamburgers and egg sandwiches were best sellers. Though the store closed about 6:00 P.M., the fountain remained open until 10:00 on Friday nights to capitalize on the end-of-week *pau hana* crowd.

Until the 1960s, Yoneji's customers continued to enjoy home delivery services. Owen Yoneji remembered the routine. Since the store's clientele included many working people, he'd often arrive at an empty house, unlatch the door, carry in the box of groceries, and leave it on the kitchen table, taking the time to place perishable items in the ice box. If payment was not already waiting under a ketchup bottle on the table, he would leave a bill there before he departed the house, relatching the door on his way out. The inventory within the store sometimes seemed a jumbled collection of items unavailable elsewhere, sought-after items such as camphor for linen closets and stovetop rice cookers, with a lip that kept the rice water from boiling over the edge of the pot.

In 1988 the old Yoneji's structure was razed and a new one constructed. The building setback, originally to accommodate a gas pump, was retained to allow parking in this space-deprived neighborhood. Today, Yoneji's operates as a food wholesaler and leases out offices on the street-front side of the building. Though the new façade does not replicate the old, it was designed to complement the style of the historic buildings along the block.

THE FAIRVIEW TRACT BEHIND RICE STREET

More than a generation ago, in 1977, the Kaua'i County Council adopted its Lihue Development Plan. It had been conceived by Honolulu consultants who were perhaps unappreciative of the organic character of this neighborhood, which had been built and continues to be run by local entrepreneurs and patronized by residents. The plan recommended that "the area presently bound by Rice, Kalena, and Kress Streets, and some adjacent area across Kalena Street should be completely redeveloped," because such a solution "would be a meaningful step in creating a competitive and enlarged shop area where there are now marginal businesses, obsolete structures, and insufficient parking."[76]

Among the "marginal businesses" so easily dismissed by 1970s urban planners are establishments that continue to be operated by the founders' families. In addition to Yoneji's, they include Tanaka Plumbing, founded by Shigezo Tanaka, a tinsmith at Nāwiliwili who moved to Kalena Street and opened the plumbing supplies store that still bears the family name, and the Lihue Barbecue Inn.

Lihue Fishing Supply and Kalena Fish Market, 2007.

Masaichi Sasaki, who had worked for Grove Farm and later served as chauffeur for Gaylord Wilcox, opened the Barbecue Inn on Kress Street shortly before World War II. The restaurant began to thrive after Pearl Harbor, when hordes of military personnel stationed on Kaua'i brought steady patronage to its tables. The more than 40,000 troops who spent time on the island were a hungry bunch: the four restaurants open for trade in Kapa'a in 1941 mushroomed to twenty-three in 1944, and "hot dog wagons sometimes netted $100 a day."[77] For many years the Sasaki family, like others in this area and similar locations around the islands, lived behind the restaurant. Sasaki's son Henry and daughter-in-law Mildred later ran the business. Since Henry Sasaki's death in 2006, Mildred has carried on with one of her daughters, Donna Muramoto, the third Sasaki generation involved in the Barbecue Inn.

At the end of Kress Street stands the Lihue Christian Church, which was officially organized in 1900 as the Lihue Japanese Church. Services had begun before the turn of the twentieth century on the grounds of the Hale Nani estate in a cottage used for what was called the Young People's Christian Association (where an Episcopalian clergyman had also held monthly services in the 1880s). The house was moved a half mile to the site of the

Lihue Christian Church, 1975. Harvey Tam, Kaua'i Historical Society

current campus when Mary Sophia Rice made it available to the Japanese congregation. In 1916 the first chapel was built, along with a dormitory to accommodate boys from beyond Līhu'e who attended Kauai High School. A social hall followed in 1924. Probably a result of the large number of first-generation Japanese immigrants among the three-hundred-member congregation, Rev. Paul Osumi was among the leaders of the Japanese community forcefully interned after the United States entered World War II. Elsie Wilcox led a group of citizens, including her sister Mabel, William Henry Rice and his brother Charlie, to pressure—ultimately unsuccessfully—the military governor for Osumi's release.[78]

The wood-and-stone chapel at the front of the campus was dedicated in 1957. It embodied the spirit of devotion exhibited during "Operation Moss Rock" the previous year, when dedicated men of the congregation personally hauled the stones donated by Grove Farm from lands on the south shore to make the chapel a reality. The social hall was rebuilt in 1997 after Hurricane 'Iniki destroyed the old structure. The Lihue Christian Church officially changed affiliation from Congregational Christian to United Church of Christ in 1964. It describes itself today as a "progressive mainline congregation with beliefs rooted in the Lutheran, Calvinist, Reformed and Congregational traditions." Community involvement, with an emphasis on education and youth, has been an ongoing mission at Lihue

Hamura Saimin, 2008.
Nancy J. Budd

Christian. In 1967 the first day-care center on Kaua'i licensed by the Department of Social Services was opened there. Both 'Ae Kamali'i Preschool and the Wilcox Adult Day Care Center now have homes on this campus.

Other businesses that once thrived in the Fairview Tract are but memories today, with new enterprises having taken their place. The Lihue Fishing Supply once housed Ideal Cleaners. In the building next door, Akimoto Store, a sundries, seeds, and bread shop, preceded Flowers Forever. Sadamitsu Store at Kalena and Halenani was replaced by Jack Wada Electronics, now Kauai Electronics, Inc. KQNG Radio took the place of a small hotel and Matsuda's jewelry shop on Halenani Street. Further along the block, longtime restaurant Ma's Place closed in 2007. Kauai Realty moved to the corner lot at Halenani and Kress from the old Central Service Station on Rice Street. It followed Harry's Appliances, which had itself replaced Kauai Super Market. Robert's Jewelry, named for founder Robert Ozaki, originally sold clothing, shoes, and accessories in the building as well as jewelry. Across from Hamura Saimin, an institution on Kaua'i, are the parking lot and offices of the company that started it all, William Hyde Rice, Ltd. This location was once the site of the slaughterhouse on these former dairy lands.

FIVE

ON THE MOVE

Paradises from the past are seldom useful as anything but rulers by which to measure the failures of the present, the failures that paradises of the future seek to fix.

—Rebecca Solnit, *Storming the Gates of Paradise*

The Automobile Era of the twentieth century transformed the relationship between people and place on Kaua'i. The membranes separating each self-contained, uniquely defined community became increasingly permeable as roads improved and cars became increasingly accessible—and created problems of their own.

Sharing the road on the main street, 1920s style. private collection

A drive in the past lane must look to the pavement itself for an understanding of the development of central Līhu'e. From its historic origin at what was casually called the "main Lihue corner" in front of the Isenberg memorial, Rice Street descends 200 feet over the mile and a half it travels to the mouth of Nāwiliwili Valley. There, it becomes Nāwiliwili Road and begins a climb up the west side of the valley from the harbor. Near the top, at what is now Halekō Road but used to be the last segment of Nāwiliwili Road, the route curves east, drops into the valley and past the former mill site, and returns to the main Līhu'e corner and Rice Street once again. A hundred years ago traveling around the four-mile, elliptical path was termed "going around the block."[1]

THE AUTOMOBILE ERA DAWNS

The concepts of far and near are relative, dependent on speed, time, and accessibility. Today, in a modern car, the four-mile journey can be completed in eight minutes without once exceeding the speed limit. An unburdened pedestrian moving with determined briskness could possibly make the circuit in an hour. Back when conveyances were limited and many of the island's roads were little more than rutted tracks rendered occasionally treacherous by storms, the effort of land travel kept most people close to home. "But at least you have bad roads," Paul Isenberg wrote his Līhu'e family in 1895, "formerly we had none."[2]

Daniel Paul Isenberg, who lived on O'ahu and raised thoroughbred horses at Wai'anae, no doubt caused a sensation when he shipped his car to Kaua'i while on a visit in 1905.[3] Two years later, seventy-four-year-old Grove Farm plantation owner G. N. Wilcox became the first Kaua'i resident to actually own an automobile:

G. N. Wilcox gave his first car, a two-cylinder horseless carriage steered with a tiller, to John A. Hogg. Lucy Wilcox, Grove Farm Homestead Museum

> It was a steam car, a motor car they called it. I gave it to Hogg—he was the telephone man, had a pair of horses, but it was hard for him to get around to repairs a long way off. It was really a small steam engine burning gasoline, with a boiler. Yes, I drove it a little. But I soon gave it up.[4]

Six people owned cars on the island in 1908, seventy-four in 1910, ninety-two (plus ten motorcyclists) by mid-1911. The new vehicles garnered considerable attention from the public and the press. When officials in early 1912 drove from Hanapēpē to Kapa'a and back to Līhu'e in three and a half hours and still managed stops for school inspections in

The elliptical path pictured in 1974, from town to the harbor and back around the other side of Nāwiliwili Valley, was once termed "going around the block." Hawai'i State Archives

each of the towns, the *Garden Island* enthused that such a trip "would have been out of the question without a machine." H. D. Wishard, Līhu'e resident and longtime Kaua'i Board of Supervisors chair, registered the island's 134th car when he bought a new Hudson that April.[5]

Not everyone on Kaua'i was as convinced as Wishard about the advantages of the automobile. That same month the *Garden Island* reported, tongue firmly in cheek, that quite a few businessmen "have not entirely forgotten the staying qualities of the horse, and who remain his staunch friend regardless of fancy gas machines."[6] Their numbers included bank manager Frank Crawford, Sheriff William Henry Rice, and Rev. J. M. Lydgate. Among the Kaua'i drivers "who have forsaken the noble animal for the mechanical monster" were the rest of the Rice brothers—Charlie, Philip and Arthur—along with their father, William Hyde Rice, Rev. Hans Isenberg, and several members of the Wilcox clan.

The future was unequivocally on the side of motorized vehicles, and in 1912, when Lihue Plantation was in its great period of town building, it

Rev. Hans Isenberg abandoned "the staying qualities of the horse" and became the second owner of an automobile on Kaua'i after G. N. Wilcox registered ownership of the first two. Kaua'i Museum

The route to the Lihue Plantation mill and into town from the west, 1887. Roads on Kaua'i in that period were not unlike those across the United States. "Outside the business districts, roads dwindled to little more than wagon ruts," observed Earl Swift in *The Big Roads.* "Out in the sticks, a sprinkling of rain could turn them to bogs; their mud lay deep and loose, could suck the boots off a farmer's feet." Mixed in that stew was a generous amount of manure from the local beasts of burden. When this picture was taken, horses in America's largest city, New York, were contributing 2.5 million pounds of manure and 60,000 gallons of urine *every day.* On this main Kaua'i travelway, with a preponderance of working oxen, mules, and horses around it—a thousand oxen at Lihue Plantation alone—the fly-buzzing stench of the road must have been appalling. Hawai'i State Archives

donated ten feet of land along the main street so that the road could be widened. In turn, the County agreed to pay all costs for moving and rebuilding the stone wall that ran along the roadway from William Hyde Rice's Hale Nani estate to the Lihue Hotel (now the site of Kalapaki Villas). The County also gave permission to the plantation in 1913 to erect poles for electrical lines around Līhu'e on the condition that all work was done to the county supervisors' satisfaction, and that if the roads were widened in the future "the said poles, where they interfere with traffic, shall be removed at the expense of the company, and that the poles may be used for public purposes."[7]

By the end of 1915 a total of 367 automobiles, trucks, and motorcycles had been registered on Kaua'i.[8] A quarter of them were Fords, 16 percent Buicks, and 11 percent Cadillacs, followed by lesser numbers of Overlands, Hudsons, Studebakers, Chevrolets, and two dozen other makes. Included in the mix were four Stevens-Duryeas, expensive limousines developed by Frank Duryea, who in 1896 with his brother Charles had produced the first commercial automobile in the United States.

Gradually the horse riders converted—or were converted. In 1917 several members of the congregation at Lihue United Church bought Rev. Lydgate a green, five-passenger Dodge to ease his duties to reach distant parishioners. According to his son William,

In 1924, evidence of equestrian use was still visible in the town core. Although several haphazardly parked automobiles are visible around the county building, stables and a grazing horse remain behind it. 11th Photo Sec., Hawai'i State Archives

The Von Hamm-Young company sold the aristocratic Packard, which they advertised in a 1930 issue of the *Garden Island*. Former Garden Island Motors president Hobey Goodale remembered that until the 1950s or '60s Waimea Garage was the dealer for Chryslers and later Volkswagens; Otsuka's in Kapa'a for Nash; Garden Island Motors for Ford, Mercury, Lincoln; Von Hamm-Young for American Motors, Dodge, and Packard; Kōloa for General Motors. *Garden Island* collection

however, "Father was a dreadful driver" who never learned to coordinate the clutch, gear, and throttle timing needed to shift gears, though "he seemed oblivious to all this mismanagement, and the faithful old Dodge stood up well under the punishment." Lydgate identified the automobile as the instrument "that profoundly changed life at the parsonage," giving the family "a mobility undreamed of in our horse and buggy days." When the worldwide influenza outbreak of 1918 and 1919 came to Kaua'i, the minister was able to travel into remote valleys around Līhu'e and notify health authorities about those he found to be ill. He also traveled occasionally to Mahelona Hospital near Keālia to conduct religious services for the tuberculosis patients there. And the benefits of the automobile were not all work related; the Lydgates' ability to travel by car to Kōloa for Sunday church services in a third the time the trip had previously taken meant enjoyment of much more beach and swimming afterward. J. M. Lydgate bought an Essex roadster (a division of Hudson) for his work after he left the ministry and became a land agent for Kaua'i. After his father's death in 1922, Lydgate's oldest son, John Mortimore Jr., traded in the family Dodge for a Hudson, "a big and elegant car that had the latest in technology: windows that rolled up."[9]

ROAD CONSTRUCTION

The task of transporting the new machines in the first decade of the twentieth century was more than the roads of that era could manage. Shortly after Wilcox purchased the island's first car, his niece Elsie noted in her diary that they had had to change tires eighteen times in one three-day period.[10] In 1906, with considerable financial assistance from the Territory, the County instituted an ambitious eleven-year program to macadamize the main belt road and several laterals leading from it.[11] When two dozen members of Congress visited the island the next year, reporter Ernest Acheson wrote to the Washington, Pennsylvania, *Observer* that Kaua'i enjoyed "eighty miles of good, wide, carriage roads. . . . All the bridges and culverts are of concrete. . . . This system is being extended every year."[12] The process was completed on the Līhu'e-to-harbor circuit within a couple of years.

By the end of 1912 the roads between Hanamā'ulu and Waimea had been macadamized. The *Garden Island* credited the excellence of that work to Kaua'i car owners having registered the largest number of automobiles, per capita, of any of the Hawaiian islands. The route north to Hā'ena was finished in 1917.[13] That year the Territorial Senate, in its published *Senate Journal,* noted the superior road building that had taken place on Kaua'i: "With the exception of the County of Kauai, the several county governments have neither adopted nor pursued any consistent road policy."[14] The reason it identified for this island's success: "The County of Kauai alone has adopted the proper system of appointing a competent road engineer, and placing the entire responsibility and execution of road construction and upkeep in his hands."

Halekō Road, 1910.
Jerome Baker, Hawai'i State Archives

The capable hands that the Senate referenced were those of Joseph Hughes Moragne (1864–1937). Born and educated in Alabama, Moragne began work as Kaua'i's engineer in the early years of the Territory. He proceeded to engineer both the macadamizing and the upkeep of the Kaua'i belt road, its connectors, and bridges around the island. According to the *Senate Journal,* Moragne's work and the commitment of Kaua'i to fund its roads meant "existing roads have been kept in repair and all surplus has gone into regrading and extending, year by year, the macadamized roads. As a result, Kauai has the best and most economically administered roads of any county in the Territory."[15] Moragne did not make government work his sole occupation. Several plantations utilized his talents, among them McBryde Sugar Company, for whom he developed the Wainiha power plant's water collection system, and Grove Farm, where he designed the first reinforced concrete bridge in Hawai'i at Hulē'ia in 1909, among other innovations.[16] Lihue Plantation hired Moragne in 1919, and during his eighteen years working for the company he developed a remarkable and vast irrigation system throughout its acreage.

Macadam surfacing in the early territorial period might have been state of the art but it was not without maintenance issues. A type of road construction developed in mid-eighteenth-century Scotland, macadam used layers of broken stones laid in tight patterns and covered with small stones to create a hard surface. Early attempts in Līhu'e to stabilize the macadamized surfaces with applications of oil rendered the roads dangerously slick in rainy weather, especially on grades such as existed on lower Rice Street. That practice was abandoned. However, macadamized roads that were left untreated tended to ravel in dry weather. To prevent deterioration, water carts were used for a while to wet the road surfaces down, a successful system until the point at which more roads than cart capacity rendered the practice prohibitively expensive. By 1917 the favored method of upkeep was to position a man (known as a cantonier) to patrol and maintain each two-mile segment of

The road between Līhu'e and Nāwiliwili, ca. 1915. The county building is in the background at right, with Frank Crawford's property immediately in front and to the left of it. Lihue Hotel cottages stand along the road to the left of the cart passing by. Kaua'i Museum

road. The only shortcoming of the cantonier arrangement, Moragne believed, was the difficulty of securing "the services of intelligent men who are also industrious; the two good qualities do not seem to combine frequently enough in the labor available."[17] (He himself had strong incentive beyond his inherent capabilities to be industrious: in 1915 the County Board of Supervisors had voted to give Moragne a 5 percent commission on all road and bridge work in the county.)

During the Depression-era 1930s, available federal funds precipitated another

significant period of road and bridge building around Kaua'i. One of the projects was the construction of the Lihue Mill Bridge and an adjoining section of roadway *mauka* of the plantation mill.[18] Their completion eliminated the need, for the first time in the area's history, to loop south around the mill on Halekō Road when heading west from town. The new transportation route *mauka* of the factory passed over the area where the pond that once drove factory operations had been located.

The island's primary roads achieved dignity in 1938 when they were formally given

Joseph Moragne, in the foreground wearing a dark hat and white shirt, was county engineer during the great road construction project of the early territorial period. He is walking in front of a portable rock crusher used in the macadamizing process. Mary Moragne Cooke

names by the County Board of Supervisors. Prior to that time maps listed "Government Road" or the "Government Belt Road" and people spoke colloquially of "main street" in Līhu'e. They chose the name Kaumuali'i for the belt road west of Līhu'e to honor the last *ali'i nui* of Kaua'i—although that name had placed fourth in the community vote: Roosevelt Highway won as the most popular choice. The government belt road north became Kūhiō Highway, with the stretch from the Isenberg monument to Hanamā'ulu initially labeled Isenberg Street. The main road through Līhu'e became William Hyde Rice Street. The road originally carved out of land between the old Crawford residence and the Nāwiliwili side of the county building's lawn was named Hardy Road to honor Judge Jacob Hardy (1827–1915); it made a left turn *mauka* around the courthouse and met Isenberg/Kūhiō.[20]

Some of the streets were labeled with numbers in Hawaiian. One and two, 'Akahi

THE POETRY OF BRIDGE WORK

Construction of the Lihue Mill Bridge was challenging because of the depths necessary to be dug to support the foundations. Territorial Highway Department construction supervisor Robert Belt expressed his anticipation of inspecting the excavations in a poem:

PRAYER OF THE INSPECTING ENGINEER

Sometimes I've picked the narrow view and held you pretty close,
I've hammered at you daily and perhaps I've been verbose
In urging you to do the job just as the Book decrees—
Well, that's what I get paid for. Will you not excuse it please?
Today I must descend into a hole you've dug for me.
Some forty feet below the ground and narrow as can be,
To see if you've got bearing for the bridge you're going to build,
And if it's all the same to you I'd rather not be killed.
Upon a little piece of board, tied to a rope, I'll sit
The while your men will lower me into the dankish pit.
The sound of pumps will pound my ears and drown my muffled cries,
And flashes of a misspent youth will pass before my eyes.
Hand over hand your sturdy men will pay the lifeline out
While inch by inch and foot by foot they ease me down the spout.
If someone's hand should slip, my chance would not be worth a dime.
There's just one prayer that comes to me at such a ticklish time:
"I HOPE YOU FELLAS LIKE ME!"[19]

Finishing touches were made to the Lihu'e Mill Bridge in 1936. Tom Fujii, Kaua'i Historical Society

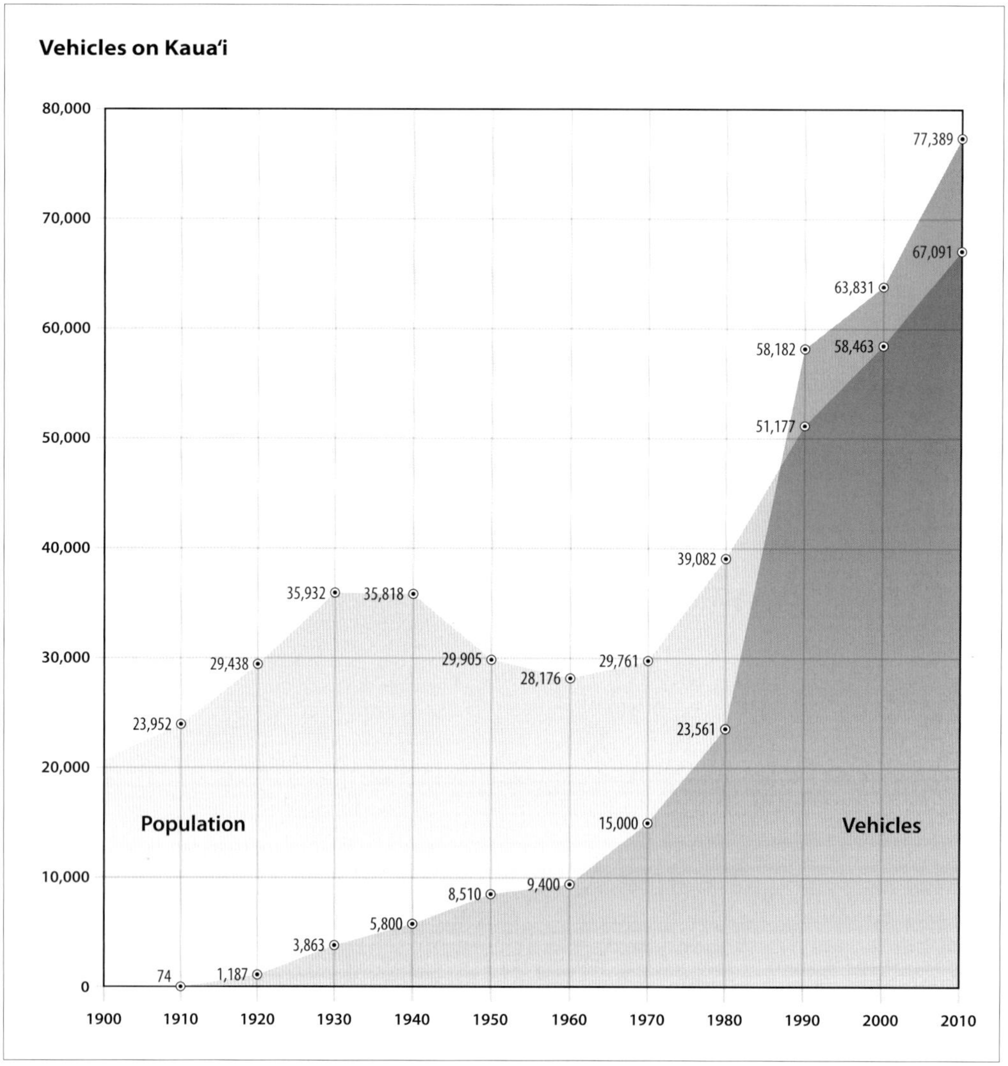

During the 1900s, vehicle ownership on Kauaʻi rose from zero to more than one for each resident on Kauaʻi.

and ʻElua, were assigned to the streets parallel to Kūhiō between Hardy and Ahukini that constituted the Lihue Town Tract. Numbers three through seven (ʻEkolu, ʻEhā, ʻElima, ʻEono, and ʻEhiku) identified streets in the Isenberg residential tract *mauka* of today's Kūhiō Highway. On the other side of town, the road through the Hale Nani business tract on the Nāwiliwili Stream side of Rice Street became eight—ʻEwalu—and the traditional driveway from Rice Street to the armory (now the State Office Building) behind the county building became ʻEiwa (nine). ʻUmi (ten) later replaced the name Hardy on the block between Rice Street and the courthouse when Hardy was rerouted to continue in a large curve north of the courthouse and around Wilcox School before meeting Rice Street.

By 1940 about 5,800 vehicles were registered on Kauaʻi, a ratio of one for every six residents.[21] True, not every vehicle belonged to an individual or family. Island companies—plantations, stores, garages, and other businesses—owned a significant percentage of the total number. Enough households still lacked personal vehicles that Wilcox Hospital, which opened in 1938, included nurses' quarters to enable employees to live on the premises during their work week. Various opportunities to live in town were provided for Kauai High School students as well.

After World War II, as the first homes *makai* of the county building began conversion to commercial enterprises, the Board of Supervisors decided to expand the roughly

Hawaiian Bitumuls Co. laid a "free sample" of the new surfacing material, hot mix asphalt, on Rice Street, March 6, 1952. J. P. Errett, Kauaʻi Historical Society

thirty-five-foot-wide Rice Street another ten feet. Supervisor Anthony C. Baptiste Jr. was opposed to the plan. It should be widened twenty feet instead of the proposed ten, he argued: "Lihue is the county seat, and I feel that the street should be fixed to take care of traffic for the next thirty years." Many business and home owners along Rice Street testified otherwise, contending that the road was already wide enough for a "country town." Additionally, owners on the south side of the street had previously surrendered land for sidewalk improvements and were resistant to losing further property to roadway. Finally, in January 1946, after several deferrals, the supervisors agreed in a three-to-two vote to take fourteen feet from each side of the street as setbacks for road and sidewalk expansion. One disgruntled landowner was heard to mutter "bunch of thieves!" as he left the meeting. (In 1968 the county bought another 4516 square feet of land, part of "the old Crawford home," in a condemnation action for additional widening of Rice Street.)[22]

Meanwhile, road construction materials were improving. The early water-bound macadam paving gave way to a superior construction called penetration macadam as the standard road surface treatment on Kaua'i. That method, too, became obsolete. In 1952, Hawaiian Bitumuls Co. installed a "hot mix" asphaltic concrete plant next to Grove Farm's rock crusher at Halfway Bridge. The new surfacing method was stronger, faster to lay down, smoother than the penetration pavement, and less expensive to repair. It had reportedly been adopted already as a standard road material on O'ahu, Maui, and Hawai'i. The county celebrated by using hot mix to widen Rice Street from Lihue Store to the old railway underpass, approximately where Ace Hardware is located today.[23]

DEMOCRATIZATION OF THE AUTOMOBILE

Vehicles registered on Kaua'i numbered 8,510 in 1950.[24] The nearly 150 percent increase during the decade was especially significant, since the island's population actually declined almost 20 percent between 1940 and 1950. As statehood approached, so many of their customers could drive between towns that brothers H. S. and Fukutaro Kawakami, who ran stores in Waimea and 'Ele'ele, respectively, decided to merge as a way to avoid competing with each other.[25] The number of cars cruising around Kaua'i and rolling down Rice Street continued to increase dramatically. In the eight years between 1960 and 1968, vehicle registration jumped almost 44 percent, from 9,400 to 13,500 vehicles, or a ratio of one vehicle for every three residents. (The figures for all of Hawai'i are even more impressive: a 180%

In keeping with the automobile's growing dominance and the resulting need for fuel, gasoline supplier Central Service Station was positioned at the main Līhu'e intersection of Rice Street and Halekō Road (above). Standard Oil leased it from 1946 to 1963. During the 1960s Līhu'e redesign, the old Central Service was transformed into shops and offices, and the gas station moved to the center of town (below), directly across from 'Eiwa Street. Tom Fujii, Kaua'i Historical Society

When work was needed on Rice Street in 1974, consultants Kutaka, Portugal and Ibara, Inc., proposed long-term improvements to widen the road to a uniform 56 feet and to clean up and protect electrical, cable TV, and telephone lines by laying them underground as water pipe trenches were being dug. The County rejected those recommendation as too expensive. It chose simply to reconstruct the 40- to-50-foot-wide street from the top of the road to the Kalena-Hardy intersection and to resurface the roadway to Kapule. Had the consultants' plan been approved, it might have mitigated the impact of Hurricane 'Iniki in 1992.

increase in the number of registered vehicles between 1960 and 1970, or nearly one car for every two people in the state.)[26]

By 1987 there were 40,000 vehicles registered on Kaua'i, slightly more than one per resident and too many for Rice Street to be imagined any longer as a slow road in a sleepy country town. In an attempt to ease the congestion on what had become the island's busiest county-owned street, a third, "turning" lane was configured in the center of Rice, a solution that turned out to be akin to using a teaspoon to fill an empty radiator. "Rice Street is still a mess," the upstart newspaper of the time, the *Kauai Times,* headlined in 1988.[27] It quoted the warning by Mayor Tony Kunimura that the situation would grow worse before it got better, "because people keep coming to the island to live and visit."

In 2003, when the latest Rice Street upgrade was completed, 70,000 vehicles were registered on Kaua'i. The two-year project included widening the street to four lanes between Halekō Road and Ace Hardware, expanding the intersection near Ace, improving drainage, landscaping with Florida kou trees (*Cordia sebestena*), and adding curb cuts to conform to Americans with Disabilities Act regulations. The County Department of Public

After the 2003 Rice Street reconfiguration, candlestick bollards were installed to prevent left-hand turns onto Kele Street by the post office. In 2013 the historic crosswalk across Rice Street was restored, and the County is completing plans to signalize the intersection.

Works preserved a hint of the road's history by retaining a section of old cut-stone curbing still visible in front of the Kaua'i Museum.

The overall results of the project for the town were mixed. For a while, more cars could move through the area without precipitating traffic jams, but speed, inattention, and the slalom ride occasioned by parking spaces confusingly positioned intermittently along the street created hazards—and collisions—in the center of town. After seven crashes occurred outside the post office within the first months of the project's completion, the County installed a "fence" of effective if unsightly breakaway, reflectorized, median delineator poles, also known as candlestick bollards. Only a few years later the Department of Public Works began investigating new possibilities to ease the problems along the road. In 2013 the County began to explore enhancing traffic flow by removing some on-street parking and temporarily returning Rice Street to three lanes as well as blocking off 'Eiwa to through traffic by closing its Rice Street access. Meanwhile, the number of registered vehicles continued its climb: 88,836 were recorded in 2012 for a population estimated at less than 69,000.

SAFETY AND TRAFFIC

Irresponsibility behind the wheel did not begin with the 2003 Rice Street redesign. Reckless driving and "the tendency to undue speed" were issues even at the dawn of the automobile era. In 1917 county supervisors passed the first laws to set speed limits and to designate horn and nighttime head and tail light usage. A *Garden Island* editorial about the ordinance recommended that the County hire "one or more traffic officers for each populous district, mounted on motor cycles, who will patrol the highways and promptly arrest all who neglect or contravene the law."[28]

In 1921 the newly formed Kauai Automobile Club installed go-slow signs in English and Japanese at the accident-plagued corner near the front of Lihue Grammar School, where the Nāwiliwili road turned toward Līhu'e and also intersected the road leading west to Kōloa and beyond. To slow the hot-rodders down, the County inserted unmarked bumps and dips in that location and elsewhere, a traffic-calming mechanism that was not without its own perils. After more than enough experience with them, the members of the Lihue Business and Professional Women's Club wrote a letter to the Board of Supervisors in 1924 suggesting that the dips be painted white to increase visibility and ensure "greater safety to the public." The dips became a highlight of at least one travel writer's visit. In a 1930 tourist guide to the islands, he cautioned that on Kaua'i

> the county fathers hit upon a most novel plan to shoot these reckless motorists up to heaven. At all strategic and dangerous places on the road where cars should slow down to five miles or less an hour, either mounds or dips have been built which will wreck any motor passing over them faster than a walk, besides murdering its occupants. All I can say is "Beware"—and remember that in this [tropical] climate it is easy to forget![29]

In 1934 the Board of Supervisors decided to remove the road dips and bumps. Bernice Hundley, supervising principal of Kaua'i schools, protested. Grove Farm manager E. H. W. Broadbent also objected, testifying that he couldn't remember a single accident at the Lihue School corner since the bumps had been in place, "whereas previous to their installation, there had been so many smash-ups that the place became known as Calamity Corner." Supervisor Aguiar blamed the decision to remove them on the wishes of E. S. Wheeler, a U. S. Bureau of Roads official. Aguiar claimed that Wheeler feared loss

To control increasing traffic at the main Līhu'e corner, a man stood in a gazebo and hand-operated stop and go signs, 1931. William J. Senda, Kaua'i Museum

of future federal aid for road projects if the County didn't comply. The *Garden Island* suggested that Aguiar's dislike of such traffic calmers actually dated back to 1926 when, late for an appointment in Waimea, he and fellow supervisor Henry Peters had sped over a bump in Puhi. "Before they knew it," the paper chortled, "Peters went flying up, nearly thrusting his head through the top of his car, and Aguiar found himself nearly making a hole in the windshield."[30]

In 1931 the County stationed a man in a gazebo in the middle of the main Līhu'e intersection. His job was to control traffic by wielding a hand-operated stop sign. He was eventually replaced by permanent stop signs planted at the corners of the road.

More than a few Kaua'i residents despaired of fast-increasing urbanization in 1973 when Līhu'e's first two traffic lights appeared farther down Rice Street, at its intersections with 'Umi and Hardy streets. Other than two lights installed to warn drivers of haul cane trucks crossing public roads in Kekaha and Kōloa, these were the first two traffic signals on the island. Many others have since been installed, although in the twenty-first century the County is considering other traffic-calming options that may increase flow through intersections, such as a planned traffic circle at Hardy and 'Umi streets.

As a tangent to traffic, the question of parking inevitably arises in automobile-based planning discussions about central Līhu'e. Early in the automobile age, drivers took a casual approach to leaving their vehicles around town, with diagonal parking in front of Lihue Store, some parallel parking along Rice, and vehicles randomly left in grassy areas around town. In 1924 employees petitioned the Board of Supervisors for a garage to be constructed near their work at the county building. In 1929, Ordinance No. 25 gave police the authority to designate parking on the main streets of villages and towns around the island "in order to prevent congestion."[31] As road changes have occurred since then, parking

Parking at Lihue Store or Tip Top could be a challenge, even during the Depression years of the early 1930s. William J. Senda, Kaua'i Museum

possibilities have also varied. In late 2013, some street parking was still available in central Līhu‘e. Spaces continue to be positioned parallel to the roadway, and they remain free of charge. But for residents habituated to pulling up to, or at least very close to, the doorway of their in-town destination, parking has become a driving issue in critiques of the town's potential roadway changes.

The motor vehicle, an endless source of fascination. Corstorphine, Kaua‘i Historical Society

The solutions of one era often become the problems of the next: the love affair with the automobile and the freedoms it brings is an apt example. As America and its Kaua‘i microcosm have transitioned from the Automobile Era into a digital age, thinkers and planners continue to grapple with the negative impacts of cars, among them pollution, traffic woes, and the expense of road maintenance. One measure of the grip that automobile ownership has taken on this island population is that both a Līhu‘e civic center master plan created in 2003 and a town core design plan begun at nearly the same time highlighted traffic issues in central Līhu‘e, as did the County's general plans in 1961, 1970, and 2000. The 1970 report described a "vital" need for a Līhu‘e bypass from Hanamā‘ulu to Puhi; the 1977 regional plan for Līhu‘e didn't just comment on congestion and inadequate parking, it suggested the development of bike paths and mass transit systems. Proponents of current "smart growth" and "complete streets" concepts continue to advocate approaches that will move people out of their cars and herd the vehicles themselves into fewer, more centralized locations. Dedicated bicycle lanes, concentration on public transportation vehicles, and better provision for walkers and wheelchairs are all part of the continuing discussion about community livability. Meanwhile, sidewalks in central Līhu‘e, where they exist at all, have been compromised by the various road widenings of the past century, adding to the county seat's reputation as a pedestrian-unfriendly town.

SIX

AROUND THE BEND

The dreams and the hard work of many men and women have finally brought us here today. It has been long in coming.

—**Lyndon Johnson,** at the signing of the Housing and Urban Development Act, 1968

Hardy Street's distinctive curve outlined new opportunities for Līhu'e to grow and expand as a century of sugarcane fields transitioned to both public and private development after World War II and statehood.

Raising ceremonial shovels at a 1964 groundbreaking for the Molokoa subdivision: Stanley Raymond and Clinton Childs, Lihue Plantation representatives; Tetsuro "Rosey" Maeda and Yoshio Hiranaka, Kauai Builders, Inc.; Hans Hansen, Lihue Plantation manager; Yoshiko "Dimples" Kano, Lihue Plantation real estate clerk; Rev. Kenneth Daugherty; Paul Muraoka, Lihue Businessmen's Association president. Joe Shiramizu, *Garden Island* archives

When Līhu'e Town's vast changes in the 1960s become a topic of current conversations, residents of a certain age usually describe the dramatic transformation of the Lihue Store and Tip Top into the shopping center at the town crossroads. Often overlooked are the building contributions made to the town by tourism, unions, arts, culture, education, sports, and residential living.

TRAVELERS BECOME TOURISTS

The raspberry sorbet-colored façade of the Motel Lani at the corner of Rice and Hardy streets camouflages the last remaining home in the old Rice Street neighborhood. The Kauai Public Library Association, Ltd., originally bought this lot and built a modest residence on it for the town librarian. In 1957 the property was sold to Benzo and Mutsume Asakura, who in turn sold it to Hisa Sato six years later, the year the motel was established. In 1966, Wallace and Janet Naumu purchased it. Although Wallace died in an accident after Hurricane 'Iwa in 1982, Janet continued as Motel Lani's proprietor.

The Kauai Library Association provided a modest house for the town librarian until the 1950s. The Motel Lani was established there in 1963. Kaua'i Museum

A casual glance at this property offers little evidence of the visitor industry's current economic dominance in Hawai'i, but the shift from agriculture to tourism as the state's cash crop was already under way by the time the Naumus bought the Motel Lani. In addition to the motel's ten rooms, several other hotel facilities offered central Līhu'e accommodations in 1966. Hale Lihue, now the Kauai Palms Hotel, offered twenty rooms in the Fairview tract, and the Tip Top Cafe and Motel had opened a two-story, fourteen-room facility on 'Akahi Street, the former site of owner Mitchell Ota's home. Almost fifty years later the Tip Top continues to provide accommodations for budget travelers and student groups.[1]

Other Līhu'e lodgings from that era exist only in memory, including the Hale Pumehana on 'Elua Street, which featured twenty rooms configured in a cottage setting; the Hale-Ka-Lani with six rooms; and the Hi-Way Motel with nine. Gone too are the ten-room Palm Haven in the former Moragne house on Rice Street and its six-room annex at the old Crawford residence on the corner of Rice and 'Umi, two of a "chain" of converted homes developed by Richard and Mae Martin as the Happy Holiday Resorts, which also included the old Horner beachfront mansion and a mountain estate in Wailua. As tourism on Kaua'i began to increase substantially, up 22 percent between 1965 and 1966, another 15 percent the following year, more accommodations were on the way. At the time, Kaua'i was considered to have an insufficient number of "lower priced rooms geared to the group traveler on economy tours" but catered instead to "middle and upper price ranges," a characterization that evolved as the industry expanded.[2]

During the century after Hawai'i's first Western tourist stepped ashore at Waimea in 1778, paid transient lodgings did not exist on Kaua'i. Instead, residents typically opened their homes to travelers. Queen Emma exemplified the practice while on a processional trip to Kaua'i and Ni'ihau with her new husband Alexander Liholiho (Kamehameha IV) two months after their marriage. The young queen wrote her father from Grove Farm plantation in a letter datelined "Lihue, Widemann's August 31 1856."[3] Her letter described the royal party's progression with an "escort of four or five hundred natives" from Kōloa to Līhu'e, where they stopped for more than a week. Grove Farm owner Hermann Widemann housed the king and queen, along with Liholiho's personal secretary and two of Emma's companions. Other members of the entourage lodged at Governor Kanoa's "houses on the beach at Nawiliwili."

Nineteenth-century resident Mary Sophia Rice, wife of early Lihue Plantation manager William Harrison Rice, vividly remembered, "There were neither boarding houses nor hotels on Kauai in that day, and the few white residents literally kept open house."[4] She

The Palm Haven, across from the current Kalapaki Villas, was originally the Rice Street home of Joseph and Mary Moragne. It later became the home of their son William and his family. From left: Honey Girl, the Moragne's spaniel, with Katie, wife Jean, Bill, Mary, William, and Sally. William J. Senda, Mary Moragne Cooke

recalled that providing accommodations for guests often occurred at "the inconvenience of the family who were turned out of their beds for the wayfarers." Bishop Thomas N. Staley, writing in 1868, considerably widened the aloha reception in Hawaiʻi beyond Rice's characterization of hospitality as provided exclusively by "the few white residents." He not only assured readers that "life and property in the Hawaiian Islands are as secure as in any part of the civilized world," but that the visitor "who turns into a native house in the wildest and most remote parts even of Hawaii, is sure to meet with a kind and hospitable reception."[5]

On the receiving end of the arrangement, 1870s sojourner Charles Nordhoff lamented the necessity of imposing himself upon island residents after he landed via schooner at Waimea:

> It is one of the embarrassing incidents of travel on these Islands that there are no hotels or inns outside of Honolulu and Hilo. Whether he will or no the traveler must accept the hospitality of the residents, and this is so general and so boundless that it would impose a burdensome obligation, were it not offered

> in such a kindly and graceful way as to beguile you into the belief that you are conferring as well as receiving a favor. Nor is the foreigner alone generous; for the native too, if you come with a letter from his friend at a distance, places himself and all he has at your service. When we had reached our friend's house, I asked my conductor, the policeman, what I should pay him for the use of three horses and his own services. He replied that he was but too happy to have been of use to me, as I was the friend of his friend. I managed to force upon him a proper reward for his attention, but I am persuaded that he would have been content without.[6]

As the nineteenth century matured and the sugar industry blossomed, the intrepid explorers of the early days gave way to business travelers representing commercial interests both large and small. Near the turn of the century, a few hotel-like lodgings for drummers—traveling salesmen "drumming up" business—began to open their doors in populated areas such as Kōloa and the waterfront village of Nāwiliwili. The sea change in hostelry on Kaua'i occurred in 1890, when Charles W. Spitz (1854–1942) opened the Fairview Inn at what was then considered the edge of Līhu'e but is today a mere couple of blocks down Rice Street, where Kalapaki Villas stands.[7]

The Fairview Inn, ca. 1895. Kaua'i Historical Society

Spitz is not well remembered today, but the Budapest-born entrepreneur was an early and restless pioneer on the Garden Island. He had arrived in Hawai'i in 1880 and initially worked at Kilauea Plantation, then as a shop clerk in Hāna, Maui. He struck out on his own in 1886 and established a store at Nāwiliwili four years before opening the hotel. Afterward, at the turn of the century, he established the first wholesale liquor store on Kaua'i (it closed with the advent of Prohibition). Identifying another emerging market, Spitz expanded into the automobile business in 1912 with the establishment of Nawiliwili Garage. Charlie Rice, along with a few other investors, bought the garage and its Ford dealership from Spitz in 1923—it would become Garden Island Motors—and they moved the business into a new concrete building in the commercial strip along Kūhiō Highway. By then Spitz had moved to Honolulu and was engaging in business enterprises there.

William Henry Rice purchased the Fairview in 1894 after a stint in service as its manager. For nearly half a century, until he leased the business to his son-in-law, Wayne Ellis, in 1941, Sheriff Rice was also hotelier Rice, the guiding light of Lihue Hotel. The *Garden Island* frequently referenced the Fairview Inn/Lihue Hotel (Rice changed the name in the early 1920s), which it considered "a credit to the town." In 1913 it called the hotel "the first sky scraper on Kauai" after Rice constructed a third-story addition on the original building. Over the years Rice would make many other improvements that the newspaper publicized. He bought his brother Arthur's adjacent home and created an annex in 1921, then built an administration building and dining room in 1925. By then several cottages were located on the grounds of the hotel, which housed long-term tenants as well as transient guests. A pavilion at the rear of the administration building provided a setting for numerous social events of the day, including dances, banquets, club meetings, and bridge parties. After Rice died in 1945 his family sold the property to Inter-Island Steamship Navigation Co.[8]

With Inter-Island's steamer *Hualalai* leaving weekly from Nāwiliwili Harbor and the expectation of a new Līhu'e airport in 1949 to accommodate its company-owned Hawaiian Airlines, the hotel purchase seemed an ideal fit for Inter-Island's vertical integration business format. In a conscious effort at product branding before it embarked on a major public relations campaign, Inter-Island changed the hotel's name to the Kauai Inn to parallel the company's Kona Inn on Hawai'i. The company also updated the 15-acre site: the main building and cottages were renovated, and two new redwood buildings added twenty-four rooms; grounds were also relandscaped with tropical flowers, a broad lawn, and a freshwater swimming pool. Before statehood in 1959, the Kauai Inn announced a million-dollar

After buying the property in 1945, Inter-Island changed Lihue Hotel's name to Kauai Inn as a coordinated branding effort with its Kona Inn on Hawai'i. Travel in those days was still a pastime for the privileged, as reflected by the hotel room count: 1,200 total in all of Hawai'i. That number is compared to 9,872 units in 2011 on Kaua'i alone.
Tom Fujii, Kaua'i Historical Society

expansion, designed by Honolulu architect Theodore Vierra, to include "a new main building with lobby, shops, cocktail lounge and dining room and lanai," a pool double the size of its predecessor, and an adjoining "500 capacity convention hall."[9] The plan was scrapped after the Charles Rice property on Kalapakī Bay became available. Initial discussions between Rice and Inter-Island Resorts president Walter Dudley Child were in the $150,000 price range when a second bidder, Halekulani owner Clifford Kimball, entered the scene. After Rice asked the competitors to submit sealed bids, the sale price reached $813,000.[10]

By the time of that purchase, a successful federal antitrust suit had broken up Inter-Island Steamship Navigation Company into four separate entities: Inter-Island Resorts, Ltd., Inter-Island Steam, Hawaiian Airlines, and Overseas Terminals.[11] Inter-Island Resorts divested its real estate on Rice Street and trucked the Kauai Inn structures to the Kalapakī site for use there. Late in the 1960s it sold them to a Phoenix-based partnership, which moved them once again, reuniting the venerable structures and the Kauai Inn name at Niumalu, where it exists to this day.[12] By then Inter-Island Resorts was successfully operating its massive new Kalapakī Bay hotel, the Kauai Surf.

If the Lihue Hotel/Kauai Inn served as the premier lodging and social gathering place

Inter-Island Resorts participated in the Kaua'i Kamehameha Day parades with its own float. The front design features the Kauai Surf's distinctive mask imagery. Kaua'i Historical Society

of the territorial period, the Kauai Surf sparkled as the island's high-rise glamour spot of the early statehood years, a counterpoint to the brilliant fantasy of a Polynesian paradise known as the Coco Palms a few miles away. Before 1959 the relatively few and mostly privileged visitors to the island had frequently looked to immerse themselves in island society. As late as 1958, when Dudley Child Jr. announced the planned Kauai Inn expansion, he said that the aim of the $25,000,000 project was to retain an informal "country club" atmosphere.[13] But the dawn of the jet age democratized travel. After twenty-plus years of population decline on Kaua'i—due in part to the decreasing need for workers on the ever-more-mechanized plantations and the lack of other employment opportunities—tourism shone as a beacon of promise for the island. The new vacationers were a diverse lot, but a common ambition was to frolic in sand and surf.[14] Kalapakī, with its long beach and calm, protected bay, was made-to-order for the experience. The Kauai Surf's opening in 1960 signaled the visitor industry's transition from a pocket change segment of Kaua'i's economy to its cash crop of the future. The first increment of the 352-room Kauai Surf, the largest hotel built on a neighbor island up to that time, was celebrated with great fanfare. Hawai'i governor William F. Quinn officially cut the *maile* rope with Child to welcome their five hundred invited guests into the new hotel, which included the island's first passenger elevator among other enjoyments.[15] A couple hundred more rooms were gradually added, along with a new lobby and nine new holes to complete an eighteen-hole golf course.

The glamour gradually faded, however, and twenty years later Inter-Island Resorts was in trouble. Lacking other options, the company "put itself on the auction block" in 1982.[16] Hemmeter Investment Co. seized the opportunity to acquire both Maui Surf and Kauai Surf, paying $94 million for the privilege in 1984. The "Hemmeter" in the investment company's name stood for Christopher Bagwell Hemmeter (1939–2003), who had been developing hotels in Hawai'i since the early 1970s. Alternately admired, envied, and despised for his successes and his excesses, Chris Hemmeter was named *Hawaii Business* magazine's 1977 "business man of the year."[17] With his remake of the Kauai Surf into the Westin Kauai, he introduced a mega-resort to the low-key, rural Garden Island. Hemmeter's promise of great revenues for county coffers (an estimated $200 million annually in the resort's heyday—and also the island's largest employer) convinced the Kaua'i Planning Commission to waive the island's sacrosanct four-story building height limit, which had been enacted after Inter-Island constructed the Surf. The commission allowed the erection of a ten-story building, along with a wedding chapel, stables for several dozen horse-drawn carriages, a health spa, conference center, dining areas galore, and "more marble and fiberglass columns than can be found anywhere else in Hawaii."[18] Speaking at a Kaua'i Chamber of Commerce meeting during the resort's construction, Hemmeter announced to the audience that his goal was for guests to spend their entire Garden Island stay without ever moving beyond the boundaries of his flamboyant playground.

When it opened in 1960, the Kauai Surf became the island's only high-rise hotel and the largest hotel built on a neighbor island. Harvey Tam, Kaua'i Historical Society

The $202 million transformation of the Kauai Surf into the Westin Kauai was completed in 1987. Architectural historian Don Hibbard summed up a common view of the results:

> In his exuberance, Hemmeter overextended himself and with the Westin Kauai and Hyatt Regency Waikoloa pushed the edges of credibility, transparently offering an overwhelming, ersatz opulence skirting the fringes of plausibility. . . . Glitzy, teetering on the gauche and garish, Hemmeter's later

Sculpture at the bridge to Kaua'i Lagoons.

hotels' emphasis on all-encompassing amazement overshadowed the essence of Hawai'i.[19]

Among Hemmeter's admirers was former governor Ben Cayetano, who tipped his hat to Hemmeter years later as the person most responsible for changing "the nature of resort development in Hawai'i."[20] Many Kauaians lamented that change, however, believing that the Westin had superimposed a Disneyesque veneer on an island much loved for its natural beauty. They feared that his creation had ushered in a new era of travel trade values in which the landscape of Kaua'i provided little more than a backdrop for artificial delights.

The year after the Westin Kauai opened, Hemmeter's name appeared on the *Forbes* list of America's four hundred wealthiest people, but his success would prove chimerical. Though the Kaua'i resort was apparently able to meet its operational expenses, property owners Hemmeter/VMS Kauai Co. II had already defaulted on a $194 million loan in 1992 before Hurricane 'Iniki dashed forever its hope of future glory.[21] The bank foreclosed. Hemmeter left Hawai'i in 1990 for greener pastures on the mainland. Although he maintained that he made money on the Westin Kauai, he declared personal bankruptcy in 1997,

Kaua'i Marriott, 2008.

blaming it on government corruption after a casino deal failed in New Orleans. Liquidation figures at the time showed Hemmeter with more than an $87 million debt. Hemmeter succumbed to cancer in 2003; he died in California at the age of sixty-four.

Two years later Marriott International bought the property for $51.3 million. It repaired hurricane damage, refurbished some hotel units, and reconfigured others into timeshares.[22] In 2006, Marriott Vacation Club International unveiled a billion-plus dollar development plan for the adjacent Kauai Lagoons, once part of the 850-acre Hemmeter dream. (Initially an equal ownership joint venture with Hawai'i developer Kevin Showe, the Marriott Vacation Club International bought out Showe in 2007.) Although parts of the project were mothballed after the economic convulsions late in 2008, the development reflects the most recent evolution of the travel industry: vacation property ownership. The company's ten-year development plans prescribed 750 units of pricey timeshare "villas," multimillion dollar condos, and even more exclusive vacation "estates."[23]

ILWU

The Hawai'i International Longshoremen's and Warehousemen's Union conceived a territory-wide building program shortly after World War II when it received an unexpected windfall from a settlement with thirty-one sugar plantations for violations of the U.S. Fair Labor Standards Act. ILWU regional director Jack Hall explained to attendees of an all-island joint meeting in 1950 that, since the union had been awarded more than anyone had expected in the settlement, its attorneys had given the group $135,000 from their own fees! According to Hall, the ILWU's "Building of Our Own" project was important not only to construct a permanent headquarters for officials' administrative work and members' recreational activities but also to create "a monument to the stability of our union in these islands." To finance the program, members each contributed fifteen dollars via a twenty-five-cent-a-month assessment.[24]

The regional headquarters in Honolulu opened on February 2, 1952, shortly followed by buildings at Hilo, Honoka'a, and Wailuku. In 1954, Lihue Plantation's parent company, American Factors, offered the ILWU land at Ahukini or Hanamā'ulu for a Kaua'i center, and several private individuals made sales offers of their own properties. One was Mrs. Clem Gomes, whose husband had defeated incumbent Elsie Wilcox and won the Kaua'i Senate election in 1940 with the aid of Hall and the union.[25] The local leadership, intent on establishing its presence in central Līhu'e, dismissed those offers and countered with

Architect's rendering of the Kaua'i ILWU building. Alfred Preis, ILWU Local 142 archives

others. One site the union unsuccessfully sought to purchase was land situated directly *mauka* of the courthouse at the corner of Hardy and 'Umi streets (a lot that later became an American Factors Contractors Association showcase home in Lihue Plantation's Molokoa subdivision).[26] Finally, on May 6, 1955, American Factors agreed to sell a parcel across from the proposed War Memorial auditorium to the ILWU Memorial Association. The price for nearly an acre of land was fifty cents per square foot plus half the expense of constructing a paved road from Rice Street to the lot.

In July the union's building and planning committee compiled a list of recommendations for the Līhu'e headquarters that included space for offices and a conference room as well as a kitchen, barbecue pit, and "luau shade" for outdoor recreational use.[27] A dormitory for twelve beds, common at the time in union buildings, was included to accommodate leadership temporarily on island as well as workers on their way home to the Philippines and elsewhere. Construction bids were solicited for the building, and local contractor Alfred Nobriga won the contract. The ILWU stipulated that materials be obtained from either Kauai Commercial Co. or American Factors, both unionized businesses.

The structure presents an unusual profile for Kaua'i: the A-frame roof of the conference room emerges from the flat roof of the building's main section, rises to an apex, then drops almost to the ground on the opposite side. That feature may have inspired the dedication program's description of the building as "ultra-modern" and the *Lihue Plantation News* report of its having "the effect of a modern building in Mexico City or Rio do Janeiro or Miami."[28] Other defining characteristics of the design included the expansive use of glass to create the wall along the Hardy Street side of the conference room and the 2,300 square feet of lime rock (purchased from Grove Farm) used to face the concrete block walls along the front and portions of the side of the building.

ILWU regional director Jack W. Hall at a "defense-of-the-union" picnic, Hanamā'ulu Beach, 1952. ILWU *Dispatcher*

Among those taking part in the dedication ceremony on April 27, 1957, was ILWU International secretary-treasurer Lou Goldblatt. He congratulated the membership on their new home while warning that "the only way to keep a union building is to be prepared to trade it for a picket shack if you have to." (The 128-day ILWU strike of twenty-six plantations by 13,700 worker began the following February.) Jack Hall, the keynote speaker, thanked Lihue Plantation manager Keith Tester for his patience and assistance in locating the land, then stressed the theme of unity within ILWU membership, a concept that County Board of Supervisors chair Anthony Baptiste broadened to unity throughout the community. Tester acknowledged that the union had grown to be part of the island, though he recognized the inherent differences between workers and owners. "Let us dedicate [the new building] in the hope that it will play a part in bringing a sincere understanding of the basic problems and the troubles of labor and management," he proposed. Telesforo C. Manipon, Lihue Plantation's ILWU Local 142, Lihue Unit, chair, gave his address in Ilocano.[29]

Alfred Preis, right, with Janina, his wife, and Erica, their daughter, at the opening of Hale Hapaiko Hall, the 1957 addition to the ILWU headquarters in Honolulu. With them is United Press bureau chief Charles Bernard. ILWU Local 142 archives

Absent from the dedication, but instrumental in the ILWU's long-term vision of union buildings on every island, was Alfred Preis (1911–1993). The Austrian-born architect arrived in Hawai'i after fleeing Nazi Germany in 1939. After the December 7, 1941, attack on Pearl Harbor, Preis and his wife were yanked from their Honolulu home and interned for three months as suspected enemy aliens, along with others from Germany or German-annexed countries. After being released Preis joined Hart Wood's firm, then established his own office in 1943. He became the ILWU's architect of choice about the time the union conceived its territory-wide building plan. Preis

THE STATE FOUNDATION ON CULTURE AND THE ARTS

Alfred Preis was a fine architect, but he remains high on many lists of Hawai'i's twentieth-century visionaries for another reason: his success in making culture and the arts an acknowledged, government-supported priority in the state. To accomplish this end, Preis was part of a core group that included then-governor John A. Burns and Maui businessman Masaru "Pundy" Yokouchi. Together in 1965 they conceived and successfully convinced Hawai'i legislators to establish the State Foundation on Culture and the Arts with a mission "to promote, perpetuate, preserve, and encourage culture and the arts, history and the humanities as central to the quality of life of the

people of Hawai'i." Preis was the SFCA's first and longest-serving executive director, a position he held from 1965 to 1980.

From his earliest days here, Preis appreciated both the breadth of cultural diversity and the range of artistic talent in Hawai'i. In 1967 he was instrumental in creating the state legislation that mandated 1 percent of the cost of every new state building to be used to purchase public art (the first such law in the nation, one that twenty-six other states have since enacted). Those funds became the basis for the Art in Public Places program, a combination of both commissioned works included as intrinsic parts of building sites and purchased, relocatable pieces such as paintings and moveable sculptures displayed on a rotating basis in state facilities. The total value of the program to Hawai'i remains incalculably greater than the sum of its parts. The ever-growing collection includes more than 6,200 pieces by over 1,500 artists, a legacy to Hawai'i's citizens of the future.

A fundamental component of Preis's longtime vision, a public museum for the collection, became a reality nine years after his death. The Hawai'i State Art Museum opened in 2003 in Honolulu's capitol district in the historic Armed Services YMCA building, which was later owned by Christopher Hemmeter and served as company headquarters during the developer's heyday in Hawai'i. Today, changing exhibits can be seen there, and others are present in schools and government offices, buildings, and lawns on Kaua'i and across the state.[31]

Wai'ale'ale–Waiola, *located at Hardy and 'Umi streets, is a Hawaiian basalt and stainless steel sculpture, created in 1996 by Ralph Kouchi as part of* Art in Public Places, *a program of the State Foundation on Cultural and the Arts. The differing answers to "What is art?" have generated controversy about more than one piece over the years. Former Kaua'i legislator Tony Kunimura, never a man known for verbal delicacy, once critiqued a particularly controversial painting as "junk, pure junk!"*

The USS Arizona Memorial was designed by Alfred Preis.

designed the Honolulu regional headquarters in 1952 and its addition in 1957 as well as the Hilo, Wailuku, and Līhuʻe structures.

Today Alfred Preis the architect is best known for his design of the Arizona Memorial at Pearl Harbor, completed in 1962. According to Jan Peter Preis, the memorial was, for his father, "a dedication to everything that America stands for: peace and freedom and prosperity."[30]

SALVATION ARMY

Hawaiʻi's building boom of the 1960s dramatically changed the footprint of central Līhuʻe even as it transformed Waikīkī and the landscape elsewhere in the fiftieth state. Heavy demand for construction materials substantially inflated prices, which in turn affected many construction plans, including the Salvation Army's blueprints for its Hardy Street community center. The proposed project's estimated building costs rose more than 225 percent between 1967 and 1969, forcing the organization to request an extension on its building permit while it revised its blueprint for the 50,000-square-foot parcel. By the time the center's groundbreaking took place in January 1970, the twelve units of planned senior housing had been scrapped. The final layout of the facility, designed by architect Hiroshi Abe, was identical to centers on O'ahu and Maui.[32]

Among the dignitaries who lifted the first shovelsful of dirt at the groundbreaking was Richard Sloggett, Kaua'i Salvation Army's advisory board chair. For Sloggett, contributing time and resources to the organization was a family tradition. His father Henry Digby Sloggett and aunts Elsie and Mabel Wilcox had been board members in 1924 when the Salvation Army built its community hall on Kūhiō Highway on land leased from Lihue Plantation. The three had followed the lead of their uncle George Norton Wilcox, whose gifts to the Salvation Army in Hawai'i over the years totaled hundreds of thousands of dollars.

Envoy Larry Groenleer (left) and Capt. Mitham Clement with Mayor JoAnn Yukimura in front of the Salvation Army disaster canteen. Salvation Army

The Wilcoxes were not alone among missionary descendants to recognize the value of the organization's work and its potential to "do good" here. The Central Union Church in Honolulu had initially invited the Salvation Army to come to the islands in the late nineteenth century because "thousands of immigrants were pouring into Hawaii to work in the plantations in the 1890s."[33] The congregation "realized the serious need for a 'spiritual organization with a social aim . . . a social organization with a spiritual aim' to work with the young and old of all nationalities in Hawai'i." By 1897 a mission station was established on Kaua'i.

Dora Rice Isenberg, another missionary descendant who served on the advisory board with Digby Sloggett and the Wilcox sisters, bequeathed Molokoa, her Līhu'e home on German Hill past the Lutheran church, to the group in 1950. When Lihue Plantation sought to further its commercial development along Kūhiō Highway in the 1960s, the Army, as adherents call themselves, traded that Molokoa

George Norton Wilcox was a successful, multidimensional businessman, but many people remember him most respectfully as an unstinting philanthropist. The Salvation Army was one of the many recipients of his generosity over the years. In 1922, for example, he gave the Salvation Army a significant donation to build a boys' home in Kaimukī and establish the Waioli Tea Room in Mānoa, an innovative restaurant conceived as a place to train young girls in the food and service industry. Wilcox's gifts continued throughout his long life. Grove Farm Homestead Museum home for the current lot across town in the new Molokoa subdivision. The plantation subsequently demolished the Isenberg homestead to plant cane, and it leased the former Salvation Army community hall lot on Kūhiō Highway to Pizza Hut, which constructed its own trademark restaurant on the site. The Salvation Army built its new community center on Hardy Street with spaces for educational and cultural activities, Ladies League meetings, social welfare services, community room, preschool, day-care center, recreational facilities and a chapel, where Sunday services continue to be held.

According to Capt. Mitham Clement, formerly of Kaua‘i, the Army's advisory board serves as "the army behind the Army" and acts as a liaison with the community. Service remains the Salvation Army's primary community outreach activity, with the religious basis of that service acknowledged in its theme, "heart to God and hand to man." The preschool and day-care activities have been discontinued in Līhu‘e, but the Salvation Army carries on its outreach with the soup kitchen, counseling, other family and social welfare assistance, and Christmas red kettle and bell ringing (a tradition that began in San Francisco in 1891).

KAUAI WAR MEMORIAL CONVENTION HALL

County planners envisioned a public auditorium on the eastern edge of the town core a generation before the first bulldozer arrived on the scene to begin site preparation. By the mid-1950s, when the ILWU was searching for downtown space, the proposed "War Memorial Auditorium Site" was already plotted on some maps. Indeed, at the building's dedication on December 4, 1964, County Board of Supervisors chair Raymond Aki reminded all who had gathered to celebrate the occasion that the County had begun planning and "putting up funds" for a civic auditorium thirty years earlier.[34]

The great billowing tent of a structure, with its moss rock columns and central, gridded, exposed aggregate façades, was designed by Honolulu architect Clifford F. Young. He had made a name for himself collaborating with internationally renowned architect I. M. Pei on the East-West Center's Jefferson Hall administration building (now the Hawaii Imin International Conference Center) on the University of Hawai‘i campus in Honolulu.[35] Young remembered that the convention center advisory committee formed to oversee the War Memorial creation knew about his participation on the East-West Center project, which was completed in 1962. After seeing the award-winning design on a Honolulu site visit, they were convinced that Young was the man for their job.[36]

The Kauai War Memorial Convention Hall was completed in 1964.

In those early, optimistic days following statehood, the Kaua'i Board of Supervisors returned Young's initial blueprints because they "provided for a seating capacity of only about 800." The county leaders "felt this was not realistic because the average audience on Kauai for musical and auditorium type programs is about 1,000 people." The revised plan discarded a former mezzanine configuration and instead placed lobby, lounges, and seating all on a single floor. The construction utilized a double-arched roof, created by intersecting two large "glulam" beams—glued, laminated lumber—to span the broad interior space efficiently. The *Honolulu Star-Bulletin* claimed that the convention hall design would create "the first structure of its type in Hawaii" to utilize such a system.[37]

The community's wait through the Great Depression, World War II, and statehood for the convention center to become reality heightened the excitement about opening day. In addition to the midday dedication ceremony, with obligatory speech making, general congratulations, and the "breaking" of a *maile* lei, the Honolulu Symphony inaugurated the auditorium that night by performing selections by Robert Schumann, Felix Mendelssohn,

The Neal S. Blaisdell Arena and Kauaʻi's convention hall were both dedicated to the memory of Hawaiʻi's war heroes. Both were completed shortly after the 1964 New York World's Fair opened, and both share with some of its pavilions the curved shapes reflective of a segment of modernist architecture. Such forms captured public imagination in Hanna-Barbera's 1962-1963 animated *Jetsons*, with its round, futuristic world of Orbit City.

Georges Bizet, Otto Nicolai, and Spartaco Monello. The orchestra's appearance was made possible by the efforts of the Mokihana Club, the culmination of a decade in which it had tirelessly sponsored "Little Symphony" school concerts. In November 1964 the Mokihana newsletter announced, "Kauai has moved up in the music world. This year there will be a full Symphony of 45 musicians coming for the annual concert." It proudly noted that with so many musicians participating, "we can drop the 'little' in the Symphony Concerts and henceforth be called the 'Honolulu Symphony' in all publicity." The same issue of the newsletter urged members to host one of the musicians in a spare bedroom, which was a common outer island practice of the time. Before its evening Convention Hall performance for the general public, the symphony performed at the three island high schools, financed by a legislative appropriation.[38]

Although the auditorium was the dominant segment of the building's layout, the design included a central lobby conceived to provide exhibition space, two smaller meeting and event rooms, a kitchen, and a manager's office. The Kauai Art Group utilized the lobby area to exhibit its first juried show, judged by art luminaries Isami Doi, Harvey Tam, and John Gregg Allerton.[39] For the "homeless" arts community, the Convention Hall promised a new and exciting space to display the range and variety of talent on Kauaʻi. The *Garden Island* shared those hopes. Its December 5, 1964, editorial suggested:

> Kauai has every right to be proud of its new auditorium which now has been formally opened and dedicated. The unit was constructed as a convention hall. The reason for this, of course, is to justify the use of State funds in its construction. Realistically, however, it is well known its use for convention purposes will be of a minor nature compared with other uses to which it will be put.
>
> Actually its real use will be more on the cultural side than anything in the field of economic development. It is in this area also that its real contributions to the community will be made. . . .
>
> There are many avenues in this area that should be explored. The assistance of all interested organizations should be secured. The University

Deborah Pratt, Lela Morgan, and Mary Wilson were among the Mokihana Club members who planned and sponsored the Honolulu Symphony at the War Memorial's dedication on December 4, 1964.
Kaua'i Historical Society

of Hawaii, The East West Center, and Bishop Museum are examples of the contacts that should be made toward making the greatest possible use of the new structure. . . .

At the same time the entertainment field should not be overlooked. The auditorium offers facilities that have been sadly lacking in the past. The auditorium can open a great new field in all phases of entertainment from the classics to the popular. The use and development of local talent is a field that will need exploring as well.

Emory Griffin-Noyes, Mercedes Johnson, and Chloe Stokes, students of Kauaʻi Academy of Dance, perform the *Nutcracker* at the Convention Hall, 2006.
Tommy Noyes

> The auditorium should be a challenge to the community and to all concerned with it. Steps should be taken toward meeting the challenge. The time to begin is now.[40]

A few years later, dreams held by the arts community for a secure, periodic exhibit space at the convention center had faded. According to former Kauai Art Group president Carol Ann (LeGoullon) Davis, use of the building for exhibitions and display became almost impossible because of the lack of support by an early director of the facility. Meanwhile, the Kauai Surf at Kalapakī created a smaller convention space for the hotel's growing business trade that became available to local musical and theatrical groups. As the resort era blossomed, other meeting and convention facilities sprang up. When the Kauaʻi Community College Performing Arts Center opened in 1995, with its state-of-the-art light and sound systems, it emerged as the preferred, though not always affordable, location over the thirty-year-old War Memorial's auditorium, at least for smaller events that needed less seating than the latter's thousand-person capacity.

The meeting rooms and lobby at the Kauai War Memorial Convention Hall were *the* place in its early days to hold wedding receptions, graduation parties, baby luaus, and other celebratory functions. Though no longer considered the glamour spot on the island, it remains a popular rental space for such events. According to Eddie Sarita, director since 1999, reservations to use one or both of the rooms—with occasional spillover into the main lobby area—must sometimes be scheduled nearly a year ahead of an event. The visual arts community has not returned, but auditorium usage continues; commercial concert promoters utilize the space for a variety of musical and theatrical performances, and the hall enjoys considerable usage by local school bands, drama groups, chorales, dance troupes, and *hula hoʻike*.

A CENTURY OF TENNIS AND OTHER SPORTS

The *Garden Island* sports column heading, 1911.
R. Yardley, *Garden Island* archives

Sports have traditionally played as popular a role on Kaua'i as they do elsewhere. Hawai'i, the island state, celebrates its life-giving connection to the ocean with the popular recreations of swimming and surfing. Eight outrigger canoe clubs around the island currently participate in competitive paddling, which was named Hawai'i's official team sport in 1986.

On land, baseball enjoys a particularly interesting history in Hawai'i because of its close links to the early development of the rule-driven game we know today as "America's pastime." According to the National Baseball Hall of Fame, Alexander Joy Cartwright Jr. (1820–1892), "The Father of Modern Base Ball . . . carried baseball to Pacific Coast and Hawaii in pioneer days." Cartwright had been a founder in the 1840s of the New York Knickerbockers, a team that established set rules for the game. Then,

A German bowling club maintained two lanes in central Līhu'e, near the current post office, early in the twentieth century.
Kaua'i Museum

tantalized by the California gold rush in 1849, he trekked from his hometown of New York City to San Francisco, but he soon moved on to Honolulu and made it his home (he is buried at O'ahu Cemetery). Though children in Hawai'i had long played loosely structured bat-and-ball games, an official league in Honolulu, with teams using the regulations of the California National Baseball Convention, which included nine innings, first appeared in the 1860s after Cartwright's arrival.[41]

On Kaua'i in the early twentieth century, the *Garden Island* spearheaded efforts to organize an islandwide baseball league. A Līhu'e team became one of seven to participate that first season, the others being Makaweli, Kilauea, Eleele, Koloa, Kawaihau, and Homestead. At season's conclusion, the newspaper commented on the collegial atmosphere the games engendered, bringing "the people of our island closer together . . . to cause them to realize more fully, the value of a united citizenship for the advancement of the welfare of a community."[42] Beyond the paper's catholic philosophy of unity—and at another point in

Longtime *Garden Island* editor Charlie Fern at his desk. Fern loved sports; he also knew that reporting on games sold newspapers. Mike Ashman, Kaua'i Historical Society

history—Americans of Japanese ancestry started their own league in 1929. In 2013, Kauai AJA Baseball wrapped up its eighty-third season with six teams: the Hanapepe Rivermen, Kalaheo Farmers, Kapaa Homesteaders, Lihue Townies, Makaweli Indians, and Waimea Tsunami.[43]

In August 1911, as that first baseball season drew to an end, the *Garden Island* broadened its support of sports, suggesting that other games be organized—a boxing tournament, a lawn tennis tournament, or a polo game played at the Hulēʻia field "between the Kauai and Cavalry teams on New Year's Day, the army men to be the guests of our local team."[44] The aristocratic sport of polo was, in fact, well enjoyed on Kauaʻi, with the four Rice boys among the avid participants. Arthur Rice played as a member of the Hawaiʻi polo team in 1913, when it captured the prized Bourne Cup from California's San Mateo Polo Club. Other team members included Walter Dillingham and Harold Castle from Oʻahu, and Frank and Sam Baldwin of Maui.[45]

After he began working for the paper in the early 1920s, Charlie Fern continued the *Garden Island* enthusiasm for sports. Later that decade he formed a barefoot football league on Kauaʻi. Līhuʻe joined the competition with two teams, the Lihue Planters and the Lihue Townies. Eventually, the different weight-class Lihue Ramblers and Lihue Sugar Babies would also spar in the rough-and-tumble game that thrived into the 1950s. "An Ode to Charlie Fern," a poem read during the 1982 barefoot football reunion to honor Fern on his ninetieth birthday, characterized the game they used to play with "No helmets, no pads, no shoes, no cleats / Only our bare 'feets.'"[46]

A variety of organized youth athletics, both school-related and independently run, have flourished alongside adult games. During World War II, when the army took over the Kauai High School gym, *kamaʻāina* Hobey Goodale remembered playing basketball with his pals "almost every weekday evening" in games with the medics stationed there. After the soldiers left, Goodale and his teammates joined a newly formed league as the Surfriders, "because most of us surfed at Kalapaki."[47]

In 1936, the plantation formally organized its own sports organization, the Lihue Plantation Athletic Association, and two years later the company dedicated the newly constructed Isenberg Recreational Center. It included a gym, an 11-acre ball field, a 440-yard track, and four tennis courts.[48] In his 1939 "biography" of King Cane, John Vandercook wrote of plantation competitions as having "a fine disregard for the Hawaiian climate," noting that they followed a mainland schedule: autumn football, winter basketball, spring baseball, "and tennis the year round."[49]

The Lihue Plantation Athletic Association became a member of the Kauai Athletic Union after the latter was founded in 1937. The KAU included groups such as Kauai High, the YMCA, and the Lihue Townies as well as the sugar and pineapple plantation teams. KAU committees coordinated boxing, swimming, basketball, softball, and volleyball (with twenty-nine teams) in addition to tennis. In 1938 the KAU voted to establish a committee of seven women to "encourage Women's Sports for Kauai" in addition to the traditional men's.[50]

The game of tennis had been enjoyed in the center of Līhuʻe Town since 1913. The *Garden Island* announced that July that with the completion of a double lawn tennis court, "any one imbued with sufficient tennis spirit to raise a racket is welcome to the use of the court whenever he may wish."[51] The courts are visible at the top edge of the large field in the 1924 photo on pages 228–229; a well-used baseball field can be seen to their right.

They proved consistently popular, and in 1952 lighting was installed to extend

The Puhi Girls Softball Team won the league's 1938 Kauaʻi championship. Standing from left: Danny Peters, Kokichi Fujii, Gussie Texeira, Janet Thain, Mary Peters, and Kazumi Yoshida. Kneeling: Dorothy Silva, Castellina Ibis, Lulu Alcover, Sumie Yoshida, and Magdalina Kolo. Seated: Beatrice Texeira, Frances Texeira, Marjorie Texeira, and Josephine Ibis. Tom Fujii, Grove Farm Homestead Museum

The public tennis courts can be seen immediately behind the Kaua'i Museum (it was the library then) in this 1954 aerial. To the right is the Historic County Building. At lower left is the main Līhue corner, with Lihue Store on one side and the Tip Top partially visible on the other. Alan Fayé Jr., Pacific Skyways competitions across the nets beyond sundown. After the plantation unveiled its town redesign a decade later, the County assumed the responsibility to provide a new pair of public courts for the ones being displaced. It constructed them on Hardy Street between the elementary school and the convention center. Lihue Plantation contributed the fencing, poles, netting, and lighting fixtures, materials they recycled from the well-used courts that had held pride of place in the center of town for forty years.[52]

THE MOLOKOA SUBDIVISION: HOUSING IN TRANSITION

The 300-acre master plan included residential and industrial components in addition to the frequently cited commercial center. In early 1961, C. Hutton Smith, president of American Factors and Lihue Plantation, described the proposed housing subdivision as containing a hundred lots, with several hundred more available in the future "should the need arise." The tract was located between Hardy Street and Ahukini Road opposite the Elsie H. Wilcox Elementary School. Later that year George Houghtailing, a founding member of Community Planning, Inc., the plantation's consulting firm, submitted plans to Kauaʻi County engineer Calvin Ching for "Lihue Homes, Unit I, comprising 71 lots with areas ranging from 7,500 square feet to 12,300 square feet." Houghtailing's cover letter requested preliminary subdivision approval.[53]

Modified ranch-style homes, promoted as the "all-Hawaii" house, characterized Lihue Plantation's 1960s planned residential community.

Houghtailing was prominent in Hawai'i planning circles. He had worked for almost two decades at Honolulu's public works department and planning commission before stepping into the position of planning director for a dozen years. According to a Community Planning and Engineering corporate profile, Houghtailing "was instrumental in establishing Honolulu's Planning & Traffic Commission in 1945" and assisted Kaua'i and the other Hawai'i counties to create "planning and permitting departments and programs to generate land-use master plans for their respective islands."[54]

The master plan proposal was one that modern-day "smart growth" planning advocates would appreciate, a residential community situated within walking distance of elementary school, shopping, library, and government offices. Residents' workplaces would potentially be located nearby as well, since the proposed industrial park was positioned just east of the subdivision. But the concepts that seem eminently logical today ran contrary to Kaua'i County and Hawai'i State general plans of the time, and it created a "public furor" over worries that "residents will flock to buy homes in Lihue and thus vacate other towns." Business owners elsewhere on the island feared that what promised to become a boom for Līhu'e could bankrupt them. Concern was particularly acute in Kapa'a, where American Factors had announced the closing of its Hawaiian Canneries the previous year, causing considerable trepidation about that region's economic future. Some critics urged the plantation not to sacrifice prime sugarcane production for the Līhu'e development but to lease equivalent acreage instead "to either the Kapaa cannery effort or Kilauea Plantation before new unemployment problems cripple the Island's economy." Planning director David F. Wong also suggested an alternate site for the industrial area, acreage adjacent to the mill, where he felt that problems of air pollution blanketing the town and automobiles congesting it would be avoided.[55]

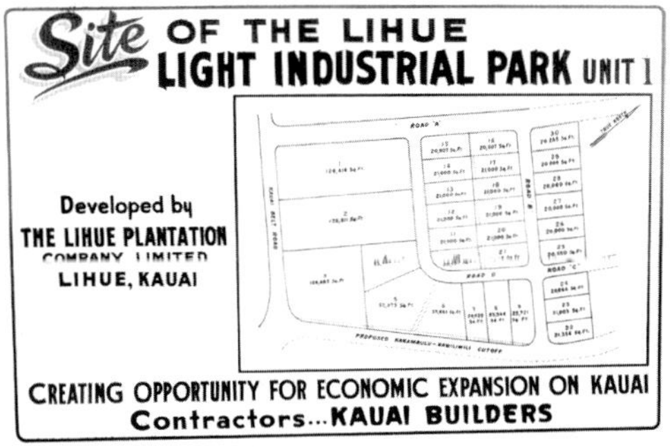

Construction sign at the Lihue Light Industrial Park, on acreage at the Nāwiliwili side of town, promised to provide many new opportunities for business establishments and a work destination for nearby homeowners. Kaua'i Historical Society

To counter the plantation's residential proposal, Wong presented a plan in which the subdivision site was positioned west of town, *mauka* of Kaumuali'i Highway. That land was fallow, and development there would generate new taxes for the county while retaining the income from the existing cane lands in town. George Houghtailing championed the central Līhu'e location. He maintained that the plantation's approach provided an "orderly development of the area adjacent to the existing city, whereas the County's plan would 'leapfrog' more than a mile outside of the existing city."[56] He also stressed the increased county expenditures for road maintenance and other services, such as utility lines and school buses, which Wong's suggestion would incur. The Kauai Planning and Traffic

Commission ultimately favored the Lihue Plantation master plan, and the new subdivision moved forward.

The main road through the project extended 'Umi Street, which fronted the courthouse and police station, across Hardy Street to Ahukini Road. The plantation named the other three streets in the tract after varieties of sugarcane: Pua'ole, Uahiapele, and Uluhui. The contractor for the subdivision, Kauai Builders, began site preparation in mid-1963 to transform the historic cane land—among the earliest cultivated by the fledgling Peirce and Company more than a century previously—into a lively new neighborhood. On December 13, 1963, Lihue Plantation manager Hans Hansen sent a letter to the County requesting final approval for the Lihue Homes, Unit I, "Molokoa."[57]

The plantation offered the subdivision's fee-simple lot-and-home packages exclusively to company employees for a period of time before opening sales to the general public. Ground was broken for the first home—a parsonage for Lihue Baptist Church—in the winter of 1964. Its construction was a cooperative project between the plantation and Kauai Technical School.[58] Twenty-four more had followed by the time the 1964 Lihue Plantation annual report was published (in 1965), of which "8 have been sold and applications for purchase of 15 others received."

The shift toward promoting home ownership to workers was a conscious one. Unionization in 1946 had ended the practice of plantation-supplied housing, and the company gradually began to release acreage for fee-simple purchase. During the late 1940s, eighty-one lots in the Isenberg tract, *mauka* of the Kūhiō Highway commercial district, were made available "as an encouragement to employees to own and build their homes." Employees did purchase more than half of those lots, and after twenty-one houses had been completed in 1950 the company newsletter declared the project "a great success."[59] Total lot and house costs reportedly ranged between $7,500 and $85,000 (slightly less than one-tenth the value of 2013 dollars), with company physician Samuel R. Wallis's home representing the skewed high figure in the range. The 1964 annual report explained further: "As new houses are occupied, older plantation houses are vacated and, where rehabilitation is uneconomical, these houses are demolished or sold with the understanding that they be relocated."[60] By the mid-1960s, the company's policy manual noted that few plantation rentals were still in service.

The waiting list for homes in Molokoa had swelled to 350 families when plans for the second increment of approximately two hundred lots began.[61] Unlike the first segment, in which the company developed the subdivision, Amfac (the name changed from

The Isenberg and Molokoa subdivisions supplanted plantation camps of the past. Kaipu Camp served as company-provided housing for some of the Grove Farm laborers. Other plantation camps, such as Lihue Camp, the Kilipaki and Korean camps, Rice Camp, and Puhi Camp, existed near the mill and in other areas near work. Grove Farm Homestead Museum

American Factors in 1966) sold the entire parcel as a single unit. In July 1967 the Molokoa Village Development Company, Ltd., owned by Edward K. Jensen and Robert J. Prosser, acquired the land. Before the tract could take shape, however, the County and developer had to overcome a significant blockage: inadequate sewerage. Līhu'e's existing system was already operating near capacity and could not accommodate the additional demands of a couple hundred more homes. In order to proceed with the subdivision, the developers agreed to pay 52 percent of costs to build a new system. Federal funding and a smaller state contribution would provide the balance of funds. Although the road to completion held other infrastructural impediments, the company received the approvals it needed to create Molokoa Unit II, one of the first residential areas on Kaua'i to feature underground utilities. In the initial year of sales, more than half of the two-hundred-plus lots were sold, most of them to local folks.[62]

Molokoa Unit III received tentative subdivision approval in 1984 but would struggle through thirteen years of requests for extensions before achieving final approval in 1997.

Water, problems with effluent from the Lihue Plantation mill's waste, roads placement, park dedication lands, and school bus stops were all complications along the development path for Unit III, but a significant factor in the delay was Amfac's own internal upheavals. By 1984 the company's two decades of diversification and international corporate acquisitions were coming back to bite the company. During the final quarter of 1984, Amfac withheld stock dividends for the first time in its sixty-six years.[63] After JMB Realty Corporation bought Amfac in November 1988, the Molokoa project got "lost in the shuffle."[64] The once powerful member of Hawai'i's Big Five could not complete Molokoa III, even under its new ownership; shortly after Hurricane 'Iniki in 1992, Amfac/JMB sold the subdivision acreage to Okada Trucking Company, Ltd., which eventually finalized the plans for its development.

In preparation for the Molokoa subdivision, the last sugarcane crop was harvested in May 1962. In the distance are the low lines of Wilcox School, the police station, courthouse and, behind the trees, the county building. Kaua'i Historical Society

Some companies doing business nearby provided homes for their managers in the Lihue Town Tract. One was S. H. Kress and Co. A 1937 letter in the Hawaiian Sugar Planters' Association archives announced the approval of the Kress purchase of the 15,000-square-foot Lot 34, Block A, for $525. National Building Museum

The Molokoa I homes on the *mauka* side of 'Umi Street backed up against the Lihue Town Tract, which had been developed in the 1930s and '40s. It included the two streets, 'Akahi and 'Elua, between Kūhiō Highway and 'Umi. Much like the "Elite Street" properties sold on Rice Street in the 1910s, Lihue Plantation offered the Lihue Town Tract lots in fee simple to the general public rather than utilize them for employee housing there. Individuals such as Ah Sau Ahana, deputy county auditor, and Katsutaro Yamasaki, a Bank of Hawaii employee, purchased lots and by 1936 were constructing homes in the subdivision. Corporations also bought lots to provide residences for their executives: Consolidated Amusement Company built a home for its local theater manager in the tract, as did S. H. Kress and Company. The plantation stressed that these 100- by 150-foot lots were to be used exclusively for residential purposes, though county planners in later decades encouraged business development. Today, many of the homes have been converted to or entirely replaced by commercial structures, especially on 'Akahi Street.

The modified ranch-style homes built in Molokoa I belong to a different generation than those in the historic Lihue Town Tract. They are based on designs conceived in the 1940s by the Hawaiian Sugar Planters Association's director of architectural services,

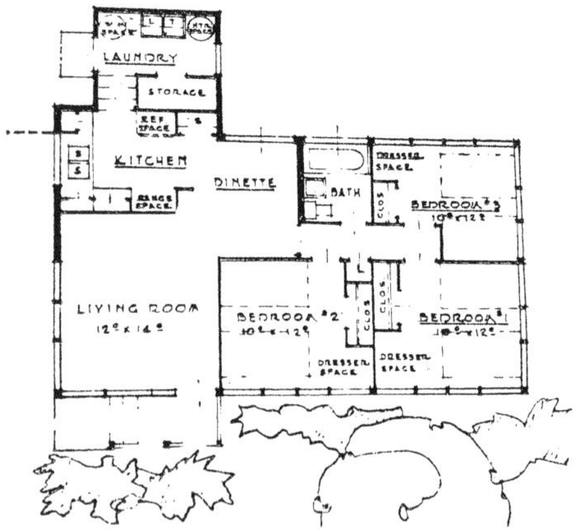

Sketch of All-Hawaii house plan. Hawaiian Sugar Planters' Association archives

Theodore A. Vierra (1902–1987).[65] Vierra graduated from Kamehameha Schools in 1919 and received a degree in architecture from Harvard University. In addition to his work with HSPA, Vierra designed the Memorial of the Pacific at Punchbowl and several buildings at Kamehameha Schools: Keawe Gym, Pākī Hall, the seventh and eighth grade dormitories, Ruth Ke'elikolani Swimming Pool, and the Bernice Pauahi Bishop Administration Building. After Inter-Island bought Lihue Hotel and rebranded it as Kauai Inn, the company hired Vierra to expand the property with four new buildings and 102 rooms. He may have been an architect for the Kauai Surf as well.[66]

Emphasizing affordability, Vierra created a three-bedroom house plan, with variations, in such a way as to capitalize on standardized materials of the day and efficiency of construction. It was promoted as "ultra-modern" and marketed as the "all-Hawaii" house. Several Hawai'i companies utilized or adapted the plans, with Kahului serving as the pioneer location. That Kahului Town's first 166 homes were sold in four days when they were offered in 1953 was an indication of the style's success—and the hunger of the population for home ownership. On Kaua'i, Amfac was not alone in its experimentation with the all-Hawaii home; McBryde also utilized the design in its 'Ele'ele subdivision.[67]

Even untrained observers can easily distinguish between the plantation vernacular homes of earlier days, including those in the Lihue Town Tract, and the tropical adaptation of ranch-style homes built in Molokoa I.[68] The former typically presents a boxy appearance, with hip roof (sometimes double-pitched), tongue-and-groove walls, double-hung and slider windows, nine-foot (or more) ceilings, and frequently a French door entry with sidelights. The ranch homes, by contrast, are rectangular and low, with a shallow gable roof (pitch and gravel being a typical material), living room picture windows, and jalousies. The yards, too, differ markedly, with the earlier homes surrounded by considerably more trees and shrubbery, and many still retaining the character-defining short hedges that line the tract's two streets. Manicured lawns with carefully pruned greenery is the dominant landscaping style in the newer subdivision. Probably the most striking difference between Lihue Town Tract and Molokoa I is the relationship of the family automobile to the residence; the 1930s and 1940s homes tucked detached garages away at the back of the property (a vestige of horse and carriage days), whereas the carport became the preeminent feature in many of the planned dwellings in the later era.

Many families in the neighborhood once flew carp on Boys Day, May 5, in celebration of their sons. A few still continue the tradition.

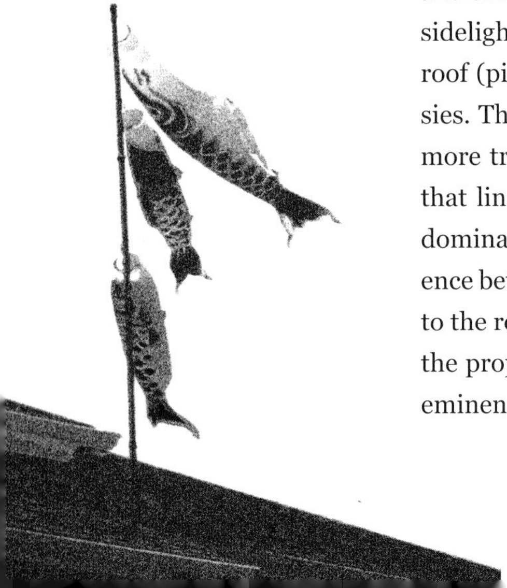

Molokoa II and III present yet another construction style. Property buyers in those subdivisions chose their own house designs and contractors. Combined with a new accessibility to inexpensively produced building materials and furnishings from Asia, the result is a more cosmopolitan, less Hawaii-specific appearance to those neighborhoods.[69] The size of houses and their footprint on the Unit III lots have also changed dramatically. By 1995, when the subdivision's restrictive covenants were written, the *minimum* size of a residence was 1,200 square feet of interior floor space, "exclusive of servants' quarters, garage, and workshop"—half again larger than the 'Umi Street homes. Forbidden in the subdivision is "asphalt felt rolled, pitch and gravel, corrugated iron, or any metal roofing," once a standard in Hawai'i.[70]

As another generation gradually replaces the original homeowners in the first Molokoa neighborhood, several traditional elements are disappearing. Fewer carp fly above homes to celebrate a household's sons during the Japanese festival of Boys' Day each May 5, and the water jugs that once lined carefully manicured 'Umi Street lawns as a deterrent to dogs have almost completely disappeared.

Jugs of water were once a common sight at the edge of lawns. Homeowners hoped they would scare away dogs who saw their reflections in the glass.

EDUCATING THE CHILDREN

The Lihue Grammar School, predecessor of the Elsie H. Wilcox Elementary School, was built on the Puhi side of the Lihue Plantation mill. It was founded in 1881 as a public English school with a principal and one assistant responsible for the eighty-seven enrolled students. Two years later enrollment had grown by eleven and the school hired a second assistant, who taught in the Hawaiian language.[71]

By the early 1920s the campus, then forty years old, was dilapidated enough for the Mokihana Club's Health Committee—Mary Rice, Helen Lydgate, Dora Isenberg, and Anna Wilcox—to pressure county supervisors into providing a new school. They complained, "Our present school (LIHUE) is a miserable make shift, in size, entirely inadequate, unsanitary in every way. Our community is heartily ashamed of it."[72] Underscoring the problem's severity they noted, "Were it not for the use of four rooms in the Japanese school, 260 of the Lihue children would not be able to have any schooling." The ladies' efforts were rewarded; a new campus, constructed across the street from the old one, opened in the spring of 1923. Three years later an English Standard section, a territory-wide, segregated system to "protect the good speech habits of a minority of the pupils," was moved from Kauai High

OPPOSITE PAGE
Esther Kawakami performed with her class during May Day celebrations at the Elsie H. Wilcox Elementary School, 1972. Esther Kawakami-Williams

to Lihue Grammar School.[73] Dubbed the Annex, it effected a two-tier educational system that continued until the 1950s.

During the middle of the Depression, enrollment exceeded a thousand students taught by a faculty of thirty-four. The ten-acre campus included twenty-three buildings and two vegetable gardens, along with assorted chickens and pigs. Another three acres across Halekō Road housed teachers' cottages. Periodically, discussions took place about whether the school's proximity to the mill caused health problems, whether the site was too "off center," away from the main Līhu‘e population, and whether the tiny Huleia School should be closed, with a replacement elementary school constructed at Puhi.[74] The first two questions took years to resolve, but in 1946, shortly after World War II, Huleia School did close, and its students were shifted to the Līhu‘e campus.

By 1952 the leading edge of the Baby Boomer generation swelled enrollment to 1,200 students. The campus was once again deteriorated and inadequate. All of the buildings suffered from mildew, dry rot, and the accumulation of mill-generated soot on roofs and eaves. Government officials heard parents' complaints that the tremendous amount of grime dropping on the school grounds was an unsanitary nuisance to the clothes and

Book Week was an exciting event for teachers and children, with many creating imaginative representations of characters in their favorite books. A *Honolulu Star-Bulletin* story about the event on Kaua‘i in 1928 reported, "Barley bags, soap boxes and baby carriage wheels were quickly thrown together to impersonate the Dog of Flanders and his milk cart." Lihue Public Library

bodies of their children. In his privately printed *Autobiography*, John Corstorphine recounted the effects of the mill ash at Lihue Grammar School when he was a student there in the 1930s:

> The sugar cane brought into the mill by cane car still had some leaves and other burnable material on it which was handled at the mill. There was a great, huge, tall smokestack to carry away the smoke and other burning byproducts. The smoke it handled. The by-products were a different story. The ash produced by the burning process was not gray, nor powdery as you might imagine; it was black and in large pieces, somewhat brittle and sometimes as much as six inches long. If the mill had been working over the weekend, I would come back to school to find a find a black covering over the grass, walks, roofs, trees. Every surface had black on it. It looked like the result of a "scorched earth" policy. After recess the barefooted children all had black feet, clear up to their ankles. If you were unlucky enough to fall on the playground, you were automatically multicolored, red from the color of the underlying dirt, green from the grass and black from the ash.[75]

The school's location next to the mill, the regional center of industry, sometimes compromised the teaching environment as well as personal hygiene. The screech of trains hauling cane into the factory, the fierce hiss of escaping steam from its power plant, and the din of the massive grinding machinery created disruptions that could defeat teachers' best efforts in the classroom. Additionally, public officials were concerned about the hazardous traffic conditions at the busy intersection of Nāwiliwili and Halekō roads. And though money was available to construct a new kindergarten classroom (the first kindergarten class had opened in October 1945), there was no room for another building at the existing thirteen-acre site, nor for a playground more expansive than the 40- by 60-square-foot plot already utilized for that purpose.

Declaring itself "unqualifiedly ready" to find another location for the school, the Board of Supervisors suggested acquisition of the cane land immediately south of G. N. Wilcox Memorial Hospital, where Walmart now stands. In 1954 the County and Lihue Plantation settled on a different location closer to the town center, next to the newly completed police station where sugarcane was still growing on the Nāwiliwili side of the courthouse. (A decade later the Kauaʻi Community College also became a candidate for the Walmart

Lihue Grammar School performance. William J. Senda, David Alexander

location, but the state ultimately opted to accept a donation of Grove Farm land in Puhi for the campus.) Negotiations shifted from a land exchange to a cash settlement, which prompted brothers Charlie and Harold Rice to toss a cherry bomb into the discussion. Declaring the plantation's sales price of $10,000 per acre a "holdup," the brothers argued that Lihue Plantation should make a gift of the acreage for the school site as a way "to make friends," especially since a large percentage of the students were children of its employees. Harold Rice went so far as to accuse American Factors of wanting "to bleed" the county.[76] When the company dismissed such an idea, the brothers shifted to the position that the existing school site was actually ideal except for its proximity to the mill, which should be condemned as a public nuisance.[77] By the time, in 1959, that County and plantation settled on a compromise price of about $125,000 for the fourteen acres, the new school had been designed, built, and operational for more than a year.

While the land fight was being waged, a parallel battle erupted over what the new school should be called. In 1955, Senator Noboru Miyake submitted a resolution to the Territorial Senate to name it the Elsie H. Wilcox Elementary School as a way to honor the recently deceased, "beloved and public spirited daughter of Hawaii" for her noteworthy

The distinctive outline of the Elsie H. Wilcox School is easily identifiable in this mid-1960s aerial of central Līhu‘e. The domed roof of the Convention Hall is visible at right, and the developing Molokoa subdivision is to the left of the school. The State Office Building had not yet replaced the armory, nor had the round building supplanted the Tip Top. A hint of the Līhu‘e Airport runway can be seen near the top of the photo, beyond the fields of sugarcane. Hawaiian Sugar Planters' Association contributions to the field of education.[78] Approved unanimously by both the Senate and the commissioners of public instruction, the name was unprecedented on Kauaʻi, where schools had heretofore been identified by the names of their surrounding communities. The Territory's decision was unappreciated by the Kauai County Board of Supervisors, who proceeded to install a plaque identifying the new facility as the Lihue School. The disagreement found its way to the attorney general in 1959. He issued a formal ruling that the school commissioners, the territorial-level group who had adopted the Elsie H. Wilcox name, was the body that held the legal authority and responsibility to make the naming decision. Resistance was inevitable, and it came almost immediately from supervisor Tsuneto Kunimura (later, a state representative, then mayor, and often affectionately known as "Uncle Tony"), who declared, "Legally or otherwise, it is still Lihue School." Kunimura demanded, "Has the plaque been changed?" He threatened, "If they have, there is going to be some fireworks."[79] Ultimately the pyrotechnics fizzled, and the Elsie H. Wilcox Elementary School, or simply Wilcox Elementary, is how most refer to the institution today.

The architect of the new facility, Ernest H. Hara (1909–2006), was a noted school designer. An alumnus of Punahou, Hara graduated from the University of Southern California in 1935. He spent six years in the office of Claude A. Stiehl, then worked for a year with C. W. Dickey before becoming a field engineer for the Army Corps of Engineers between 1942 and 1945. After the war Hara established his own architectural firm, one of the first Asian Americans to do so in Hawaiʻi. In 1956, as the Līhuʻe school plans were in progress, Hara's reputation was significant enough for him to be invited to speak at Stanford University's fifth annual School Planning Institute, where he shared his perceptions about "Trends in Planning Schools in Hawaii."[80] The University of Hawaiʻi recognized his achievements by creating an annual Ernest H. Hara, FAIA, Distinguished Service Award to "honor outstanding lifetime service to the architecture profession." He also won the 2002 Medal of Honor from the American Institute of Architects/Hawaii State Council for his career-long efforts to advance the profession and develop connections between east and west, particularly between Japan and Hawaiʻi.[81]

The new campus, with its parallel rows of concrete block buildings connected by breezeways, is a classic example of postwar, Eisenhower-era school design, just as many older schools' 1920s bungalow-type classrooms were typical of their day. The administration building was positioned at the front of the school adjacent to the horseshoe-shaped entryway, a convenient dropoff point for the increasing numbers of children whose parents had begun driving them to school. The cafetorium was located next to the parking lot

Public schools were not the only institutions to offer educational opportunities in Līhu'e. Next to the Lutheran church on the hill *mauka* of the mill, a German school operated between 1883, when this photo was taken, and 1918. Initially students were taught in German, though later the first language was changed to English. Anti-German hysteria during World War I effectively shut down the school, which at its height enrolled more than one hundred students. A Japanese-language school also operated near the Līhu'e cemetery until World War II. The Immaculate Conception Catholic Church built a school in the Isenberg tract where students were taught for many years in the second half of the twentieth century. Kaua'i Museum

by the police station, and the county park on the Rice Street side of the school became the children's playing field.

Until statehood in 1959 the Territorial Department of Public Instruction and its commissioners maintained responsibility for policy decisions and operations, including teacher hiring and firing. School construction and maintenance, however, had been a local function since the formation of the Hawai'i county government system in 1905. To the counties, therefore, fell the decisions about where schools would be built as well as how the burden of paying for facility expenses would be met (enough to consume five-sixths of the total real property tax revenues in 1958).[82] Although more finances for building and maintenance were clearly needed than this rural island's local taxes could supply, the County was loathe to relinquish its powers to the new State of Hawai'i. County Board of Supervisors chair Anthony Baptiste, with members Tony Kunimura and Raymond Aki, testified against the change before the House of Representatives, as did the Kaua'i district and school building superintendents. Despite their arguments that county-level maintenance of school facilities was more efficient, the Hawai'i Constitution established that the state would control all aspects of the public educational system, including its

Elsie Hart Wilcox (1874–1954) was the third of six children born to Sam and Emma Wilcox and the niece of Grove Farm owner G. N. Wilcox. She was appointed Commissioner of Education in 1920 and served in that position until her election to the Territorial Senate in 1932. Despite pressure from others of her class, owners and managers of agricultural businesses who saw no profit in educating their future workforce, Wilcox championed broad, progressive, public school standards for all the children of Hawai'i. She was also a "professional volunteer" who founded the YWCA on Kaua'i and served on the boards of numerous organizations concerned with education and social welfare in Hawai'i. Elsie Wilcox died while the new elementary school in Līhu'e was under construction, and it was named for her as a fitting tribute to her dedicated efforts. Hawai'i State Archives

facilities. The change created the most centralized educational operation in the nation. A tangential result is that today in Hawai'i, where county revenues no longer pay the costs of public education, property taxes are lower than the national average whereas the aggregate of state taxes, which do fund our schools, rises above it.

Enrollment at Wilcox School has periodically risen and declined during its sixty-plus years on Hardy Street. Hanamaulu School students began attending Wilcox after that institution was closed in 1963. (The population growth in Hanamā'ulu and Wailua led to the opening of a new elementary school in Hanamā'ulu, King Kaumuali'i, in 1990.) In 1967 and 1968, the eighth and seventh graders, respectively, were transferred from the elementary school to Kaua'i High, which then became Kaua'i High and Intermediate. When Chiefess Kamakahelei Middle School opened in Puhi, sixth graders transferred there. Currently, over nine hundred students attend Elsie H. Wilcox Elementary School in kindergarten through fifth grades.

LIHUE PUBLIC LIBRARY

Frank Lloyd Wright may not have visited Kaua'i, but the philosophical principles of the man often described as America's foremost twentieth-century architect are embodied in the Lihue Public Library. Rhythmic space. Integration of light. The assumption of spirituality in architecture. It's all there, standing as testimony to Wright's design principles and created by one of his lifelong disciples, Stephen Noboru Oyakawa (1921–1980).

The architect was born to Zensho and Kame Oyakawa, immigrant hog farmers from Okinawa. A graduate of the University of Illinois, Oyakawa "walked through destiny's door in 1944, when sculptor Isamu Noguchi introduced him to Frank Lloyd Wright in New York."[83] He spent the next fourteen years as one of Wright's famed Taliesin fellows, learning and working at the master's elbow and integrating himself in Wright's total-immersion, apprenticeship community. A 1958 *Honolulu Star-Bulletin* interview quoted Oyakawa as acknowledging that he "learned to cook well, dance, play several musical instruments, sing, sculpt and do ceramics" in his life at Taliesin; his longtime draftsman and kindred spirit, Charles Saiki, would later remember the quality of Oyakawa's Japanese teriyaki. Along the way Oyakawa also absorbed Wright's preference for "honest arrogance" over "hypocritical humility," not a typical sentiment in Hawai'i.[84]

After returning to Honolulu to assist with family matters and set up an architectural practice in the islands, Oyakawa displayed that preference when he vocally skewered contemporary Hawaiian architecture. A 1958 *Star-Bulletin* article titled "Honolulu: 'No Color, No Imagination, and, Bad Design Sense,'" quoted Oyakawa as complaining, "The idea of being honest with the materials and the feeling they are to convey is remarkably lacking in most of Waikiki." Although builders sought to invent "an atmosphere of paradise," he said, they managed to create instead "a beastly tourist trap scene." Oyakawa was hardly alone in his assessment. When Vladimir Ossipoff, Hawai'i's premier midcentury architect, became president of the Hawai'i Chapter of the American Institute of Architects six years later, he declared a "War on Ugliness" as the theme of his term. (Ossipoff's vice president that year was Wilcox School designer Ernest H. Hara.)[85]

One Hawai'i architect whom Oyakawa did appreciate was Hart Wood, the creator of Līhu'e's original library building on Rice Street. He described Wood's First Church of Christ Scientist in Honolulu as "a beautiful building. Gracious and charming."[86] Perhaps Oyakawa's use of lava rock in the new library's tapering exterior walls was a respectful nod to its 1924 Rice Street predecessor, which features the material with such success. Or it

might have been simply the best choice to embody "organic architecture" in the building, a concept he had learned from both Wright and his own Buddhist philosophies. Saiki described the approach as "pertaining to the existence of life."[87] Oyakawa's son Allen, himself a Taliesin fellow, remembered that everything his father did had a reason. "He thought about everything, it had meaning, it had to relate to something."[88] That is not to say no consideration was given to practicalities. The building was constructed in nine-foot segments, an unusual choice when considering typical board and other material lengths but understandable given standard, three-foot-multiple library shelving systems. Oyakawa, who fondly remembered his Saturday evening socials around a dancing fire at Taliesin, might have thought his inclusion of a moss rock fireplace in the front conference room was practical too, but that feature, which was part of his original blueprints, was omitted in the final construction of the building.

The Lihue Library, completed in 1969, was the third state library branch Oyakawa designed, after ʻAiea and Liliha on Oʻahu. They were all built with money from the Federal Library Service and Construction Act, an element of President Johnson's vast Great Society programs. Those funds were earmarked to improve public library services and facilities in rural and other underserved areas. Improve it did. The new facility was

Lihue Public Library architect Stephen Oyakawa studied with Frank Lloyd Wright as a Taliesin fellow from 1946 to 1961. A devotee of the famed architect, Oyakawa campaigned unsuccessfully for Wright to design the Hawaiʻi capitol. Pictured in 1955 with Wright and other apprentices, Oyakawa is the fifth man from the right. Seated from left: John Howe, Wright, Wright's grandson Eric Lloyd Wright, Wesley Peters, John Amarantides. First five standing diagonally from left: Mark Heyman, Eugene Masselink, Raja Aederi, James Pfefferkorn, Alan Wool. Standing immediately right of Wright: Ling Po, David Dodge, Thomas Casey, Donald Brown. Standing to the right of Eric Wright: Oyakawa and Kenneth Lockhart. John Engstead, Frank Lloyd Wright Foundation

Thelma Hopper Hadley (1902–1987) served as Kauaʻi librarian for forty-four years. She began her career in 1927, three years after the Hart Wood building on Rice Street was completed, and she was still at the library's helm when the new facility on Hardy Street was dedicated in 1969. Kauaʻi Historical Society

triple the size of the old, with space for 80,000–100,000 volumes. It also included a landscaped reading lanai and space for the two bookmobiles that regularly transported part of the collection to patrons offsite. However, the quantum leap between the old building and the new was not its size but its technology: the incorporation of library-to-Wilcox School TV conduits, an audio "listening room," music carrels, and other state-of-the-art innovations. "The new sophisticated machines," Oyakawa had told a statewide conference of the Hawaii Library Association in 1965, "would soon be changing the storage of knowledge in libraries."[89] In his design of the Lihue Public Library, the architect practiced the technological innovations he preached, with much fanfare and appreciation by the community. It has been said that the building was designed in the shape of a book, but the graceful curved roof extending the length of the building hints at a soaring wave of knowledge that the new technological capabilities promised to wash across the school, Līhuʻe Town, and beyond.

Times change; all new things grow old. The rows of magazines that patrons once enjoyed have been whittled down to but a few; movie DVDs and ebooks are now available, along with Internet access on dedicated computers. In 2013 the Lihue Library was closed for several months to renovate and modernize the facility for its current patrons, but the need continues for additional space to house books, media, equipment, and services in the twenty-first century.

Lihue Public Library, 2005.

THE MERGER OF FAITH, POLITICS, AND POWER

The imprint of European and Asian influence in the development of central Līhu'e is considerable, but little is evident of the long tenancy of the Hawaiian people on this land. Two institutions that provide an opportunity to reflect on the complex responses of the Hawaiian monarchy to the challenges of their era are the public health office and St. Michael and All Angels Episcopal Church. According to historians Ralph S. Kuykendall and A. Grove Day, "One of the important developments—perhaps the most important—in the reign of Kamehameha IV was the establishment of the Episcopal Church in the kingdom, an event that held political as well as religious significance."[90]

An Episcopal affiliation (the British form is Anglican) was comfortable for the king, Alexander Liholiho. He had long been impressed by the liturgy, hierarchy, and formality of the denomination, which he had experienced years before at religious monuments such as Trinity Church in San Francisco and Westminster Abbey in London. Queen Emma also felt at home in that faith, having been reared in the household of her English grandfather, Dr. T. C. B. Rooke, who held ardent British sympathies. The couple used the Episcopal ritual at their wedding, and both king and queen wanted their only child, Prince Albert Edward Kauikeaouli Kaleiopapa a Kamehameha, to be baptized in the Anglican Communion and raised in its traditions.[91]

King Kamehameha IV and Queen Emma are memorialized in a stained-glass window, designed by John Wallis, at the entry to the cathedral of St. Andrew, Honolulu.

On the other hand, the move to import British clergy and their religion doubly disturbed the American-based Congregational missionaries, who had heretofore dominated the religious life of the islands and who feared that Anglican influence on the monarchy would compromise their own political leverage as well as dilute American supremacy in the kingdom. Maria Rice Isenberg, in Honolulu for treatment of her tuberculosis, expressed some of the antipathy felt toward the Anglicans by the Congregationalist missionaries and their families. In a December 20, 1863, letter home, shortly after the death of Kamehameha IV, she wrote:

> The other day the Queen told Bishop Staley that someone had told her the cause of the King's death was his forsaking the Protestant Missionaries, his old friends. Of course the Bishop was fearfully angry and said no one should be admitted to talk with the Queen. . . . Many of the Natives say that the influence

> of the English Clergy did induce the King to drink, and so hastened his end. But the common impression is that Prince Lot, the new King, will take very much the same course as his Brother.[92]

In New England, home of the missionary board, the *Boston Daily Advertiser* decried the introduction of an English Episcopal mission: "We do not *insinuate*—we charge that this Mission is a part of a long-standing intrigue to make British influence paramount in a group of Islands which, politically, are the key which will hereafter control the Pacific."[93] The Yankees had strong economic ties with Hawai'i, but they were also well aware that British sympathies lay with the rebel South in the American Civil War years, 1861–1865.

From the perspective of the Hawaiian monarchs, American influence in their kingdom was growing alarmingly, not only in religious and political matters but in economic ones as well. A strong effort to annex Hawai'i to the United States had exerted considerable pressure on Kamehameha III in 1853–1854. He died before signing any agreement, but his heir, Liholiho, was mindful of the continuing risks to his country's independence. He feared "that the great preponderance of American interests, including the missionary interest, would lead to the overthrow of the monarchy, annexation to the United States, and ultimate extinction of the Hawaiian race." (Perhaps, too, the aristocratic prince veered more strongly away from America after a trip there in 1849, when a conductor tried to force him off a train leaving Washington, D.C., because of his color.) To diffuse that threat Kamehameha IV sought to reduce the missionary influence in his cabinet, to create a reciprocity treaty with the United States rather than submit to annexation, and to maintain Hawaiian sovereignty by obtaining a guarantee from America and the major European powers to respect the country's independence. The introduction of the Anglican church worked hand in hand with those ends.[94]

In 1861, Britain's Queen Victoria herself granted the royal license for the Archbishop of Canterbury to consecrate the Reverend Thomas N. Staley as bishop of the new missionary diocese in Hawai'i. Tragically, preparations for his departure and the long voyage around Cape Horn delayed Staley's arrival until October 1862, eight days after the death of cherished Prince Albert, lovingly referred to as "the hope of Hawaii." Despite their crushing loss, Liholiho and Emma pushed on with their plans. Before his death in 1863, the king translated the denomination's *Book of Common Prayer* into Hawaiian and commissioned the construction of the Episcopal Cathedral of St. Andrew in Honolulu.

Missions were established on O'ahu, Maui, and the island of Hawai'i, but progress on

Kaua'i was slower. Episcopal services were held at Kilauea for a short while in the 1860s, and between 1881 and 1885 the Makee Sugar Company at Keālia hired an Anglican priest as plantation chaplain. After he left, however, no regular services were held until the twentieth century. And no permanent structure housed an Episcopalian congregation until All Saint's Church in Kapa'a was constructed in 1926. The Venerable Charles Crane wrote about the reason for establishing an Episcopal church in Kapa'a rather than Līhu'e. In a 1970s typed history of the founding of St. Michael's, he wrote that, to avoid an Episcopal church being established in town, "a 'comity' agreement was struck whereby if The Episcopal Church would not establish a mission in Lihue, the Congregationalists would refrain from creating a 'haole' church in Kapaa."[95]

Gradually, the dynamics changed in Līhu'e. A plan to establish an Episcopal church in town moved forward in the early 1960s, partly in partnership with the Philippine Independent Church, whose clergy and congregation were made welcome in the planning process.[96] The name "The Church of St. Michael and All Angels" was chosen because it was long and "made the letterhead look balanced" with the "Philippine Independent Church and Episcopal" listed below it on a second line. Organizers also felt "that the other-worldly nature of the name would appeal to the P.I.C. folk with their more Catholic approach to liturgy and theology."[97] The congregation was able to buy seven choice lots in American Factors' planned Molokoa subdivision, kitty-corner to the courthouse and directly across

St. Michael and All Angels Episcopal Church, 2003.

MANY PEOPLES, MANY RELIGIONS

The Līhu'e region is home to nearly twenty houses of worship representing many different religions and denominations existing in Hawai'i. The first group to land in the islands, the Congregational missionaries, stepped ashore on the Big Island of Hawai'i in 1820 and made an immediate impact.

Roman Catholic priests who arrived seven years later were not welcomed. The American missionaries considered them a challenge to their dominance, and the *ali'i* feared Catholicism as idol worship too soon after the practice had been abolished in Hawai'i. The religion made many converts, however, and after the predominantly

Catholic Portuguese began immigrating, Immaculate Conception Church was established at Kapaia in 1884. By the turn of the century, Catholicism had become Kaua'i's largest Christian religion. It is also the largest religious faith throughout Hawai'i, followed by the Church of Jesus Christ of Latter Day Saints, and Buddhism.

The first Buddhist bishops arrived in Hawai'i at the end of the nineteenth century to minister to the spiritual needs of thousands of Japanese in the islands. During the next two decades dozens of temples for the various Buddhist sects sprang up across the Territory. The Lihue Hongwanji, constructed in Kapaia Valley across the stream from Immaculate Conception, was one.

Missionaries and their descendants continued their interest in and donations to religious institutions. Lihue Christian Church on Kress Street, the Salvation Army, and St. Michael and All Angels are beneficiaries of their largesse, as is the Lihue Union (now Lihue United) Church. The Gothic Revival style building, designed by the early Ripley and Dickey partnership, was completed in 1901 on Nāwiliwili Road. Having grown dilapidated and termite ridden, it was replaced a half century later by the current structure, one of architect Hart Wood's last projects, which he designed to complement one of his first, the adjacent parish hall.

The apse of Immaculate Conception Catholic Church, Kapaia.

The original Lihue Hongwanji building at left was removed to Hanalei in the 1980s and has since been used for nonreligious purposes.

The Lihue Union Church, early twentieth century. Grove Farm Homestead Museum

Rev. Hiseki and Mrs. Mineo Miyasaki, Lihue Hongwanji, Kapaia, 1905. Kaua'i Museum

The *koa* entry doors to the church were sketched by Joseph Rozon and carved by Jerry Lujan.

from Wilcox School. The new church, designed by Honolulu architect Charles Wagner and constructed in the shape of an angel with outstretched wings, was dedicated in 1965.

By the 1980s the expanding congregation and its many outreach activities had outgrown the modest structure. The local firm of Agor Architecture was hired to design both a new church and a two-story parish house. The Reverend Jan Rudinoff, who served as parish rector for thirty years before his retirement in 2004, likes to tell people that Steve Shackleton, the Taliesin-trained "dropout Hare Krishna" designer in Agor's office, "had a dream about the building, got up and drew it. When the design was shown to the congregation not a single person complained." Ron Agor remembered, "The progressive design of the church was done intentionally to reflect the parish's progressive philosophy."[98]

Agor defined progressiveness in architecture as going "beyond conventional design with large open spaces under the roof that have no visible support posts." Steel beams and steel-reinforced concrete made such a concept possible. Two walls of sliding glass doors that dissolve the barrier between inside and out on either side of the nave, where the congregation sits, symbolize the parish's emphasis on being a welcoming community. Of particular note are the entry doors. Carved of laminated *koa* wood by Kauaʻi sculptor Jerry L. Lujan, in collaboration with artist Joseph Rozon, the doors portray a serene St. Michael, shield in one hand, spear in the other, vanquishing a writhing dragon at his feet.

The Right Reverend Donald Hart, Bishop of Hawaiʻi, consecrated St. Michael's new house of worship on February 12, 1991. An adjacent two-story, L-shaped parish hall was scheduled for dedication on September 27, 1992, but Hurricane ʻIniki rearranged those plans on September 11. For several months the building became Red Cross district headquarters; it was one of the few places during the early period of disaster relief that could offer water and phone service. Today, the upstairs spaces are leased to nonprofit organizations and small business professionals. The Jewish community on Kauaʻi utilizes the sanctuary for monthly Shabbat services and other religious holiday celebrations throughout the year.

Its position as the youngest of the island's six Episcopal churches entitles St. Michael's to the custodianship of a silver chalice and paten donated to Kauaʻi by Queen Emma herself. The two vessels, used by priest and congregation in their Holy Communion services, provide a tangible link to the Hawaiian monarchs who initially brought the denomination to these shores a century and a half ago.

HAWAI'I STATE OFFICE BUILDING

The three-story State Office Building was completed in 1969, the same year as the library, though the structures could hardly be more different. The rigidly vertical structure is the highest in town. It "raises its square whiteness in the heart of Lihue," observed the *Garden*

Līhu'e's State Building, 1975. Another 8,400 square feet of office space was added in 1980 with the enclosure of the open lanais on the third floor. Harvey Tam, Kaua'i Historical Society

Island in 1971, which noted critically, "perhaps because of its mainland look, its Hawaiian name is never heard."[99] That name is Kaeo, so called to honor the high chief who became the second husband of the *ali'i 'aimoku,* Kamakahelei, ruler of Kaua'i in the lateeighteenth century when James Cook first landed on the island at Waimea (their son Kaumualii would follow as ruler).[100]

Unlike most of lower Hardy Street, where construction in the 1950s and '60s rolled back the sugarcane fields acre by acre, this site had long held a public structure, the Lihue Armory. Calls for armories to be erected around the island began in 1915, when Europe was held tight in the death grasp of World War I. America would remain at peace for another two years, but these faraway islands were not so remote as to shelter the population from military preparations—some would call it war fever. A battalion of the national guard was organized on Kaua'i, and more than four hundred men joined up. An armory for weapon storage as well as drilling and meeting space became a priority. By the spring of 1916 land immediately behind the county building was secured, and Capt. J. H. Moragne returned from Honolulu with completed plans for a T-shaped structure to be built on the site, with offices designed for the short stem of the building and a drill hall in the long section.[101]

In October 1919, Philip Rice, who had been instrumental in forming the initial American Legion post in Honolulu, helped organize post number two on Kaua'i. By 1922, Legion membership had reached one hundred, and its activities had expanded beyond the

The *Garden Island* proudly reported in January 1923 that, to remodel the armory in Līhu'e, "a subscription was started and over $1000 was collected in the next two weeks from more that 300 different people. The subscriptions were from 25 cents to $50 and came from all nationalities. The Japanese and Filipinos were very generous in their subscriptions. . . . [The plantations] were so generous in their response that the building was assured by September. . . . This new building not only fills a long felt want in the community but demonstrates a splendid spirit of community co-operation of which we are justly proud." *Garden Island* archives maintenance of civil defense to include educational, athletic, and social work. The armory, if enlarged, could provide a fine facility to accommodate games, pageants, and public meetings. Enthusiasm for the expansion project was such that fundraising efforts exceeded the financial goal in five months. The surplus funds allowed for a number of "necessary extras," such as removable bleachers, showers and toilets, a boxing ring, and a lighting system installed by Kauai Telephonic Co. The Mokihana Club remodeled the kitchen, and the Legion's Woman's Auxiliary furnished the ladies' dressing room. The facility's conveniences made it a useful community hall: the Kaua'i County fairs were held in and around the building for many years, along with untold numbers of performances and games.

The Kauai County Fair was held at the armory for many years, including 1938, when this banner was used on letterhead. Hawaiian Sugar Planters' Association archives

During World War II the Lihue Armory served as Local Board No. 2, and it was here that the first Americans of Japanese ancestry in the Territory were allowed to volunteer for military service. Among them was Mitsuru Doi (1924–2002), a Kapaia Garage station attendant whose Japan-born father worked as a yardman for Dr. Sam Wallis. Doi was the first of fifty-eight men at the Lihue Armory to volunteer, pass the physical examination, and take the oath of induction on March 11, 1943. (Ninety-two more were inducted on March 13 at Local Board No. 1, Makaweli, then an additional seventy-one when the call was increased.) Another volunteer, Lihue Plantation engineer Shuichi "Pete" Sakamoto (1908–1988), was a thirty-four-year-old, married, Purdue University graduate with a two-year-old son. In all, nearly 1,300 Kaua'i men served during World War II, most with the 442nd Regimental Combat Team. Many returned to the island after the war and built successful careers. Forty-eight died in service to their country, and their names are enshrined at the Kaua'i War Memorial Convention Hall.[102]

Another 442nd veteran, architect Shoso Kagawa, was the designer of the State Office Building in Līhu'e. Born in Honolulu to immigrants from Hiroshima, Kagawa was a sophomore at the University of Hawai'i when Pearl Harbor was bombed in 1941. He enlisted on March 25, 1943, shortly after Doi and Sakamoto, and became part of the 442nd's 522 Field Artillery Battalion. After the war Kagawa took advantage of the G.I. Bill to attend Columbia University School of Architecture, possibly the first person from Hawai'i and first of Japanese ancestry to be admitted. After working for several years in New York, he returned to Hawai'i and opened Kagawa and Associates, Inc. Over the years he designed many public facilities—among them the Kalanimoku State Office Building in Honolulu, the Maui County Office Building, and the Duke Kahanamoku swimming pool at the

Mitsuru Doi, right, was the first American of Japanese ancestry in Hawai'i to be inducted into the army in World War II. With him was fellow inductee, Lihue Plantation engineer Shuichi Sakamoto. Library of Congress, Prints and Photographs Division, FSA/OWI Collection, LC-USE6-D-010177

University of Hawai'i at Mānoa—as well as private ones, including the Rice Shopping Center in Līhu'e. Kagawa's style reflects the strong modernist influences of his East Coast training, as do the designs of so many of the other young Hawai'i architects who studied on the continent in that postwar period.[103]

The State Building was the last major structure to rise in the heart of Līhu'e during the transformational 1960s. It created a post-statehood home for the governor's representative and several state agencies. Today these include the departments of Hawaiian Home Lands, Social Services and Housing, Land and Natural Resources, Commerce and Consumer Affairs, Child and Public Welfare, Labor and Industrial Relations, Education, Taxation, and the University of Hawai'i College of Tropical Agriculture and Human Resources Extension Service. In the twenty-first century, state government work has again spilled beyond the allotted space: the Department of Transportation and the Department of Accounting and Government Services have moved beyond the heart of Kaua'i and now reside in the Puhi Industrial Area.

Two in One, created by internationally recognized artist Gwen Lux Creighton, was commissioned by the State Foundation on Culture and the Arts in 1969 for the lawn of the State Building. The ten-foot-high, twin concrete sections of a sphere were meant to symbolize the close working relationship of state and county governments; the stepped base represented public participation in the political process. The sculpture has since been moved to the grounds of the Kaua'i Community Correctional Center. Harvey Tam, Kaua'i Historical Society

SEVEN

BACKS TO THE FUTURE

Whereof what's past is prologue, what to come
In yours and my discharge.

—William Shakespeare, *The Tempest*

I ka wā mamua, ka wā mahope, a well-known Hawaiian proverb, proposes that people place their backs to the future when seeking guidance, that they look to former times, the time "in front"—*mamua.* That way navigates wisely toward the time "behind"—*mahope,* that which comes afterward—"for the future is always unknown, whereas the past is rich in glory and knowledge."[1] The past is prologue.

Central Līhu'e, 1976. R. M. Towill Corporation

The origins of Līhu'e are rooted in the sugar industry; over time the town's core branched well beyond plantation life to encompass a dynamic mix of government, retail, human resources, and professional activities. Because Līhu'e never experienced a period of extended decline, the town today is a patchwork of historic building materials and techniques, with no single architectural style predominating.

CONSTRUCTING THE PAST

Despite the evolutionary rhythm of change in town, three significant building periods are identifiable. The first transformed it from hamlet to commanding island nucleus, the second enlarged government influence within the town, and the third remade Līhu'e into an expression of postwar modernism. All three issued from larger trends of their eras.

The first took place in the early years of the twentieth century when Lihue Plantation began creating its concrete village. The county building, Bank of Hawaii building, Lihue Store, original Tip Top, and Halekō duplexes, all constructed between 1910 and 1916, exhibited solid testimony to the town's foundation upon Western philosophical precepts as well as the plantation's power. A subtle symbol of the period is the Italian marble horse trough donated by Hans and Dora Isenberg and installed for public use and enjoyment at Līhu'e's main intersection. The elegant fountain implied that community pride of place, encouraged by such enhancements, was a priority for the company town.

The Isenbergs' actions mirrored and were likely influenced by the City Beautiful movement that emerged in America after the 1893 World's Columbian Exposition in Chicago. Its adherents believed in creating lovely urban surroundings as a form of social control, a way to inspire moral virtue. Historian William H. Wilson wrote that, although attractiveness was important in and of itself in City Beautiful philosophy, "its role in environmental conditioning was never far from the minds of its advocates. The civic center's beauty would reflect the souls of the city's inhabitants, inducing order, calm, and propriety therein."[2] City Beautiful was linked to the larger Progressive movement of the same era, which sought to reform social ills and political corruption. On Kaua'i the Mokihana Club, in which Dora Isenberg had been instrumental, illustrated some of the Progressive social welfare philosophy in activities such as its public health programs.

The second significant phase began in the Depression era as both territorial and federal governments visibly entered the Līhu'e landscape. In 1930 the Territory introduced the town to the adapted Mission Revival style that had become popular in Honolulu,

The Old Archives Building in Honolulu, on the grounds of ʻIolani Palace, was designed by Oliver Traphagen and completed in 1906. Its symmetrical features, columns on either side of a full-height porch, pediment, and dentil cornices bear a striking resemblance to the Kauaʻi County Building designed by Clinton Ripley a few years later. The style was inspired by the Columbian Exposition in 1893 and remained popular for a generation as an expression of strength, stability, and conservatism.

The Kauaʻi County Building, ca. 1916.
Helen McKaye, Hawaiʻi State Archives

California, Florida, and elsewhere. The Territorial Office Building, positioned adjacent to the county building, was followed at the end of the decade by the similarly styled circuit courthouse and the U.S. Post Office. Federal funds from the government's New Deal efforts to provide jobs and jump-start the economy also changed the routing at the historic island crossroads by cutting a new passageway between north and west sides of Kaua'i, *mauka* of the mill. Other New Deal road and bridge improvements around the island created unprecedented opportunities for residents to travel beyond their own communities and visit the go-to island center: Līhu'e. The town broadened its destination appeal near the end of the decade with the opening of Kress and other businesses along Rice Street on the Nāwiliwili side of town.

These first two periods changed the fabric of the town, but it is the work of the 1960s that defines Līhu'e today. In those early years after statehood, Līhu'e became a poster

U.S. Post Office building in Līhu'e. William J. Senda, Kaua'i Historical Society

child for the quip that the Hawai'i state bird was the construction crane (though hints of what was to come had begun in the late 1950s with the placement of the police station, ILWU headquarters and Wilcox Elementary School on the town's perimeter cane lands). The development of the Lihue Shopping Center at the island crossroads precipitated the construction of the First Hawaiian Bank and Lihue Plantation administration buildings on Rice Street as well as the Senda building at Hardy and 'Akahi. County and state construction filled in much of the rest of Hardy Street between the school and union headquarters. The State Office Building, library, convention hall, and tennis courts all took their place on the curve of the road; Molokoa homes and Salvation Army completed it.

A notable aspect of the midcentury construction within Līhu'e's few central blocks is the number of distinguished architects whose work is included there. Five of them served as presidents of the Hawai'i chapter of the American Institute of Architects: Kenneth Roehrig (Kaua'i Museum annex), Edwin Bauer (Lihue Plantation building and First Hawaiian Bank), Alfred Preis (ILWU), Clifford Young (Kaua'i War Memorial Convention Hall), and Ernest Hara (Elsie H. Wilcox Elementary School).[3] Though they never headed the Hawai'i AIA, both Shoso Kagawa (State Building) and Stephen Oyakawa (Lihue Public Library) were regionally recognized, and Lihue Shopping Center designer John Graham held national prominence. Laying the basis for much of these architects' work was former Honolulu planning director George Houghtailing, whose private urban planning firm the plantation consulted for the redevelopment concept.

By the early 1960s, Lihue Plantation's parent company, American Factors, was thinking big, looking beyond sugar for its fiscal well-being. It successfully created large residential developments on O'ahu as well as the first master-planned resort in Hawai'i, at Ka'anapali, Maui, on lands that were part of its subsidiary, Pioneer Mill. Seeking strategies to expand the vision on Kaua'i, Lihue Plantation hired celebrity architectural and planning firm John Carl Warnecke and Associates to create an ambitious development plan that addressed not only Līhu'e Town but also the neighboring regions of Nāwiliwili/Kalapakī, Kapaia Valley, Kilohana crater, and Hanamā'ulu Bay.[4] When the Līhu'e master plan began, Warnecke had already been chosen to design the Hawai'i State Capitol (with local Belt Lemmon & Lo architects), and its construction had begun. The Līhu'e area study was completed in 1966 and showcased in a spectacularly designed, grasscloth-covered, foot-and-a-half square presentation book with printed maps, illustrations from Paul Gauguin's Tahitian-period paintings, and tipped-in photographs of the study sites.

FOLLOWING PAGE
John Carl Warnecke and Associates completed a regional master plan for Lihue Plantation in 1966. Warnecke (1919–2010) had achieved renown after designing a solution for Lafayette Square, in front of the White House, that would preserve the historic buildings and texture of the square while allowing for modern government office buildings to be built unobtrusively behind them. Jacqueline Kennedy, a dedicated advocate of preservation of the square and restoration of the National Mall, is pictured with Warnecke at the project's unveiling in October 1962. A close friend and admirer of the architect, she chose Warnecke to design the John F. Kennedy memorial gravesite, with its eternal flame, after her husband's assassination in 1963. Abbie Rowe, White House Photographs, John F. Kennedy Presidential Library and Museum, Boston

GOVERNMENT PLANNING

Generating development plans was hardly unique to Lihue Plantation or American Factors. As the influence of plantations declined and that of government increased, the County prepared documents intended to guide island development. General plans in the early 1960s, 1971, 1984, and 2000 addressed the island as a whole. A Līhuʻe regional plan was adopted in 1977 and a town core design plan in 2010. All of them noted the prime agricultural land surrounding Līhuʻe, upon which any substantial town growth would encroach. They also commented on the town's shortage of housing and its traffic congestion, with differing solutions presented over time. Each in its own way offers a glimpse of the moods and concerns of their eras.

The first, "General Plans for Five Urban Areas of the County of Kauai: Waimea, Koloa, Kapaa, Hanapepe, Lihue," was completed in 1961, a year before its companion north shore plan.[5] At the time of statehood the economy and the population had been declining for more than two decades. The result, the study observed, was "rutted roads, shappy [shabby] school buildings, inadequate water systems, dilapidated park structures and by the very appearance of its government building."

Though the county held out hope that sugar and pineapple might still serve as significant income sources, with the possibility of diversification into other crops such as guava and passion fruit, it recognized the economic narrowness of an agricultural base. Kauaʻi needed another industry to take the island into the future. It set its hopes on tourism. Although the visitor count had risen 395 percent in the 1950s, the total number of people who came to the island in 1959 still totaled under 52,000. And in 1960 "there were little more than 200 rooms available as tourist accommodations on Kauai." To build a base for the industry, the plan prescribed the development of major resort concentrations at the Hanalei River mouth, Wailua Beach, Nāwiliwili Bay, Kukuiʻula and Poʻipū beaches, and the Salt Pond area at Port Allen. It recognized the need for comprehensive zoning and a subdivision regulation program to accomplish long-term goals. Like all the plans that followed, it recommended that Līhuʻe remain the island's dominant transportation, retail, wholesale, and professional services center. "Whatever the cause for diminishing land availability," the plan stressed, "some means for accommodating Lihue's growth must be found." Its suggestion for possible development along the slopes of Kilohana crater has been copied by numerous government and privately generated plans for half a century.

In 1968 the Kauaʻi County Charter was adopted into law. Not only did the charter

Travelers had been arriving in Hawai‘i from time immemorial, but the tourist industry became an economic priority—and a viable possibility—after statehood. One of the early image leaders of the industry was the Coco Palms at Wailua. It was bought by Lyle Guslander in 1953 and transformed by marketing genius Grace Guslander into a travel trade icon. Ray Jerome Baker, Kaua‘i Historical Society

change the governing structure by replacing the Board of Supervisors with a mayor and County Council, it required the preparation of "A General Plan for the Island of Kauai." That guiding document, completed in 1970 and adopted by the County Council in 1971, is considered the island's first comprehensive plan. It was designed by Eckbo, Dean, Austin and Williams in a joint venture with Muroda, Tanaka and Itagaki, Inc. Like the 1961 document, this plan discussed the need for subdivision requirements and a comprehensive zoning ordinance (the first CZO was already in preparation; it was adopted in 1972). It placed new emphasis on the importance of conservation and resource management, with open space zones "to preserve and insure visual access to unique historic and scenic resources." Included in that concept was the need to protect the essence of Kaua‘i as the Garden Island and to insist that growth be compatible with the island's unique landscape and environmental character. An exuberant population boom on O‘ahu in the 1960s led the consultants to predict a dizzying rate of growth for Kaua‘i, to 90,000 residents and 2,000,000 annual visitors by 1990. (In 2012, Kaua‘i had an estimated residential population of 68,400 and 1,085,000 visitors.) Limiting factors for the island's prosperous

1970 Kauai General Plan cover. AECOM

economic future that they identified were "disproportionate ownership of land . . . limited skills and availability of labor [and] insufficient local capital."[6]

For modern readers of the consultants' 1970 document, its most remarkable element is a cultural dynamic on Kaua'i that stunned the California planning consultants and their Honolulu partners. Their report warned that the greatest stumbling block to a bright future was the "agricultural feudalism" from which the island was only beginning to emerge. They described the power hierarchy upon which both government and the general population relied as "a paternalistic plantation fiefdom" whereby decisions were deferred to the few large landowners at the top. "The culturally derived resultant is an unconscious conspiracy between the dominant landowner/employer and the subordinate government which exploits a resigned public," a condition, they complained, that was too often shrugged away as simply "the way things are on Kauai." The consultants' frustration with acceptance of the status quo is apparent from the first page of the report. It exhorts Kauaians: "If you care about KAUAI and YOURSELF and the FUTURE but don't know what to do about it, let your education begin here with this report. READ IT with a dictionary, if necessary, but read it EXAMINE IT, ASK QUESTIONS."

The same consulting firms (with corporate names changed to EDAW Inc. and Muroda and Associates, Inc.) teamed up in the mid-1970s to create a regional study, the "Lihue Development Plan," which considered Niumalu and Nāwiliwili, Kapaia, Hanamā'ulu, and Puhi in addition to Līhu'e Town itself. In recognition of the district's increasing urbanization, the plan sought to identify the physical, social, and economic changes that were occurring and to set goals by which the district could thrive as it grew. An emphasis was placed on extensive public involvement in the planning process. The group chosen to serve on the Citizens Advisory Committee met weekly for over three months, and a questionnaire was published in the newspaper inviting others to share their views. At the time Kaua'i was experiencing the lowest residential vacancy and turnover rates in Hawai'i, and the plan recommended construction of multifamily units as a priority to ease the housing shortage. Inadequate water and sewerage remained problems to be solved, and apprehension about incipient social breakdown, with rising juvenile delinquency and drug use, were concerns newly voiced. Remarking that Līhu'e Town "lacks cohesiveness," the plan prescribed the establishment of a Special Planning Area for the core to help revitalize and beautify the area. It also recommended the creation of an appointed Lihue Improvement Committee to review development proposals and provide "continuity of public participation." Both suggestions languished.[7]

The plan's authors were optimistic that Amfac's recent sale of a significant percentage of parcels in central Līhu'e to Harry Weinberg's HRT, Ltd., would stimulate strong commercial activity. Alluding to the sale they wrote: "There are forces presently operating in this area, which are powerful and positive. They are Lihue's foremost opportunities for future improvement." The planners elucidated that on the Kūhiō Highway strip between Rice Street and Ahukini Road "the major landowner has expressed a desire to re-develop and apparently has the means to do so. The County should encourage this process and

Kūhiō Highway businesses, 1980, before the far building was prettified with the installation of hemispheric "ears" at the roof line and the middle building was embellished with a Victorian-style cornice and window-like, applied, decorative frames to its façade. T. K. Kunichika, Kaua'i Historical Society

work with him to set the pattern for commercial development in the whole district." Their assessment of the Rice Street commercial area was less positive. In their opinion it needed a heavy-handed range of treatments, from revitalization to complete redevelopment.

The next plan, the "1982 Kauai General Plan Update," was adopted in 1984. Prepared by Planners Collaborative, whose president Richard Senelly had been principal and officer in charge at EDAW, it generally validated the conclusions of the 1971 plan. Primarily programmatic rather than conceptual, it was more of an operational manual than a visionary route to the future. It assigned or clarified areas of responsibility for various administrative departments and defined zoning designations. The consultants lauded the county for good management of island growth in the 1970s. The greatest shortcoming during that period, they advised, was not "just the lack of adequate roads, sewerage, and so on"; the more important problem was "a lack of public and public official interest resulting in a lack of support, including funding." Everybody wanted good government services, the report complained, but no one wanted to pay more taxes to get them.[8]

The most recent islandwide plan, the 2000 "Kaua'i General Plan," broke new ground. Public participation had become a standard component in general and regional plans, but it played a particularly vigorous role in this process. The Citizens Advisory Committee met more than thirty times, and a series of robust public meetings also took place in each of the five planning regions around the island. The familiar issues—housing, transportation, infrastructure, tourism, agricultural lands, and commercial development—were all addressed. Harkening back to earlier plans' desire to secure open space zones that could protect historic and scenic sites, the document confirmed residents' continuing commitment to carefully preserve the island's uniquely individualized towns, buffered and defined by corridors of open space. It also reiterated the importance of maintaining the island's rural lifestyle. These and other priorities were encapsulated in the community-generated "Vision for Kaua'i 2020." The issues, policies, and possibilities that followed were based on that vision. Among them, renewal of the Līhu'e core remained a focus, one that required "additional government investment and a careful plan to attract visitors and other sources of business—especially in light of the dispersal of new government offices to the Airport area."[9]

When the 2000 general, islandwide plan was adopted, the 1977 Līhu'e regional plan was already twenty-three years old. With the shift of concentrated shopping out of town to the mall at Puhi and the demise of Lihue Plantation, the regional plan needed serious revision. For whatever reasons, however, the planning department opted not to conduct a regional update in 2004 but to create a "Līhu'e Town Core Urban Design Plan" instead. It was intended to serve as a revitalization mechanism for central Līhu'e. The consultants, PBR Hawaii, utilized a planning concept known as form-based code rather than what is sometimes termed conventional "Euclidean" zoning, which segregates land use into separate areas (such as residential, commercial, industrial) and auto-driven suburbs. The philosophy behind form-based code is reminiscent of an aspect of the City Beautiful movement of a century previous in that it focuses on physical form as a motivational impetus. Its goal is to enhance connections of people to places by regulating the visual aspects of the town's built environment—its historic urban forms and their relationship to the common space—to reverse the loss of community character, reestablish the spirit of place, and make the town once again an appealing, compact location in which to live, work, walk, and shop. The Līhu'e plan analyzed four neighborhoods in the town core: Kūhiō Highway, 'Akahi/'Elua/'Umi streets, the civic center, and Rice Street. Each was designated a Special Planning Area with regulations specific to their individual characters. The study was adopted into law by the Kaua'i County Council in 2010.[10]

INTO THE FUTURE

As this volume goes to press, county planners, consultants, and community participants have at last begun the process of updating the 1977 Līhu'e regional development plan, now thirty-six years old. The district this study encompasses is defined by the Hawai'i Revised Statutes: "from and including Kipu to the northerly bank of the north fork and the main Wailua river." Currently, agricultural and conservation lands still dominate the region *mauka* of the belt highway, though genetically modified seed corn and other agricultural and ranching pursuits have replaced some of the former fields of sugarcane. But change is ongoing.

Many sidewalks in town fall short of being pedestrian friendly.

The Department of Hawaiian Home Lands owns 526 acres immediately south of the Wailua River, including part of the ancient *ahupua'a* of Wailua.[11] About 90 percent of that property lies between Kālepa Ridge and Kūhiō Highway. DHHL has created a long-term plan for several hundred residences and agricultural homesteads for its beneficiaries there. It proposes to use the balance, situated *makai* of Kūhiō Highway—between the highway, Lydgate Park, and the county golf course—for commercial development.

Farther south, Hanamā'ulu Town is gradually stretching toward the

Kauai Beach Resort, the public golf course, and the DHHL lands. Hanamā'ulu is separated from Līhu'e by the Kapaia Valley and still distinct from its larger neighbor. It remains a somewhat cohesive community, although that unity has diminshed as former plantation workers have aged and been replaced by others lacking a shared town history. The four-hundred-forty-unit development planned for the triangle between Kūhiō Highway, King Kaumualii Elementary School, and Kapule Highway may significantly impact the town's demographics. Another large parcel, across from the intersection of Kūhiō and Kapule highways, is zoned as agricultural and conservation, but conversations have been exploring more concentrated use of at least part of that property. On the other side of Līhu'e, suburban growth is erasing the division between it and Puhi, especially as Grove Farm's subdivisions spread west and Kaua'i Community College grows. Both those developments change the population mix in Puhi from the previously dominant plantation worker neighborhoods.

A built environment that extends from the western side of Puhi to the spreading northern end of Hanamā'ulu and patchily up to the Wailua River sounds like a classic case of sprawl, a pattern antithetical to the vision that participants of the 2000 general plan worked to prescribe for the Kaua'i of 2020. Perhaps it is, especially considering that on the other side of Wailua River the Līhu'e District meets the Kawaihao District, which already sprawls from the river to the northern end of Kapa'a. That presents a challenge for contemporary urban planners who urge "smart growth," a concept embracing compact urban environments that accommodate higher population density to achieve an efficiency of scale for infrastructure as well as accessibility to goods and services. Smart growth also encourages a variety of transportation alternatives to the automobile-oriented patterns so commonly designed. At its heart smart growth champions sustainability, which places a priority on the retention of valuable agricultural lands and other natural resources as a counterpart to urban living. All of these concepts align with the priorities expressed in the 2000 general plan. They also sound a lot like the Līhu'e of yesteryear.

The challenge is to make those concepts work in today's Līh'ue District. As the island's air and water transportation gateway, seat of government, home of higher education, and concentrated commercial center, the region is certain to see a population increase; projections expect faster growth in this district than elsewhere on the island. The impact on the area and the need to accommodate change are clear. Yet the familiar problems of inadequate housing and an overabundance of traffic woes continue, and they will undoubtedly be addressed in the final plan.

A 17-mile coastal path, Ke Ala Hele Makalae, is planned from Nāwiliwili to Keālia. In the Līhu‘e District, the section around Lydgate Park has been completed. A considerable portion of the path in the Kawaihau District is already in use. From left: Tommy Noyes, Amalya, Joann, Isaiah, and Clarence Sales, 2011. David Allio, Kauai Path, Inc.

How do the district developments impact the Līhu‘e town core? The creation of Kukui Grove, with its large mall, satellite business park on one side and big box outlets on the other, drained much of the commercial vitality from Līhu‘e's traditional heart. Former Lihue Plantation land on the airport side of town, now part of Grove Farm Company, is earmarked for mixed-use development complete with its own town center, which suggests a further drain without the formulation of clear-cut, two-way connectivity between it and the historic town core. County and state governments have already moved some of their activity to that area, and the federal post office also wants to relocate from Rice Street to its sorting center adjacent to the airport. Nevertheless, government offices still dominate central Līhu‘e, and the people who fill them generate concentrated weekday activity. Most

The historical gateway to Līhu'e remains a contemporary route as well.

of those employees drive to work in the morning and empty out the area as they leave by car at *pau hana*. Many get in their autos at lunchtime too. Even in-town residents must drive elsewhere for groceries, whatever time they choose to shop, because, unlike the past, today's town lacks a diversity of commercial options.

The Līhu'e town core houses many places of honor: several historic landmarks, the oldest continuously used county building in Hawai'i, and the state's first branch bank as well as a school, library, and many other amenities that enhance everyday life. But to fulfill its role as the healthy, pulsing heart of Kaua'i, central Līhu'e cannot be simply a functional place, it must perform as a dynamically functioning one. For central Līhu'e to become again a stimulating urban arena, planners are seeking to create new desirability by finding ways to increase the density not simply of bodies but also of destinations within the town core. Looking to the essence of Lihu'e's vibrant past can help sketch a map to its lively future.

ACKNOWLEDGMENTS

Several people have made this study a better document than I could possibly have constructed on my own, though their assistance in no way lifts the burden of inevitable errors from my shoulders. Historians Andy Bushnell and Barnes Riznik read through drafts and more drafts, patiently returning thoughtful comments about each; I relied heavily on their insights. Pila Kikuchi and David P. Scott offered considerable expertise as well. After I thought the manuscript complete, a chance meeting with historian David Forbes sent me right back into research rapture among uncatalogued documents at the Hawai'i State Archives.

Claire Lundgren's many kindnesses and her knowledge of Līhu'e life and times opened doors that I could not otherwise have walked through. Nonna Cheatham, Rodney Chiogioji, Elodie Moniz, Wilbert Pereira, Marsha Shimokawa, and Jimmy Sone lent early, invaluable assistance with images to absorb and people to interview. Morton Yamasaki provided helpful details about his family and other business people in Līhu'e, as did John Lydgate for his. Lindsay Kamm provided detailed information about church history. Myles Hironaka, Shan Jimenez, and Ricky Tsuchiya made important Planning Department files accessible. Peter Nakamura, who was then county clerk, did the same with Board of Supervisors' records. David Alexander, Hobey Beck, William Curammeng, Casey Reimer, and John Wehrheim offered photos that added depth to the history.

Indispensable to the story of Līhu'e were the recollections of Nora Curammeng Albayalde, Mike Ashman, Jose Bulatao, Capt. Mitham Clement, Lois Coleman, Sam and Mary Cooke, Fred DeBusca, Spalding and Ellen Garlinghouse, Nellie Hiyane, Setsuko Isoda,

Dimples Kano, Sally Jo Manea, Kiyoto Okimoto, Suzy Frazer Patterson, Margaret Rinker, Rev. Jan Rudinoff, Anna Sloggett, Millie Wellington, Edie Wilcox, Buichi Yamasaki, Owen Yoneji, and Jiro Yukimura. Each and every one opened my eyes to new vistas when they walked me down the memory lanes of their past. Some were also able to share photos and others to identify people in unlabeled images. Grove Farm Homestead Museum director Robert Schleck provided both a wealth of historical background and also some delicious gossip about personalities; the latter had no place in this book but certainly made our discussions entertaining. Marion Penhallow not only brought past times to life, she generously donated some cherished objects as well. I am grateful to you all.

People who care for collections must contain some unique DNA that makes them such a special breed. Chris Fayé, curator at Kaua'i Museum, went well beyond the call of duty with her familiarity of the organization's collections and also with knowledge gleaned from her own sleuthing and her family's history here. Marylou Bradley at the Kaua'i Historical Society was always forthcoming with knowledge about the organization's archives, and Keith Holdeman and Larraine Moriguchi reproduced requested society images with grace and efficiency. Līhu'e librarian Carolyn Larsen, as well as Wayne and the two Lisas, provided such committed attentions to my questions that it occasionally felt like I had my own research assistants in an extensive private collection; Patrick McNally was truly the "facilitator of access to the universe of dynamite stuff" at the Hawai'i State Library's Hawai'i and Pacific section; Melissa, Darlene, and Vicky at the Hawai'i State Archives delivered documents and information with a smile; Jodie and Dore at the Hawaiian Sugar Planters' Association went out of their way to provide uncatalogued materials typically unavailable to researchers. National Tropical Botanical Garden's brilliant librarian, Rick Hanna, provided information about both rare books and editors of rare quality; Moises Madayag, the Grove Farm Homestead Museum curator, was always helpful; John Barker at Hawaiian Mission Houses found ways to make my request a reality; and ILWU librarian Rae Shiraki gifted me not only with images but also with an insightful conversation about publishing experiences.

Nancy Budd, Kiersten Faulkner, Randy Francisco, Sue Kanoho, Beth Tokioka, Curtis Tom, Sonia Topenio, and Linda Warriner helped buoy me along at various stages of this project, though they were probably unaware of the value of their support. Neil Clendennin, Barbara Curl, Palmer Hafdahl, and Laurie Ho—collectively our Līhu'e Hui—kept the faith throughout and by doing so gained the right to tease me about my slow progress in uncovering the stones of this story. Senator Ron Kouchi is responsible for initially propelling me into the study by remembering testimony I gave about the town core when he was on the Kauaʻi County Council in the 1980s. Once he recommended me to Palmer for a history talk to the Līhuʻe Business Association, the path was paved that led to this place.

Gratitude is a totally inadequate word to express my appreciation for the assistance that Hobey Goodale and his much-loved wife Nancy provided on every level it took to make this book a reality. Without you, Hobey, the task would not have been possible.

Finally, Tommy Noyes, with his patient confidence, continues to make *everything* seem possible.

NOTES

CHAPTER 1

1. William Kikuchi, interview, April 3, 2003.
2. Also written as Kalaialamea.
3. Quoted in Joesting, *Kauai,* 109.
4. William Hooper, July 18, 1838, 72, Letters to Ladd and Company, Honolulu, 1836–1840, Transcribed excerpts, Kaua'i Historical Society archives.
5. Jarves, *Scenes and Scenery,* 146.
6. Hawaiian Mission Children's Society, *Missionary Album,* 134–135.
7. Joesting, *Separate Kingdom,* 113.
8. "Post Office in Paradise," www.hawaiianstamps.com/iskauai2.html.
9. "Post Office in Paradise," www.hawaiianstamps.com/iskauai2.html; *Industrial Conditions in Hawaiian Islands,* 26; "Lihue Plantation Company," *Honolulu Star-Bulletin,* Centenary Number, 1820–1920, April 12, 1920, 127.
10. "For Sale Lihue Town-Site Lots," *Garden Island,* August 20, 1912, 3.
11. Simpich, *Dynasty,* 80.
12. Dorrance, "U.S. Army on Kaua'i," 158; Krauss and Alexander, *Grove Farm Plantation,* 318–322.

CHAPTER 2

1. Damon, *Koamalu,* 410–413.
2. Dunn, "William Little Lee," 83.
3. Marshall, "Report on Sugar."
4. Hunnewell, "Early History," 68–70.
5. A. L. Bancroft and Co., *Biography of Henry Augustus Peirce,* 15.
6. Marshall, "Letter to Rev. S. E. Bishop," 98. For Catherine Lee on her husband, see Dunn, "William Little Lee," 60–87.
7. Marshall, "Letter to Rev. S. E. Bishop," 98.
8. Maclennan, "Hawai'i Turns to Sugar," 99; see also Mollett, "Capital in Hawaiian Sugar," 13.
9. Riznik, *Waioli Mission House,* 51–58.
10. Bartlett, *Historical Sketch,* 12.

11. Dunn, "William Little Lee," 83.
12. Rice, "History of Lihue," 47.
13. James Marshall, letter to his mother, December 18, 1853, Hawai'i State Archives.
14. Damon, *Koamalu*, 769–773.
15. Barnes Riznik, "Historical Chronology," in "Grove Farm Homestead Handbook," unpublished manual for tour guides, ca. 1980, 3, Grove Farm Homestead Museum archives; see also "Summary of Collections 2004," Hawaiian Sugar Planters' Association archives; Damon, *Koamalu,* 772–773.
16. "Thousands of Trees Arrive," *Garden Island,* September 26, 1911, 1.
17. Damon, *Koamalu*, 744; see also Krauss and Alexander, *Grove Farm Plantation,* 179–184.
18. *Evening Bulletin Industrial Edition,* March 25, 1909, 1; see also Beechart, *Working,* 78.
19. Schmitt, *Demographic Statistics,* Table 1.12; Schmitt, *Historical Statistics,* 12–13.
20. Lal, Munro, and Beechert, *Plantation Workers,* 48. Oracle Education Foundation, "Timeline," http://library.thinkquest.org/J003466/bibliography/plantation_timeline.htm; Blount, "Report of U.S. Special Commissioner," 143; *Industrial Conditions,* 26.
21. Beechert, *Working,* 327.
22. Kuykendall, *Hawaiian Kingdom,* 1:144-145; see also "Lihue Plantation Is Second One to Be Started on Kauai," *Garden Island,* July 27, 1935, 15.
23. "Lihue's New Electric Power System," *Garden Island,* August 26, 1913, 1.
24. Lydgate, William A., "A Life, Volume One: Hawaii." unpublished manuscript, New York, 1985, 11.
25. Greaney, "Hawaii's Big Six," 17.
26. Hibbard and Wichman, "Historic American Engineering," 8.
27. S. M. Lowrey, Treasurer, American Factors, Limited to the Lihue Plantation Co., Ltd., September 27, 1934, Hawaiian Sugar Planters' Association archives.
28. Porteus, *And Blow Not the Trumpet,* 200; Allen, *Hawaii's War Years,* 78–85; Klass, *World War II on Kauai,* 31.
29. Wedemeyer, *Story of the Mokihana Club,* 60.
30. Klass, *World War II on Kauai,* 28–29, 50.
31. Coffman, *Island Edge of America,* 66.
32. Interviews with Līhu'e residents, 2009–2012.
33. Mollett, "Capital in Hawaiian Sugar," 32.
34. Greaney, "Hawaii's Big Six," 17–18.
35. Cooper and Daws, *Land and Power,* 213.
36. "Industry Fighting Battle for Survival," *Lihue Plantation News,* July 1961, 1.
37. James Marshall, letter to his mother, December 18, 1853, Hawai'i State Archives.
38. Interview with Grove Farm Homestead Museum director emeritus, Barnes Riznik, May 2, 2013.
39. Krauss and Alexander, *Grove Farm Plantation,* 360–378; Kauai Trains, "Hawaiian Train Timeline," www.kauaitrains.com; see also "Good Start for Grove Farm," *Garden Island,* January 18, 1958, 8; Lihue Plantation Company, Annual Report, 1956, 3.
40. Kuykendall, *Hawaiian Kingdom,* 2:144.
41. Damon, *Koamalu,* 822.
42. Damon, *Koamalu,* 847.
43. "Presenting . . . the Railroad Department," *Lihue Plantation News,* October 1952, 3; "Lihue to Truck Cane," *Lihue Plantation News,* June 1956, 1; Lihue Plantation Company, Annual Report, 1959, 6.
44. "Kapaa Debates New Cane Truck Routes; Monday Meet Shown Four Plans," *Garden Island,*

January 15, 1958, 1; "Inspecting Coral Dredge Site at Kapaa . . ." and "Trucking Phase II," *Lihue Plantation News,* June 1959, 1.

45. Lihue Plantation Company visitors' brochure, ca. 1965, Amfac, Līhu'e office, archives; see also Hibbard and Wichman, "Historic American Engineering," 13–14.
46. Suzy Frazer Patterson, interview, October 27, 2012; "Swope Summer School All Pau," *Garden Island,* August 5, 1964, sec. 1, 8.
47. Erika Engle, "Henry A. Walker, One of the Last of the 'Big Five,'" *Pacific Business News,* April 23, 2000; Amfac/JMB Hawaii L.L.C., www.fundinguniverse.com/company-histories /amfac-jmb-hawaii-l-l-c-history.
48. Cooper and Daws, *Land and Power,* 213.
49. Simpich, *Dynasty in the Pacific,* 13.
50. Lehman Brothers Collection, "Amfac, Inc.," www.library.hbs.edu/hc/lehman/chrono.html ?company=amfac_inc; Cooper and Daws, *Land and Power,* 213; Lawrence M. Fisher, "JMB to Pay $920 Million for Amfac," *New York Times,* July 27, 1988.
51. Tim Ruel, "Amfac to Quit Farming on Kauai," *Honolulu Star-Bulletin,* September 15, 2000, 1; Dan Nakaso, "Amfac Files Bankruptcy in Twilight of 'Big Five,'" *Honolulu Advertiser,* February 28, 2002, 1.
52. Lyle Tabata, personal correspondence, October 11, 2012.
53. Anthony Sommer, "Final Harvest for Sugar Fields," *Honolulu Star-Bulletin,* November 16, 2000, 1.
54. "The History of Kauai Electric," www.kauaielectric.com/information/info%20Paper -KE%20History.htmwww.kauaielectric.com/Information/Info%20Paper-KE%20History.htm.
55. "Power!" *Lihue Plantation News,* November 1957, 1.
56. "A Way Out for Electricity Costs?" *Hawaii Business,* August 1975, 61.
57. Tabata correspondence, 2012.
58. "First Farmers Set to Increase Capacity of Its Bagasse Plant," *Manila Times,* November 28, 2007, B2.
59. "Woodward Controls Work on GE Double Extraction Turbine with Enhanced Power Management Facility," *Application Bulletin: First Farmer Holding Corporation,* PM Control Systems (www.pmcontrol.com/wp-content/uploads/2012/06/FFHC-Double -Extraction-Control-Retrofit-Case-Study.pdf).
60. Atom's Picture Blog, "The Lihue Sugar Mill," http://adamspictureblog.blogspot .com/2011/01/lihue-sugar-mill.html.
61. Andy Gross, "Lihu'e and Kekaha Mills Sold," *Garden Island,* April 14, 2005, 1.
62. Kaua'i County Planning Department, "Lihue Mill Executive Summary," 2, 5.
63. "Asbestos and Scrap Removal at Old Mills, *Garden Island,* January 14, 2011, A4.
64. Lynn McCrory, personal communication, February 12, 2013.

CHAPTER 3

1. "Lihue to Have Most Modern Store Building in the Territory outside of Honolulu," *Garden Island,* March 18, 1913, 1; "A New Home for Big Store, *Garden Island*, October 15, 1912, 1.
2. "Lihue Store," *Honolulu Star-Bulletin,* April 12, 1920, 134.
3. "Irvine Watson Brings King Tut," *Garden Island*, May 15, 1923, 8; "News Flash!" *Garden Island,* March 22, 1938, 8.
4. "Are You One," *Garden Island,* May 7, 1912, 4.

5. Edith King Wilcox, interview, May 20, 2004; Holbrook and Nancy Goodale, Margie Rinker, Lois Coleman, and Spalding and Ellen Garlinghouse, interview, March 11, 2004; Mike Ashman, personal communication, March 4, 2006.
6. "The Tip Top Building," *Garden Island*, November 14, 1916, 1.
7. "Plantation Takes Over Theatres," *Garden Island,* December 28, 1920, 1; "Lihue Landmark Makes Way for Shopping Center . . . ," *Lihue Plantation News,* May 1965, 1.
8. Lihue Plantation Company, Annual Report, 1952 (unpaginated) and Annual Report, 1959, 13.
9. "Lihue Shopping Center Plan Unveiled." *Lihue Plantation News,* August 1962, 2.
10. "John Graham Jr.," Washington State Department of Archaeology and Historic Preservation, www.dahp.wa.gov/learn-and-research/architect-biographies/john-graham-jr.
11. A TV tower in Dortmund, Germany, showcased a revolving restaurant in 1959.
12. "Coral Stone Veneer for Shopping Center . . . ," *Lihue Plantation News,* March 1964, 1.
13. "Business Zones Asked for Two Firms in Lihue Residential District," *Garden Island,* July 29, 1964, 2.
14. Acheson, *Congressional Party,* 8.
15. "Kauai Telephonic Co.," *Garden Island,* December 22, 1914, 11; Kauai County Board of Supervisors Minutes Book, March 4, 1914.
16. Bendix, *Serving Hawaii,* 9.
17. "Here Is a Good Law," *Garden Island,* April 19, 1921, 8.
18. "Proposed New Home of the Kauai Telephonic Company," *Garden Island,* February 21, 1922, 1.
19. "Proposed New Home of the Kauai Telephonic Company," *Garden Island,* February 21, 1922, 1.
20. "Kauai Telephone Company, Oldest in the Islands, to Be Dissolved," *Garden Island,* March 25, 1929, 1.
21. "Hawaiian Telcom Files for Bankruptcy Protection," *New York Times.* December 1, 2008; "With Bankruptcy Over, Telcom Plans Net TV," *Honolulu Star-Advertiser,* October 29, 2010, B4; "Hawaiian Telcom Closes Deal to Buy Wavecom Solutions," *Honolulu Star-Advertiser,* December 31, 2012.
22. James Sone, Hawaiian Telcom engineer, personal communication, February 25, 2013.
23. Quoted in Damon, *Koamalu,* 548.
24. Hörmann, *Germans in Hawaii,* 57.
25. Greaney, "Hawaii's Big Six," 15.
26. Simpich, *Dynasty,* 48.
27. Simpich, *Dynasty,* 44.
28. Schweizer, *Hawaiʻi and the German Speaking Peoples,* 118.
29. Simpich, *Dynasty,* 52; Greaney, "Hawaii's Big Six," 15.
30. Simpich, *Dynasty,* 51.
31. Damon, *Koamalu,* 883.
32. Damon, *Koamalu,* 887.
33. Unsigned, undated description of structures, Kauaʻi Historical Society archives.
34. Simpich, *Dynasty,* 62; Hörmann, *Germans in Hawaii,* 9, 44.
35. "Lihue Plantation Company," Centenary Number, 1820–1920, *Honolulu Star-Bulletin,* April 12, 1920, 127.
36. Memo to Clint Childs from Henry Wedemeyer, September 16, 1965, Kauaʻi Historical Society archives.

37. "Lihue Has Fountain," *Garden Island,* May 9, 1911, 5.
38. "Bubble Bath for Larry," *Honolulu Star-Bulletin,* September 7, 1951, 2.
39. John Frederick Janssen Jr., interview by Ken Pratt, Bank of Hawaii Oral History Committee, 1986, Bank of Hawaii archives. Jannsen served as assistance manager of the Kaua'i branch before World War II. He worked with Frank Crawford and remembered "reading some correspondence to Mr. Cooke and to other people in the bank about his [Crawford's] desire to open a branch there. They approved and he opened the first branch of the Bank of Hawaii in 1903."
40. Quoted in Damon, *Koamalu,* 915.
41. "Lihue Bank Puts in Complete Radio Set," *Garden Island,* February 6, 1923, 1.
42. "Steers Pay Call on Lihue Bankers," *Garden Island,* July 24, 1924, 1.
43. "Work Begins on Remodeling Lihue Bank, *Garden Island,* March 1, 1938, 1.
44. Janssen interview, 1986.
45. *Golden Years—Hawaii,* 182.
46. "The New Lihue Post Office," *Garden Island,* May 9, 1939, 8.
47. Kuykendall, *Hawaiian Kingdom,* 3:98.
48. "Proposals for Lihue Post Office Wanted," *Garden Island,* May 15, 1923, 8.
49. *Garden Island,* May 9, 1939.
50. Dora Isenberg, as quoted in Kolva, "Lihue Post Office," 10.
51. Wedemeyer, *Story of the Mokihana Club,* 117.
52. "The Lihue Fair, a Great Success," *Garden Island,* June 24, 1905, 1.
53. "Big Moving Job Precedes Lihue Face Lifting Plans," *Garden Island,* July 11, 1962, 8. These were not the only houses moved during the central Lihue "face lifting." The article notes that three houses on Kūhiō Highway were moved to the Hanama'ulu beach road and gave a nod to the County Department of Public Works, which pioneered the highway route when it "moved several school buildings from Lihue to Kapaa."
54. "New Office under Construction . . . ," *Lihue Plantation News,* May 1964, 1.
55. "Things on Kauai—Seen, Heard and Experienced," *The Friend,* September 8, 1860, 1.
56. Swann, "Universe of Dynamite Stuff," 64.
57. "Hart Wood, Architect of Kauai Public Library," *Garden Island,* June 20, 1922, 1; "Bids Are Opened for New Library Building at Lihue," *Garden Island,* November 21, 1922, 1.
58. Correspondence with Chris Fayé, January 29, 2013, about letters in library files, Kaua'i Museum archives.
59. Hart D. Wood, letter to Robert A. Gahran, director, Kauai Museum, July 26, 1976, Kaua'i Historical Society archives; Robert Fox, "Architectural Sketch of Kauai Historical Sites," undated, Kaua'i Historical Society archives.
60. Museum Committee of the Kauai Public Library Association Ltd., "The Kauai Museum Story," fundraising flyer, ca. 1960, Kaua'i Historical Society archives.
61. Ibid.; Letter from Thelma Hadley to Sophie Cluff, December 18, 1986, Kaua'i Historical Society archives.
62. Mary Cooke, "The Kauai Museum Story," *Honolulu Advertiser,* December 11, 1960, D1.
63. Museum Committee of the Kauai Public Library Association Ltd., "The Kauai Museum Story," fundraising flyer, ca. 1960, Kaua'i Historical Society archives.
64. Ibid.
65. "Kauai Museum & Creative Arts Center," fundraising brochure, ca. 1970, Kaua'i Museum.
66. "County Fathers Provide a Home," *Garden Island,* April 9, 1912, 1.

67. "Wm. H. Rice Is Sheriff of the County of Kauai Thirty Years Yesterday," *Garden Island,* July 2, 1935, 8; see also, "Our Business Men," *Garden Island,* August 7, 1911, 1.
68. "Progress on the County Building," *Garden Island,* January 20, 1914, 1.
69. "County Building to Be Accepted," *Garden Island,* April 28, 1914, 1.
70. Transcribed copy of Governor L. E. Pinkham message of congratulations at opening of Kaua'i County Building, Kaua'i Historical Society archives.
71. Peter Wagner, "Suspect Is Sought in Kauai Bombing," *Honolulu Star-Bulletin,* September 8, 1982, A3.
72. "Social Security Kauai Office in Lihue Now Open," *Lihue Plantation News,* July 1949, 1.
73. "County Bldg. to Have New Sloping Roof," *Garden Island,* November 9, 1937, 1.
74. Hughes, *Women and Children First,* 108.
75. Correspondence, C. E. S. Burns to American Factors, Limited, June 18, 1937, Hawaiian Sugar Planters' Association archives.
76. Zalburg, *Spark,* 7, 16.
77. "Construction of New Lihue Courthouse to Be Delayed by Strike," *Garden Island,* December 1, 1936, 1.
78. Letter from Paul Townsley, president of the Kauai Chamber of Commerce, to Chamber members, September 13, 1937, Hawaiian Sugar Planters' Association archives.
79. Beechert, *Working,* 278.
80. "Completion Date for New Lihue Courthouse Set for August or September," *Garden Island,* March 23, 1937, 4.
81. "New Lihue Court House Ready," *Garden Island,* March 1, 1938, 1.
82. "Old Courthouse Slated for Renovation," *Garden Island,* August 9, 2011, 1.
83. *Civil Code of the Hawaiian Islands,* 59.
84. *Laws of His Majesty Kalakaua I,* 101 and 16.
85. "Filipino Shot by Police in a Grambling Raid, *Garden Island,* April, 1923, 1; "Keepers of Peace," *Ke Aka o Kauai* supplement, March 25, 1977, 8.
86. "In the Lihue District Court," *Garden Island,* July 17, 1923, 1.
87. Mossman, *Police Blotter,* 122; Fred DeBusca, Wilcox Hospital, interview, October 9, 2012; Cooper, *Land and Power,* 247.
88. Stanley Doi, personal communication, September 6, 2006.
89. "Health Status—Life Expectancy," Health Trends in Hawai'i, www.healthtrends.org /status_life_expect.aspx. The discovery of penicillin and development of other antibiotics would bring another surge in life expectancy during the second half of the twentieth century.
90. Schmitt, *Demographic Statistics,* 42 and 70.
91. James Marshall, letter to his father, October 23, 1853, Hawai'i State Archives.
92. Lee, "Public Health Contrasts," *Public Health Reports,* 403–404.
93. Melody Lassalle, "Leprosy and the Formation of the Molokai Colony," Island Routes, www.yourislandroutes.com/articles/leprosy.shtml; Riznik, *Mabel Wilcox,* 52. See Riznik's biography of Mabel Wilcox for an in-depth account of this extraordinary woman's life and public health efforts on Kaua'i.
94. Griffin, *Wilcox Memorial Hospital,* 18.
95. Riznik, *Mabel Wilcox,* 43.
96. Wedemeyer, *Story of the Mokihana Club,* 129.
97. Riznik, *Mabel Wilcox,* 102.

98. Nellie Hiyane, Kapa'a Public Library, interview, February 5, 2008; "14 Dead Listed at Kauai," *Honolulu Star-Bulletin,* April 3, 1946, 1.
99. Sally Jo Manea, Kaua'i Historical Society offices, interview, November 29, 2007.
100. "CDC: Kaua'i Leading Nation in Disease-Testing Integration," *Garden Island,* December 21, 2009, 1.
101. "Currently, there are 30 percent more obese than undernourished people on the planet": Lustig, *Fat Chance,* 256.
102. "Butcher Shop to Office Building," *Garden Island,* May 5, 1914, 1; see also "In Memoriam J. P. Alohikea," *Garden Island,* September 11, 1917, 1.
103. "Butcher Shop to Office Building," *Garden Island,* May 5, 1914, 1.
104. "Quotation Made on P. L. Rice Property," *Garden Island,* August 23, 1938, 1; "Lihue District Court Now in New Location," *Garden Island,* January 16, 1945, 3.
105. "Chamber Committee Disapproves Plans for New Buildings," *Garden Island,* September 15, 1936, 1.
106. "Proposed Lihue Civic Center," *Garden Island,* October 20, 1936, 1.
107. "Site Named for Pagoda, Stone Lamp." *Garden Island,* May 10, 1961, 1; see also "From Kobe," *Garden Island,* May 24, 1961, 1. Identification of donors is inscribed on a plaque in the monument compound.
108. "Dr. Rizal Statue to Be Unveiled June 19," *Garden Island,* May 7, 1979, 3; see also "No Retaliation for Damage to Dr. Rizal Statue: Malapit." *Garden Island,* April 28, 1980, 1; "Relocation Okayed, Statue Moves Out," *Kauai Times,* April 11, 1984; Alfredo Villanueva, personal communication, November 6, 2003.

CHAPTER 4

1. Z. S. Spalding, letter to Elsie H. Wilcox, July 15, 1921, Kaua'i Historical Society archives. Isabella Bird had been impressed by the same trick performed by Hawaiians on Kaua'i. During her visit in the 1870s she wrote: "Both sexes are most expert riders. Among their feats, are picking up small coins from the ground while going at full gallop, or while riding at the same speed wringing off the heads of unfortunate fowls, whose bodies are buried in the earth." Bird, *Hawaiian Archipelago,* 192–193.
2. Siddall, *Men of Hawaii,* 1:225.
3. "W. H. Rice," *Pacific Coast Commercial Record,* May 1892, 10.
4. Siddall, *Men of Hawaii,* 1:223–225.
5. Cook, *Reminiscences,* 23.
6. Fuchs, *Hawaii Pono,* 200.
7. "W. H. Rice," *Pacific Coast Commercial Record,* May 1892, 10.
8. Eyre, "Christmas on Kauai," *Honolulu,* November, 1972, 48, 73.
9. Damon, *Koamalu,* 907.
10. "'Hale Nani' Home of Rice Family Was Famed as Hospitality Center," *Garden Island,* February 28, 1968, H1-1.
11. Cole and Wichman, *Early Kauai Hospitality,* 25. Robert Schmitt *(Firsts and Almost Firsts in Hawai'i)* generously but incorrectly transferred ownership of the Līhu'e home to Josephine Wundenberg King and attributed the ice cream claim to her. King, however, lived in the Hanalei area.
12. Ronald R. Gilliam, "The Women's Air Raid Defense: Protecting the Hawaiian Islands,"

www.historynet.com/the-womens-air-raid-defense-protecting-the-hawaiian-islands.htm. Weider History Group, June 2006 [orig. *Aviation History,* May 2002]; Chenoweth and Napier, *Shuffleboard Pilots,* 36–37.

13. "Hale Nani Tract Modern Lihue Business Section," *Garden Island,* April 19, 1949, 16.
14. Interview between Carolyn Larson and Barbara Robeson, Kauai Historical Society, with Fusayo, Arnold, and Stephen Fujii (T. Fujii's wife and two sons), August 29 and November 15, 1997, Kauaʻi Historical Society archives.
15. Kerner, "Malevolent Ancestor," 210.
16. *Prophet of Tabuse,* 181; Wilson to Ogamisama, as quoted in *Prophet of Tabuse,* 182.
17. Hamrin, "Illness and Salvation," 243.
18. *Akeyuku Kami,* 31.
19. Interview with member of Kauaʻi Tensho-Kotai-Jingu-Kyo, October 10, 2012; "'Dancing Goddess' Is Here," *Garden Island,* July 7, 1965, sec II., 7; see also Nishiyama and Fujii, "Propagation and Spread."
20. Kathryn Tolbert, "Japanese Girl Is Modern Goddess," *Nashua Telegraph,* July 14, 1973, 5.
21. Kerner, "Malevolent Ancestor," 209.
22. Lois Coleman and Margie Rinker, interview, March 11, 2004.
23. "About CPB," www.centralpacificbank.com/About-CPB/Works-For-You/Overview.aspx.
24. "Derby's New Offices," *Garden Island,* May 18, 1915, 1; Correspondence, Dr. F. M. Branch to Mr. F. Weber, October 11, 1916, Hawaiian Sugar Planters' Association archives.
25. Wedemeyer, *Story of the Mokihana Club,* 176.
26. Wedemeyer, *Story of the Mokihana Club,* 195–196.
27. Wedemeyer, *Story of the Mokihana Club,* 196.
28. Sally Netzer Smithers, personal communication, June 15, 2012.
29. Quoted in Wedemeyer, *Story of the Mokihana Club,* 200.
30. "Distribution by Island," Exceptional Trees of Hawaiʻi, www.cieer.org/discoverplants /exceptionaltrees/query/text/distribution.html.
31. "Hale Kauai" advertisement, *Garden Island,* November 12, 1946.
32. Elsie H. Wilcox, letter to Nettie, September 1, 1946, Grove Farm Homestead Museum archives.
33. "Building Ordinance Needed," *Garden Island,* May 29, 1917, 8.
34. "Plantation Men Criticize Proposed Kauai Building Code," *Honolulu Star-Bulletin,* September 22, 1954.
35. "Our History," Hale Kauai, http://halekauai.com/us.
36. "Condition of Kauai Dairies," *Garden Island,* January 9, 1923, 2.
37. Fuchs, *Hawaii Pono,* 200–201; Coffman, *Island Edge,* 10–14.
38. Nora Curammeng Albayalde, interview, July 27, 2007.
39. Hughes, *Women and Children First,* 101, 147.
40. Mrs. John Rapozo, Rice collection, Kauaʻi Historical Society archives.
41. Quoted in Hughes, *Women and Children First,* 59.
42. Edith Rice Plews, letter to Tom Foster, October 4, 1932, Kauaʻi Historical Society archives. Anna Scott Sloggett identified the letter writer and recipient.
43. Wichman journal, November 20, 1932, Kauaʻi Historical Society archives.
44. H. A. Baldwin to C. E. S. Burns, July 5, 1934, Hawaiian Sugar Planters' Association archives.
45. Arthur Smith to C. E. S. Burns, May 7, 1935, Hawaiian Sugar Planters' Association archives.
46. Wenkam, *Kauai and the Park Country,* 74–78.

47. "Threat to Meet," *Garden Island,* June 15, 1937, 6.
48. "1400 Ride Busses on Sunday as Service Starts on Eastside," *Garden Island,* June 29, 1937, 1; E. E. Bodge to C. E. S. Burns, February 11, 1937, and C. E. S. Burns to E. E. Bodge, February 13, 1937, Hawaiian Sugar Planters' Association archives.

49. "Kress Officials Make Another Survey for Local Store Site," *Garden Island,* March 9, 1937, 1.
50. See Thomas, *America's 5 & 10 Cent Stores,* for a full exploration of the Kress impact on Main Street America.
51. Cassie, Norton, "Downtown's Kress Building Was Built to Last," *Berkeley Daily Planet,* August 9, 2005, 1; see also Capitman, Kinerk, and Wilhelm, *Rediscovering Art Deco.*
52. "Opening of Kauai's Kress Store Set for February 25–26," *Garden Island,* February 22, 1938, 1.
53. Kiyoto Okimoto, interview, July 6, 2006.
54. Kawakami, *From Japan to Hawaii,* 33.
55. "New Kawakami Store," *Garden Island,* August 10, 1937, 5; "New Lihue Kawakami Store Opens Door to Public This Morning," *Garden Island,* August 10, 1937, 1.
56. Kawakami, *From Japan to Hawaii,* 40, 49.
57. Kawakami, *From Japan to Hawaii,* iii.
58. Kawakami, *From Japan to Hawaii,* 64.
59. "Times Buys Big Save," *Garden Island,* May 18, 2011, 1.
60. Chenoweth and Napier, *Shuffleboard Pilots,* 40.
61. "Kawamoto Building," Old Koloa Town, Kaua'i Historical Society archives.
62. Kawakami, *From Japan to Hawaii,* 53.
63. Yamafuji, *Follow the Rainbow,* 12.
64. Mike Miyake, "Noboru Miyake," *Garden Island,* February 28, 1971, 5.
65. Mark Matsunaga, "Noboru Miyake," *Honolulu Advertiser,* January 17, 1988.
66. Yamafuji, *Follow the Rainbow,* 30.
67. Nora Currameng Albayalde, interview, July 28, 2007; Roy Miyake, personal communication, July 13, 2007.
68. The following account of the *Filipino News* and associated quotations are based primarily on the interviews with Nora Albayalde, July 27 and 28, 2007.
69. Chapin, *Guide to Newspapers,* 21.
70. *Hawaii Business and Industry* 12, no 4., 1966, 88.
71. Steele, "Tribute to a Master," 27; Sanburn, "Moment in the Sun," 85.
72. "Guadalupe: Kauai's First Lady of Fashion," *Hawaii Business and Industry,* October, 1966, 88.
73. "Community Hails Kauai's New Garment Factory," *Garden Island,* December 4, 1972, sec. B, 1–6.
74. Interview with Millicent Wellington and Jose Bulatao, Kaua'i Historical Society offices, March 22, 2005.
75. This section based primarily on an interview with Owen Yoneji and Setsuko Isoda, Yoneji's Rice Street office, August 20, 2003.
76. EDAW and Muroda, "Lihue Development Plan," 17.
77. Klass, *World War II,* 48.
78. Simpson, *Living Stones,* 25, 179; Hughes, *Women and Children First,* 154.

CHAPTER 5

1. Wedemeyer, *Story of the Mokihana Club,* 3-4.
2. Quoted in Damon, *Koamalu,* 847.
3. Hans Isenberg diary, quoted in Damon, *Koamalu,* 914.
4. Ethel Damon, unpublished notes of interviews with G. N. Wilcox, February 1927, Grove Farm Homestead Museum archives.
5. "Kauai's Automobiles," *Garden Island,* May 23, 1911, 2; editorial, *Garden Island,* January 16, 1912; "Supervisor Buys an Auto," *Garden Island,* April 23, 1912, 1.
6. "Staying with the Horse," *Garden Island,* April 23, 1912, 1.
7. "Supervisors Hold Important Meeting," *Garden Island,* June 11, 1912, 5; Kauaʻi Board of Supervisors minutes book, February 5, 1913.
8. "Registered Automobiles on Kauai," *Garden Island,* January 4, 1916, 4.
9. Lydgate, "Life," 42–46.
10. Hughes, *Women and Children First,* 46.
11. "Road Maintenance on Kauai," *Garden Island,* September 25, 1917, 5.
12. Acheson, *Congressional Party,* 8.
13. "Kauai Automobiles," *Garden Island,* April 2, 1912, 2; "Road Maintenance on Kauai," *Garden Island,* September 25, 1917, 5.
14. *Senate Journal,* 1917, 394.
15. *Senate Journal,* 1917, 394.
16. Wilcox, *Sugar Water,* 70.
17. "Road Maintenance on Kauai," *Garden Island,* September 25, 1917, 5.
18. In 2013 work was begun to rebuild that bridge, adding eight feet to its width and changing the railings and Art Deco profile of the posts on the bridge parapet to a different design with a "historic feel." A second bridge is being constructed *mauka* of the existing structure to carry westbound travelers.
19. Spencer Mason Architects, "Historic Bridge Inventory," 213. Robert Belt teamed up with Walter Collins in 1953 to form Belt Collins, the first broad-range planning, engineering, and environmental consulting firm in the Pacific region.
20. "Waimea Streets Receive Names—Await Public Approval," *Garden Island,* August 9, 1938, 1; "Main Lihue Highways Given Names," *Garden Island,* August 9, 1938, 1.
21. Ashman, *Kauai as It Was,* 8.
22. "Baptiste Favors Widening Rice Street 20 Feet," *Garden Island,* October 2, 1945, 1; "Lihue Owners Protest Rice Street Widening," *Garden Island,* October 9, 1945, 1; "William Hyde Rice Street Setback Line Measure Finally Passes Despite Last-Minute Attempt at Deferment," *Garden Island,* January 22, 1946, 10; "Rice Street Pricing Approved," *Garden Island,* February 28, 1968, 9.
23. "New Hot Mix Plant at Huleia to Give Kauai Better Road Material," *Garden Island,* March 12, 1952, sec. II, 1.
24. "Only Five More Days to Issue 1950 Car Tags," *Garden Island,* February 21, 1950, 7.
25. Kawakami, *From Japan to Hawaii,* 59.
26. Cooper, *Land and Power,* 10.
27. "Rice Street Is Still a Mess," *Kauai Times,* October 5, 1988, 1.
28. "Careless Driving," *Garden Island,* July 31, 1917, 2.
29. Griffiss, *When You Go to Hawaii,* 304.

30. "Board Votes to Reconsider on Dips and Bumps," *Garden Island,* June 26, 1934, 1, 5.
31. "Authority Given Police in Regard to Parking Cars," *Garden Island,* December 17, 1929, 1.

CHAPTER 6

1. "Plans for New Hotels Abound," *Honolulu Business and Industry,* 46.
2. "The Martins of Kauai: Innkeeping's Jacks-of-All-Trades," *Honolulu Business and Industry,* 53–54; "Strong Upsurge in Hotel Construction Seen," *Honolulu Business and Industry,* October 1967, 33.
3. Emma, Letter to "Dear Father," August 31, 1856, Bishop Museum Archives.
4. "Kauai Inn's Famous Hospitality Dates Back to Eighteen Hundreds," *Garden Island,* September 19, 1956, III-2.
5. Staley, *Five Years' Church Work,* 107.
6. Nordhoff, *Northern California,* 66–67.
7. Siddall, *Men of Hawaii,* 2:371.
8. "Lihue Hotel Sale to Inter-Island Revealed Today; Price $125,000," *Garden Island,* January 8, 1946, 1.
9. "$1 Million Kauai Inn Expansion Due," *Honolulu Advertiser,* October 3, 1958, B6.
10. Allen, *Creating Hawai'i Tourism,* 81.
11. Hayworth, Phil, "Walter Dudley Child, Jr. 1931–2004: Kauai Surf's Creator Dies on the Big Island," *Garden Island,* December 23, 2004, 1.
12. Anne E. O'Malley, "The Kauai Inn: Over 100 Years of Aloha Service," *Kauai Business and Real Estate Magazine,* September/October 1991, 44.
13. "$1 Million Kauai Inn Expansion Due," *Honolulu Advertiser*, October 3, 1958, B6.
14. See Mike Ashman's *Kauai: As It Was in the 1940s and '50s* for a charming reminiscence of life on the island during that period and many glimpses of the Kauai Inn.
15. "Kauai Surf Hotel Has Spectacular Opening," *The Double I* 1, no. 1, 1960, 1.
16. Linda Kephart, "Executive Shuffle: Turnover at the Top," *Hawaii Business* 31, no. 2, 1985, 93.
17. "Chris Hemmeter, Creator of Lavish Hawai'i Resorts," *Honolulu Advertiser,* November 28, 2003, 1.
18. Michael Flynn, "Mixed Emotions: Is the Westin Kauai a Beauty or a Beast?" *Hawaii Business,* August, 1988, 32.
19. Hibbard, *Designing Paradise,* 160.
20. "Chris Hemmeter, Creator of Lavish Hawai'i Resorts," *Honolulu Advertiser,* November 28, 2003, 1.
21. "Grand Developer Down but Not Out," *Honolulu Star-Bulletin,* October 9, 1999, A4.
22. Hawaii State Department of Business, Economic Development and Tourism, "Foreign Investment Activities," 164.
23. Blake Jones, "Marriott Acquires Kauai Lagoons Ownership," *Garden Island,* August 28, 2007, 1.
24. "Minutes," Joint Conference of Four ILWU Locals In Hawaii, January 19, 1950, 5, ILWU Local 142 archives; ILWU, "Building of Our Own."
25. Gomes, letter to ILWU, ILWU Local 142 archives; see also Hughes, *Women and Children First,* 147.
26. "Amfac Displays New Homes . . . ," *Lihue Plantation News,* September 1965. The house was built on Saturdays and Sundays

to “feature member contractors’ work.” It sits on a particularly large lot for the neighborhood, 13,359 square feet.

27. Building and Planning Committee, ILWU Local 142, Kauai Division, Minutes, July 21, 1955, 1.
28. “A Memorial to Labor Is Dedicated,” *Lihue Plantation News,* June 1957, 5.
29. “Modernistic ILWU Building Opened as Reminder of Hard Fight That Made It Possible,” *Garden Island,* May 1, 1957, 1, 8.
30. Shapiro, “Arizona Memorial Seen as a Dedication to Peace,”*Honolulu Star-Bulletin,* May 27, 2002, 4.
31. Based on information from Hawai‘i State Foundation on Culture and the Arts, “History,” http://hawaii.gov/sfca/history.html, and communication with Wanda Anae-Onishi, State Foundation on Culture and the Arts collections manager, May 3, 2013.
32. Capt. Mitham Clement, Salvation Army, interview, October 25, 2005.
33. “History,” Salvation Army, Hawaiian and Pacific Islands Division, www.hawaii.salvationarmy.org/hawaii/history.
34. “Concert Opens War Memorial Convention Hall, *Honolulu Star-Bulletin,* December 5, 1964, 1.
35. East-West Center Annual Report, 1961, 7. Architect of record Clifford Young explained in a telephone interview in 2005 that University of Hawai‘i vice president William Walter was in charge of choosing the architect for the East-West Center. He appointed Young on the condition that, since the center would be an international place, its design team should include someone with an internationally recognized name. Young, who had known I. M. Pei as a student at the Massachusetts Institute of Technology, recruited him for the job.
36. Telephone interview with Clifford Young, November 9, 2005.
37. “Plans for Kauai Hall Redrawn,” *Honolulu Star-Bulletin,* February 4, 1963, A-7.
38. “Curtain Going Up,” *Garden Island,* November 28, 1964; Wedemeyer, *Story of the Mokihana Club,* 234.
39. Pablo Michelangelo, “First Juried Art Show Proves Need for More,” *Garden Island,* December 12, 1964, sec. 1, 2.
40. C. J. Fern Jr., “Kauai’s New Auditorium,” *Garden Island,* December 5, 1964, sec. 1, 4.
41. Nucciarone, *Alexander Cartwright,* 76.
42. “Baseball Season Closes,” *Garden Island,* September 12, 1911, 6.
43. “2013 Season Wrap Up,” AJA Baseball, www.ajabaseball.com/2013-season-wrap-up/.
44. “Sunday Baseball,” *Garden Island,* August 29, 1911, 6.
45. Cisco, *Hawai‘i Sports,* 221–222.
46. Morimoto, “Barefoot Leagues,” 7; “Tony Kunimura: An Ode to Charlie Fern from the Barefoot Football Boys,” *Garden Island,* July 6, 1982, 2-C.
47. Goodale, *Hobey,* 77.
48. Catherine Pascual Lo, “Lihue Plantation and Hanama‘ulu,” Hanama‘ula Town Celebration, February/June 2005, http://poipuwebdesigns.tripod.com/id3.html.
49. Vandercook, *King Cane,* 31.
50. Kauai Athletic Union, Board of Governors minutes, February 18 and July 13, 1938, Hawaiian Sugar Planters’ Association archives.
51. “Tennis Court Completed,” *Garden Island,* July 29, 1913, 1.
52. “A Lihue Landmark for Two Generations Will Be No More . . . . Equipment Offered to Kauai County,” *Lihue Plantation News,* March 1962, 1.
53. “LP Plans Ready for Industrial Sites, Houselots,” *Lihue Plantation News,* April 1961, 1;

George K. Houghtailing, letter to Calvin Ching, September 10, 1961, Kaua'i County Planning Department archives.
54. "Our Legacy," Community Planning and Engineering, Inc., www.cpe-hawaii.com.
55. Dale Richeson, "Amfac Lihue Subdivision Plan Stirs Public Furor," *Honolulu Star-Bulletin,* July 21, 1961, 1–3.
56. Dale Richeson, "Amfac Lihue Subdivision Plan Stirs Public Furor," *Honolulu Star-Bulletin,* July 21, 1961, 3.
57. H. W. Hansen, letter to Department of Public Works, County of Kaua'i, December 13, 1963, Kaua'i County Planning Department archives.
58. "First Home Started for Lihue Tract," *Garden Island,* February 12, 1964, sec. 5, 1.
59. *Lihue Plantation News,* June 1950, 1.
60. Lihue Plantation Company, Annual Report, 1964, 14.
61. Lihue Plantation Company, Annual Report, 1965, 10.
62. "Tourism Continues to Pace Progress on Kauai," *Hawaii Business and Industry,* October 1968, 17–18.
63. "Amfac/JMB Hawaii L.L.C. History," Funding Universe, www.fundinguniverse.com /company-histories/amfac-jmb-hawaii-l-l-c-history.
64. Kauai County Planning Department, "Extension Request" memorandum, signed by Tom Shigemoto, Planning Director, January 29, 1990.
65. "3 Bedroom House Is Offered Sugar Workers for $6,000," *Honolulu Star-Bulletin,* July 31, 1953, 2.
66. Fran Dieudonne, "Noted Architect Vierra's Home Added to State Register," *Historic Hawai'i Newsletter* 18, no. 2, 2008, 3; Dieudonne, *Always Remember,* 61–62.
67. "Home Owners to Choose from 17 Different Plans," *Maui News,* July 30, 1949, 1; see also "3 Bedroom House Is Offered Sugar Workers for $6,000," *Honolulu Star-Bulletin,* July 31, 1953, 2.
68. Hurricane 'Iniki in 1992 destroyed homes in both neighborhoods; the replacements do not conform to the styles of their neighbors.
69. Thanks to architect Palmer Hafdahl for this observation about how "made in China" products have changed home building for the past generation.
70. "Declaration of Restrictive Covenants." Molokoa Subdivision Unit III. October 11, 1995, Kaua'i County Planning Department archives.
71. "School History," Elsie H. Wilcox Elementary School, http://wilcox.k12.hi.us/history.html.
72. Wedemeyer, *Story of the Mokihana Club of Kauai,* 34.
73. Fuchs, *Hawaii Pono,* 276.
74. Oren E. Long, Superintendent of Public Instruction, to Bernice E. L. Hundley, Supervising Principal, February 28, 1945, Hawaiian Sugar Planters' Association archives.
75. Corstorphine, *Autobiography,* 84.
76. Joe Arakaki, "Kauai Board in School Site Battle with Sugar Company," *Honolulu Star-Bulletin,* October 6, 1955, 4.
77. "Rice Fires New Volley at Lihue School Change," *Honolulu Star-Bulletin,* October 11, 1955, 13.
78. "Elsie Wilcox School Name Is Legal One, *Garden Island,* April 15, 1959, 1.
79. "Legal or Not, Kunimura Raps Wilcox School Name," *Garden Island,* May 13, 1959, 1.
80. Allen, *Men and Women of Hawaii,* 197.
81. "Ernest Hideo Hara, 'Diplomat Architect,'" *Honolulu Advertiser,* November 29, 2006, B1; "AIA Honors Ernest Hara, FAIA," *Building Industry,* May 2002.

82. "Giving County Job of School Buildings Urged," *Garden Island,* September 23, 1959, 1.
83. Griffin, "Līhuʻe Public Library," 109.
84. Kaizawa, "Let Wright Design Island Capitol, Honolulan Urges," *Honolulu Star-Bulletin,* December 26, 1958, 17; Charles Saiki, telephone interview, October 29, 2002.
85. "Honolulu: 'No Color, No Imagination, and, Bad Design Sense,'" *Honolulu Star-Bulletin,* December 26, 1958, 17.
86. "Honolulu: 'No Color, No Imagination, and, Bad Design Sense,'" *Honolulu Star-Bulletin,* December 26, 1958, 17.
87. Saiki interview, October 23, 2002.
88. Allen Oyakawa, interview, October 23, 2002.
89. "U.S. Aid Brightens Libraries' Future," *Honolulu Advertiser,* March 20, 1965, A8:7.
90. Kuykendall and Day, *Hawaii,* 130–132.
91. Dutton, *Episcopal Church in Hawaii,* 8; Restarick, *Hawaii,* 69; Kuykendall, "Introduction of the Episcopal Church," 136.
92. Damon, *Koamalu,* 635.
93. Quoted in Staley, *Five Years' Church Work,* 90.
94. Kuykendall, *Hawaiian Kingdom* 2:36–38; Herbert G. Gardiner, "Prince Lot Kapuaiwa Kamehameha: The First Full Blooded Hawaiian Freemason." www.phoenixmasonry.org/kamehameha.htm.
95. Ven. Charles Crane, "A Brief History of the Founding of the Church of St. Michael and All Angels, Lihue, Kauai, Hawaii," undated manuscript, 1, St. Michael and All Angels Episcopal Church archives.
96. The Philippine Independent Church was founded by a Catholic priest, Gregorio Aglipay, in 1902 during a rising tide of nationalist sentiment in the Philippines. Its theology was closest to what was considered "high church" Episcopal in the United States. "St. Paul's Church—Honolulu in 53 Years since August 12, 1959," *Ilocos Times,* October 1–7, 2012, 6.
97. Ven. Charles Crane, "A Brief History of the Founding of the Church of St. Michael and All Angels, Lihue, Kauai, Hawaii," undated manuscript, 3, St. Michael and All Angels Episcopal Church archives.
98. Rev. Jan Rudinoff, interview, February 7, 2004; Peter McClaran, "Architectural Gems Dot Kauai," *Kauaʻi Business and Real Estate Report,* June 17, 2002, 20.
99. "State Building," *Garden Island,* March 15, 1971, B1.
100. Kamakau, *Ruling Chiefs,* 95; see also Earle, *How Chiefs Come to Power,* 138–139; Galois and Colnett, *Voyage to the Northwest,* 64.
101. "Wealth of News," *Lihue Plantation News,* March 1956, 4.
102. Klass, *World War II,* 50.
103. "Celebration of Life of Shoso Kagawa, Architect," eulogy read at memorial service, March 18, 2007; Moy, "Range of Modern Architectural Resources."

CHAPTER 7

1. Kame'eleihiwa, *Native Land,* 23.
2. Wilson, *City Beautiful*, 92.
3. Hart Wood, who designed the original Lihue library (now the Kaua'i Museum), and Guy Rothwell, who designed the former police station as well as the 1936 remodel of the Bank of Hawaii, also served as presidents of the Hawai'i AIA.
4. John Carl Warnecke and Associates, "Lihue: Area Studies," Kaua'i County Planning Department archives.
5. Kauai County Planning and Traffic Commission, "General Plans for Five Urban Areas." The 1962 study, "General Plans for Hanalei area of the County of Kauai: Moloaa, Kilauea, Kalihiwai, Hanalei, Haena," was followed a year later by a water, sewerage, and drainage plan for the island.
6. Eckbo, Dean, Austin and Williams, "General Plan for the Island of Kauai."
7. EDAW Inc. and Muroda and Associates, Inc., "Lihue Development Plan."
8. Planners Collaborative, "1982 Kauai General Plan Update."
9. County of Kaua'i Planning Department, "Kaua'i General Plan," November 2000.
10. PBR Hawaii, "Līhu'e Town Core."
11. Group 70 International, "Wailua Regional Plan," 12.

BIBLIOGRAPHY

ARCHIVAL SOURCES

Bernice Pauahi Bishop Museum, Honolulu
Grove Farm Homestead Museum, Līhu'e
Hawai'i State Archives, Honolulu
Hawaiian Sugar Planters' Association, Honolulu
Hawaiian Mission Children's Society, Honolulu
International Longshore and Warehouse Union, Honolulu
Kaua'i Historical Society, Līhu'e
Kaua'i Museum, Līhu'e

PUBLICATIONS

Acheson, Ernest F. *Congressional Party in Hawaii, May, 1907 Souvenir*. Washington, Pa.: Observer Job Rooms, 1907.

Akeyuku Kami No Kuni [The paradise of Tabuse]. Tabuse, Japan: Tensho Kotai Jingukyo Honbu, 1953.

A. L. Bancroft and Co. *Biography of Henry Augustus Peirce*. San Francisco: A. L. Bancroft, 1880.

Alexander, Arthur C. *Koloa Plantation, 1835–1935: A History of the Oldest Hawaiian Sugar Plantation*. 2nd ed. Līhu'e: Kaua'i Historical Society, 1985 [1935].

Alexander, James. *Mission Life in Hawaii: Memoir of Rev. William P. Alexander*. Oakland, Calif.: Pacific Press, 1888.

Alexander, Mary C. *William Patterson Alexander in Kentucky, the Marquesas, Hawaii*. Honolulu: privately printed, 1934.

Alexander, W. D. "A Brief History of Land Titles in the Hawaiian Kingdom." *Hawaiian Journal of Law and Politics* 2 (Summer 2006).

Allen, Gwenfread E. *Hawaii's War Years: 1941–1945*. Honolulu, University of Hawai'i Press, 1950.

——. *Men and Women of Hawaii: A Biographical Directory of Noteworthy Men and Women of Hawaii,* Vol. 8. Honolulu: Honolulu Star-Bulletin, ca. 1966.

Allen, Robert C. *Creating Hawai'i Tourism: A Memoir*. Honolulu: Bess Press, 2004.

Anderson, Mary. *Scenes in the Hawaiian Islands and California*. Boston: American Tract Society, 1865.

Andrade, Carlos. *Hā'ena through the Eyes of the Ancestors*. Honolulu: University of Hawai'i Press, 2008.

Andrews, Lorrin. *A Dictionary of the Hawaiian Language*. Honolulu: Island Heritage Publishing, 2003.

Aotani and Hartwell Associates. *Kauai Urban Design Plan*. [Honolulu]: Aotani & Hartwell Associates, 1977.

Armstrong, R. Warwick. *Atlas of Hawaii*. Cartography by James A. Bier. 2nd ed. Honolulu: University of Hawai'i Press, 1983.

Ashman, Mike. *Kauai: As It Was in the 1940s and '50s*. Līhu'e: Kaua'i Historical Society, 2004.

Barrère, Dorothy B., comp. *The King's Mahele: The Awardees and Their Lands*. Hilo, private printing, 1994.

Bartlett, S. C. *Historical Sketch of the Hawaiian Mission, and the Missions to Micronesia and the Marquesas Islands*. Boston: American Board of Commissioners for Foreign Missions, 1869.

Bartram, Paul. *Overall Economic Development Plan, County of Kauai*. Boulder, Colo.: Western Interstate Commission for Higher Education, ca. 1969.

Beechert, Edward D. *Working in Hawaii: A Labor History*. Honolulu: University of Hawai'i Press, 1985.

Belknap, Jodi P. *Majesty: The Exceptional Trees of Hawaii*. Honolulu: Outdoor Circle, 1982.

Bendix, Bud. *Serving Hawaii: The First 100 Years: The 100th Anniversary of Hawaiian Telephone Company*. Honolulu: Hawaiian Telephone, 1983.

Bennett, Wendell C. *Archaeology of Kauai*. Bernice P. Bishop Museum Bulletin 80. Honolulu: Bernice P. Bishop Museum, 1931.

Bingham, Hiram. *A Residence of Twenty-one Years in the Sandwich Islands*. Rutland, Vt.: Charles E. Tuttle, 1981 [1847].

Bird, Isabella L. *The Hawaiian Archipelago: Six Months in the Sandwich Islands among the Palm Groves, Coral Reefs, and Volcanoes of the Sandwich Islands*. 2nd ed. London: John Murray, 1876.

Bishop National Bank of Hawaii. *90 Years of Banking*. Honolulu: Bishop National Bank, 1948.

——. *The First 100 Years: Bishop National Bank of Hawaii, 1858–1958*. Honolulu: Bishop National Bank, 1958.

Bishop, Sereno Edwards. *Reminiscences of Old Hawaii*. Honolulu: Hawaiian Gazette, 1916.

Blount, James H. "Report of U.S. Special Commissioner James H. Blount to U.S. Secretary of State Walter Q. Gresham." *Hawaiian Journal of Law and Politics* 1 (Summer 2004).

Bradley, Harold W. *The American Frontier in Hawaii: The Pioneers, 1789–1843*. Gloucester, Mass.: Peter Smith, 1942.

Buke Kakau Paa no ka Mahele Aina i Hooholoia Iwaena o Kamehameha III a me na Lii a me na Konohiki Ana. Honolulu, 1848.

Buker, Betty Finley, ed. *Men and Women of Hawaii, 1972: A Geographical Directory of Noteworthy Men and Women of Hawaii*. Honolulu: Star-Bulletin, 1972.

Bushnell, O. A. *The Gifts of Civilization: Germs and Genocide in Hawai'i*. Honolulu: University of Hawai'i Press, 1993.

Capitman, Barbara Baer, Michael D. Kinerk, and Dennis W. Wilhelm. *Rediscovering Art Deco U.S.A.* New York: Viking Studio Books, 1994.

Chapin, Helen G. *Guide to Newspapers of Hawai'i: 1834–2000*. Honolulu: Hawaiian Historical Society, 2000.

Cheever, David, and Scott Cheever. *Pōhaku: The Art and Architecture of Stonework in Hawai'i*, ed. Janine Shinoki Clifford and Frank S. Haines. Honolulu: Editions Limited, 2005.

Chenoweth, Candace, and A. Kam Napier. *Shuffleboard Pilots: The History of the Women's Air Raid Defense in Hawaii, 1941–1945*. Honolulu: Arizona Memorial Museum Association, 1991.

Chinen, Jon. *The Great Mahele: Hawaii's Land Division of 1848*. Honolulu: University of Hawai'i Press, 1958.

Cisco, Dan. *Hawai'i Sports: History, Facts, and Statistics*. Honolulu: University of Hawai'i Press, 1999.

Civil Code of the Hawaiian Islands, Passed in the Year of Our Lord 1859: To Which Is Added an Appendix, Containing Laws Not Expressly Repealed by the Civil Code; The Session Laws of 1858–9; and Treaties with Foreign Nations. Honolulu: Printed for the Government, 1859.

Clendeninn, Neil J. *Effects of Urban Land Use Principles and Techniques on the Growth and Development of Small Cities: Current and Potential Future Development for Lihue, Kauai, HI*. M.S. thesis, New School of Architecture and Design, San Diego, 2003.

Coffman, Tom. *The Island Edge of America: A Political History of Hawai'i*. Honolulu: University of Hawai'i Press, 2003.

———. *I Respectfully Dissent*. Honolulu: University of Hawai'i Press, 2012.

Cole, Dora Jane Isenberg, and Juliet Rice Wichman. *Early Kauai Hospitality: A Family Cookbook of Receipts, 1820–1920*. Līhu'e: Kauai Museum Association, 1977.

Conde, Jesse C., and Gerald M. Best. *Sugar Trains Narrow Gauge Rails of Hawaii*. Felton, Calif.: Glenwood, 1973.

Cook, Chris. *Kaua'i County Manual for Hawai'i's Visitor Industry for Kaua'i County Visitor Industry*. [Līhu'e]: Program Advisory Committee and Tourism Training Council, Department of Labor and Industrial Relations, 1997.

———. *Kaua'i, the Garden Island: A Pictorial History of the Commerce and Work of the People*. Virginia Beach, Va: Donning, 1999.

Cook, John. *Reminiscences of John Cook, Kamaaina and Forty-Niner*. Honolulu: New Freedom Press, 1927.

Cooper, George, and Gavan Daws. *Land and Power in Hawaii: The Democratic Years*. Honolulu: Benchmark Books, 1985.

Corstorphine, John L. *The Autobiography of John L. Corstorphine: Memories of a Hawaiian Childhood*. Privately printed, ca. 2008.

Damon, Ethel M. *Koamalu: A Story of Pioneers on Kauai and of What They Built in That Island Garden*. 2 vols. Honolulu: privately printed, 1931.

———, ed. *Letters from the Life of Abner and Lucy Wilcox 1836–1869*. Honolulu: privately printed, 1950.

Daws, Gavan. *Shoal of Time: A History of the Hawaiian Islands*. Honolulu: University of Hawai'i Press, 1968.

Dieudonne, Fran. "*Always Remember—You Are Hawaiian": A Biography of Theodore A. Vierra, AIA: His Life and Architectural Career: 1902–1987*. Encinitas, Calif.: Neptune House, 2011.

Donohugh, Donald. *The Story of Koloa: A Kauai Plantation Town*. Honolulu: Mutual, 2001.

Dorrance, William H. "The U.S. Army on Kaua'i, 1909–1942." *Hawaiian Journal of History* 32 (1998).

Dunn, Barbara. "William Little Lee and Catherine Lee, Letters from Hawai'i 1848–1855." *Hawaiian Journal of History* 38 (2004).

Dutton, Meiric K. *The Episcopal Church in Hawaii: Ninety Years of Service: 1862–1952*. Honolulu: Missionary District of Honolulu, Protestant Episcopal Church, 1952.

Dye, Bob, ed. *Hawai'i Chronicles III: World War Two in Hawai'i, from the Pages of* Paradise of the Pacific. Honolulu: University of Hawai'i Press, 2000.

Dye, T. S., and Elaine H. R. Jourdane. *Archaeological Assessment for the Proposed T-Mobile West Hickam-Iroquois Point Cell Site No. HI 186P, 6376 Ibis Avenue, Pu'uloa, 'Ewa, O'ahu Island, TMK:(1)9-1-001:034 por*. Honolulu: T. S. Dye and Colleagues, Archaeologists, 2006.

Earle, Timothy. *How Chiefs Come to Power: The Political Economy in Prehistory*. Palo Alto, Calif.: Stanford University Press, 1997.

Eckbo, Dean, Austin and Williams. "A General Plan for the Island of Kauai." Prepared by the joint venture of Eckbo, Dean, Austin and Williams and Muroda, Tanaka & Itagaki, Inc., for County of Kauai, State of Hawaii. 1970.

EDAW Inc. and Muroda & Associates, Inc. "Lihue Development Plan." 1976.

Elsie H. Wilcox Elementary School. *Wilcox Elementary School, 1881–1981: Centennial Memory Book*. Līhu'e: Wilcox Elementary School, 1981.

Emerson, Oliver P. *Pioneer Days in Hawaii*. New York: Doubleday, 1928.

Emmet, Boris. *The California and Hawaiian Sugar Refining Corporation of San Francisco, California: A Study of the Origin, Business Policies, and Management of a Co-operative Refining and Distributing Organization*. Stanford Business Series 2. New York: AMS Press, 1970 [1928].

Fitzpatrick, Gary L. *The Early Mapping of Hawai'i*. Honolulu: Editions Limited, 1986.

Fornander, Abraham. *Fornander Collection of Hawaiian Antiquities and Folk-lore: the Hawaiian Account of the Formation of Their Islands and Origin of Their Race with the Traditions of Their Migrations, Etc., as Gathered from Original Sources by Abraham Fornander*, Vol. 4. Honolulu: Bishop Museum Press, 1916–1917.

———. *An Account of the Polynesian Race, Its Origins and Migrations and the Ancient History of the Hawaiian People to the Times of Kamehameha I*. Rutland, Vt.: Charles E. Tuttle, 1969 [1878, 1880, and 1885].

Foster, William, com. *Decisions at Chambers by Single Justices of the Supreme Court of the Hawaiian Islands*. Honolulu: Hawaiian Gazette, 1889.

Fuchs, Lawrence. *Hawaii Pono: A Social History*. New York: Harcourt, Brace and World, 1961.

Fung Associates, Inc. "Hawaii Modernism Context Study." November, 2012. Manual prepared for Historic Hawai'i Foundation symposium, "Hawai'i Modernism: A Symposium on Identification, Evaluation and Preservation of Our Recent Past," January 21, 2012.

Galois, Robert, and James Colnett. *Voyage to the Northwest Side of America: The Journals of James Colnett, 1786–89*. Vancouver: University of British Columbia Press, 2004.

Golden Years—Hawaii: Issei, Nisei and Sansei, Biographical Record of Japanese Ancestry. [Honolulu]: 1976.

Goodale, Hobey. *Hobey*. Privately published, 2011.

Greaney, Edward. "Hawaii's Big Six: A Cyclical Saga." In *The Encyclopedia of Hawaii, a 1976 Bicentennial Project*. Honolulu: University of Hawai'i Press, 1977.

Griffin, Pat L. *Wilcox Memorial Hospital in the Twentieth Century*. Līhu'e: Wilcox Health Foundation, 2000.

———. "The Līhu'e Place Name on Kaua'i." *Hawaiian Journal of History* 46 (2012).

———. "Līhu'e Public Library." In *Pōhaku: The Art and Architecture of Stonework in Hawai'i*, coordinating authors David Cheever and Scott Cheever, ed. Janine Shinoki Clifford and Frank S. Haines. Honolulu: Editions Limited, 2003.

Griffiss, Townsend. *When You Go to Hawaii: You Will Need This Guide to the Islands*. Boston: Houghton Mifflin, 1930.

Grimshaw, Patricia. *Paths of Duty: American Missionary Wives in Nineteenth-Century Hawaii*. Honolulu: University of Hawai'i Press, 1989.

Group 70 International. "Wailua Regional Plan." Prepared for Department of Hawaiian Home Lands. December 2009.

Gulick, Orramel, and Ann E. Gulick. *The Pilgrims of Hawaii*. New York: Fleming H. Revell, 1918.
Halford, Francis J. *Nine Doctors and God*. Honolulu: University of Hawai'i Press, 1954.
Hamrin, Tina. "Illness and Salvation in the Tensho-Kotai-Jingu-Kyo—the Dancing Religion of Hawaii." In *Japanese New Religions,* ed. Peter B. Clarke. Richmond, Surrey, Great Britain: Curzon Press, 2000.
Hawaii State Department of Business, Economic Development and Tourism. "Foreign Investment Activities in Hawaii and the United States, 1954 through 1998, by Country." Honolulu: Department of Business, Economic Development and Tourism, February 1999.
Hawaii State Department of Planning and Economic Development. *The Hawaii State Plan*. Honolulu: Department of Planning and Economic Development, 1978.
Hawaii State Department of Transportation Highways Division Planning Branch. "Annual Traffic Summary, Island of Kauai." Honolulu: Department of Transportation Highways Division, 1960–1971.
Hawaiian Historical Society. *Fortieth Annual Report of the Hawaiian Historical Society for the Year 1931*. Millwood, N.Y.: Kraus, 1978.
Hawaiian Mission Children's Society. *Missionary Album: Sesquicentennial Edition, 1820–1970*. Honolulu: Hawaiian Mission Children's Society, 1969.
Hibbard, Don. *Designing Paradise: The Allure of the Hawaiian Resort*. Princeton, N.J.: Princeton Architectural Press, 2006.
Hibbard, Don, Glenn Mason, and Karen Weitze. *Hart Wood: Architectural Regionalism in Hawaii*. Honolulu: University of Hawai'i Press, 2010.
Hibbard, Don J., and Wendy Wichman. "Historic American Engineering Record: Lihue Plantation Company Sugar Mill Building." National Park Service, U.S. Washington D.C.: Department of the Interior, 2008.
Hilleary, Perry E., ed. *Men and Women of Hawaii*. Honolulu: Honolulu Business Consultants, 1954.
Hobbs, Jean. *Hawaii: A Pageant of the Soil*. Palo Alto, Calif.: Stanford University Press, 1935.
Holman, Lucia Ruggles. *Journal of Lucia Ruggles Holman*. Special Publication 17. Honolulu: B. P. Bishop Museum, 1931.
Hörmann, Bernard L. *Germans in Hawaii*. Honolulu: German Benevolent Society, 1989.
Hughes, Judith. *Women and Children First: The Life and Times of Elsie Wilcox of Kaua'i*. Honolulu: University of Hawai'i Press, 1996.
Hunnewell, James F. "Early History of the Present House of C. Brewer & Co., Limited." *Hawaiian Almanac and Annual for 1896*, 68–73.
Ii, John Papa. *Fragments of Hawaiian History*. Edited by D. Barrère. Honolulu: Bishop Museum Press, 1983.
ILWU. "Building of Our Own: A Central Headquarters for the ILWU in Hawaii by 1951." ILWU Honolulu, 1949.
Indices of Awards Made by the Board of Commissioners to Quiet Land Titles in the Hawaiian Islands. Honolulu: Star-Bulletin Press, 1929.
Industrial Conditions in Hawaiian Islands. Washington: Government Printing Office, 1913.
Jarves, James J. *Scenes and Scenery in the Sandwich Islands*. Boston: James Munroe, 1844.
Jay, Robert. *Architecture of Charles W. Dickey: Hawai'i and California*. Honolulu: University of Hawai'i Press, 1992.
Joesting, Edward. *Tides of Commerce*. Honolulu: First Hawaiian, 1983.
——. *Kauai: The Separate Kingdom*. Honolulu: University of Hawai'i Press and Kauai Museum Association, 1984.

John Carl Warnecke and Associates. "Lihue: Area Studies for Lihue Town, Hanamaulu Bay, Kauai Surf Area, Kilohana Crater, Kapaia Valley." Honolulu: John Carl Warnecke and Associates, 1966.

Kamakau, Samuel M. *Ruling Chiefs of Hawaii.* Rev. ed. Honolulu: Kamehameha Schools Press, 1992.

Kame'eleihiwa, Lilikalā. *Native Land and Foreign Desires.* Honolulu: Bishop Museum Press, 1992.

Kanahele, George S. *Emma: Hawai'i's Remarkable Queen.* Honolulu: University of Hawai'i Press, 1999.

Kaua'i County Planning Department. *Kaua'i General Plan.* Līhu'e: Kauai Planning Department, 2000.

——. "Lihue Mill Executive Summary: Conceptual Master Plan." Unpublished paper. July 2005.

Kauai County Planning and Traffic Commission. "General Plans for Five Urban Areas of the County of Kauai: Waimea, Koloa, Kapaa, Hanapepe, Lihue." Lihue: Kauai Planning and Traffic Commission, 1961.

Kauai Outdoor Circle. *Kauai Outdoor Circle Indoor Cookbook.* Honolulu: Tongg, 1979.

Kawakami, Harvey Saburo, with Tom Coffman. *From Japan to Hawaii: My Journey.* Privately published, 1976.

Kent, Noel J. *Hawaii: Islands under the Influence.* New York: Monthly Review Press, 1983.

Kerner, Karen. "The Malevolent Ancestor: Ancestral Influence in a Japanese Religious Sect." In *Ancestors,* ed. William Newell. Mouton. The Hague: Mouton, 1976.

Klass, Tim. *World War II on Kauai.* Lihue: Prepared for the Kauai Historical Society by the Westland Foundation, Portland, Ore., 1970.

Kolva, J. J. "Lihue Post Office." National Register of Historic Places nomination, U.S. Department of the Interior, National Park Service, August 1988.

Korn, Alfons K., ed. *The Victorian Visitors.* Honolulu: University of Hawai'i Press, 1958.

Krauss, Bob, and William P. Alexander. *Grove Farm Plantation: The Biography of a Hawaiian Sugar Plantation.* 2nd ed. Palo Alto, Calif.: Pacific Books, 1984.

Kuykendall, Ralph S. "Introduction of the Episcopal Church into the Hawaiian Islands." *Pacific Historical Review* 15, no. 2 (June 1946).

——. *The Hawaiian Kingdom,* Vol. 1: *1778–1854, Foundation and Transformation.* Honolulu: University of Hawai'i Press, 1980 [1938].

——. *The Hawaiian Kingdom,* Vol. 2: *1854–1874, Twenty Critical Years.* Honolulu: University of Hawai'i Press, 1978 [1953].

——. *The Hawaiian Kingdom,* Vol. 3: *1874–1893, The Kalakaua Dynasty.* Honolulu: University of Hawai'i Press, 1967.

Kuykendall, Ralph S., and A. Grove Day. *Hawaii: A History, from Polynesian Kingdom to American State.* Revised ed. Englewood Cliffs, N.J.: Prentice-Hall, 1961.

Lal, Brij V., Doug Munro, and Edward D. Beechert. *Plantation Workers: Resistance and Accommodation.*Honolulu: University of Hawai'i Press, 1993.

Laws of His Majesty Kalakaua I. King of the Hawaiian Islands, Passed by the Legislative Assembly at Its Session 1888. Honolulu: Gazette, 1888.

Lee, Richard K. C. "Public Health Contrasts in Hawaii, 1850–1953." *Public Health Reports* 69, no. 4 (April 1954).

Lihue Plantation Company, Limited. *Annual Reports.* 1950–1966.

Liliuokalani. *Hawaii's Story by Hawaii's Queen.* Rutland, Vt.: Charles E. Tuttle, 1964.

Lo, Catherine. *Lihue Lutheran Church Centennial Album.* Līhu'e: Lihue Lutheran Church, 1981.

Lustig, Robert H. *Fat Chance: Beating the Odds against Sugar, Processed Food, Obesity, and Disease.* New York: Hudson Street Press, 2013.

Maclennan, Carol A. "Hawai'i Turns to Sugar: The Rise of the Plantations Centers, 1860–1880." *Hawaiian Journal of History* 31 (1997).

Malo, David. *Hawaiian Antiquities*. Honolulu: Hawaiian Gazette, 1903 [1898].
Marshall, J. F. B. "Report on Sugar." *Transactions—Royal Hawaiian Agricultural Society* 1, no. 4 (1853).
——. "Letter to Rev. S. E. Bishop," *The Friend* 47, no. 4 (1889).
Maurer, Oscar. *Three Early Christian Leaders of Hawaii*. Honolulu: Hawaiian Evangelical Association, 1945.
Mollett, J. A. "Capital in Hawaiian Sugar: Its Formation and Relation to Labor and Output, 1870–1957." *Agricultural Economics Bulletin 21* (Hawaii Agricultural Experiment Station, 1961).
Morgan, Theodore. *Hawaii: A Century of Economic Change, 1778–1876*. Cambridge, Mass.: Harvard University Press, 1948.
Morimoto, Lauren Shizuyo. "The Barefoot Leagues: An Oral (Hi)Story of Football in the Plantation Towns of Kaua'i." Ph.D. diss., Ohio State University, 2005.
Mossman, Georgia. *Police Blotter Kaua'i Style*. Honolulu: Booklines Hawaii, 2000.
Moy, Tonia. "The Range of Modern Architectural Resources in Hawai'i, 1939–1979." Experts at the Palace lecture series, Honolulu, February 28, 2013.
Nellist, George F., ed. *The Story of Hawaii and Its Builders*. Honolulu: Honolulu Star-Bulletin, 1925.
——. *Women of Hawaii,* Vol. 1. [Honolulu]: E. A. Langton-Boyle, 1929.
——. *Women of Hawaii,* Vol. 2 [Honolulu]: E. A. Langton-Boyle, 1938.
Nishiyama, Shigeru and Takeshi Fujii. "The Propagation and Spread of Tenshô Kôtai Jingûkyô with Japanese-American Society on Hawaii Island." Tokyo: Institute for Japanese Culture and Classics, Kokugakuin University, 1991.
Nordhoff, Charles. *Northern California, Oregon, and the Sandwich Islands*. Berkeley, Calif.: Ten Speed Press, 1974 [1874].
Nucciarone, Monica. *Alexander Cartwright: The Life behind the Baseball Legend*. Lincoln: University of Nebraska Press, 2009.
Okihiro, Gary Y. *Island World: A History of Hawai'i and the United States*. Berkeley: University of California Press, 2008.
Okino, Gary Y. *Cane Fires: The Anti-Japanese Movement in Hawaii, 1865–1945*. Philadelphia: Temple University Press, 1991.
PBR Hawaii. "Līhu'e Town Core Urban Design Plan Draft Report." Honolulu: PBR Hawaii, 2006.
Peterson, Barbara Bennett, ed. *Notable Women of Hawaii*. Honolulu: University of Hawai'i Press, 1984.
Planners Collaborative, with Richard A. Moore, Wilson Okamoto & Associates, VTN Pacific, William H. Liggett. "1982 Kauai General Plan Update: Summary of Findings and Recommendations." Honolulu: June, 1982.
Porteus, Stanley D. *And Blow Not the Trumpet: A Prelude to Peril*. Palo Alto, Calif.: Pacific Books, 1947.
Prophet of Tabuse. Tabuse, Japan: Tensho-Kotai-Jingu-Kyo, 1954.
Pukui, Mary Kawena. *'Ōlelo No'eau: Hawaiian Proverbs and Poetical Sayings*. Honolulu: Bishop Museum Press, 1983.
Pukui, Mary Kawena, and Samuel H. Elbert. *Hawaiian Dictionary*. Honolulu: University of Hawai'i Press, 1986.
Pukui, Mary Kawena, Samuel H. Elbert, and Esther T. Mookini. *Place Names of Hawaii*. Honolulu: University of Hawai'i Press, 1974.
Report of the Governor of Hawaii to the Secretary of the Interior, 1928. Washington, D.C.: United States Government Printing Office, 1928.
Report of the Governor of Hawaii to the Secretary of the Interior, 1930. Washington, D.C.: United States Government Printing Office, 1930.

Restarick, Henry B. *Hawaii 1778–1920 from the Viewpoint of a Bishop*. Honolulu: Paradise of the Pacific, 1924.
——. *My Personal Recollections: The Unfinished Memoirs of Henry Bond Restarick, Bishop of Honolulu, 1902–1920*. Honolulu: Paradise of the Pacific Press, 1938.
Riznik, Barnes. *Waioli Mission House: Hanalei, Kauai*. Lihue: Grove Farm Homestead and Waioli Mission House, 1987.
——. "From Barracks to Family Homes: A Social History of Labor Housing Reform on Hawai'i's Sugar Plantations." *Hawaiian Journal of History* 33 (1999).
——. *Mabel Wilcox, R.N.: Her Legacy of Caring*. Lihue: Grove Farm Museum, 2005.
Rybczynski, Witold. *Last Harvest*. New York: Scribner, 2007.
Sakamoto, Dean, ed. *Hawaiian Modern: The Architecture of Vladimir Ossipoff*. New Haven, Ct.: Yale University Press, 2007.
Sanburn, Curt. "A Moment in the Sun: When Honolulu's Splashy, Flashy and Bold Prints Took the Fashion World by Storm." *Hana Hou: The Magazine of Hawaiian Airlines* 16, no. 1 (February/March 2013).
Schmitt, Robert C. "Automobile Ownership in Hawaii before 1931: Dates and Data." *Hawaii Historical Review* 2, no. 10 (January 1968).
——. *Demographic Statistics of Hawaii: 1778–1965*. Honolulu: University of Hawai'i Press, 1968.
——. *Historical Statistics of Hawaii*. Honolulu: University of Hawai'i Press, 1977.
——. *Firsts and Almost Firsts in Hawai'i*. Honolulu: University of Hawai'i Press, 1995.
Schütz, Albert J. *The Voices of Eden: A History of Hawaiian Language Studies*. Honolulu: University of Hawai'i Press, 1994.
Schweizer, Niklaus R. *Hawai'i and the German Speaking Peoples*. Honolulu: Topgallant, 1982.
Senate Journal: Ninth Legislature of the Territory of Hawaii, Regular Session, 1917. Honolulu: Hawaiian Gazette, 1917.
Siddall, John W., ed. *Men of Hawaii*, Vol 1. Honolulu: Honolulu Star-Bulletin, 1917.
——. *Men of Hawaii*, Vol 2. Honolulu: Honolulu Star-Bulletin, 1921.
Simonds, William A. *The Hawaiian Telephone Story*. Honolulu: Star-Bulletin Printing, 1958.
Simpich, Frederick, Jr. *Dynasty in the Pacific*. New York: McGraw-Hill, 1974.
Simpson, Steven J. *Living Stones: The History of the Līhu'e United Church*. Lihue: Nina M. Magoun, 2000.
Sinclair, Isabella. *Indigenous Flowers of the Hawaiian Islands*. London: S. Low, Marston, Searle, and Rivington, 1885.
Soehren, Lloyd. *A Catalog of Kaua'i Place Names including Ni'ihau, Lehua and Ka'ula: Compiled from the Records of the Boundary Commission and the Board of Commissioners to Quiet Land Titles of the Kingdom of Hawaii*. Honolulu: privately published, 2002.
Solnit, Rebecca. *Storming the Gates of Paradise: Landscapes for Politics*. Berkeley: University of California Press, 2007.
Spencer Mason Architects. "Historic Bridge Inventory: Island of Kauai." Honolulu: State of Hawai'i, Department of Transportation, Highways Division, 1989.
Staley, Thomas N. *Five Years' Church Work in the Kingdom of Hawaii*. London: Rivingtons, 1868.
Standiford, Les. *Last Train to Paradise: Henry Flagler and the Spectacular Rise and Fall of the Railroad That Crossed an Ocean*. New York: Crown, 2002.
Steele, Julia. "Tribute to a Master." *Hana Hou: The Magazine of Hawaiian Airlines* 15, no. 6 (December 2012–January 2013).

Sterling, Elspeth P., and Catherine C. Summers, comps. "Sites of Oahu." Anthropology Department, Bernice P. Bishop Museum, Honolulu, 1978.

Stewart, Charles S. *Journal of a Residence in the Sandwich Islands during the Years 1823, 1824, and 1825*. Honolulu: University of Hawai'i Press, 1970 [1830].

Swann, Alice. "The Universe of Dynamite Stuff." *Hana Hou: The Magazine of Hawaiian Airlines* 16, no. 1 (February–March 2013).

Swift, Earl. *The Big Roads: The Untold Story of the Engineers, Visionaries, and Trailblazers Who Created the American Superhighways*. New York: Houghton Mifflin Harcourt, 2011.

Takaki, Ronald T. *Pau Hana: Plantation Life and Labor in Hawaii, 1835–1920*. Honolulu: University of Hawai'i Press, 1983.

Teggart, Frederick J., ed. *Around the Horn to the Sandwich Islands and California 1845–1850, Being a Personal Record Kept by Chester S. Lyman, Sometime Professor of Astronomy and Physics in Yale University*. New Haven, Conn.: Yale University Press, 1924.

TenBruggencate, Jan. *Lihue Mill: Grinding Cane and Building Community, One Hundred Fifty Years of Sugar Processing along Nāwiliwili Stream*. Lihue: PAHIO Development and Lihue MS, 2011.

Thomas, Bernice. *America's 5 & 10 Cent Stores: The Kress Legacy*. New York: John Wiley and Sons, 1997.

Tracy, Joseph. *History of the American Board of Commissioners for Foreign Missions*. New York: M. W. Dodd, 1842.

Tregear, Edward. *The Maori-Polynesian Comparative Dictionary*. Christchurch, N.Z.: Whitcombe and Tombs, 1897.

Tuggle, H. David, and M. J. Tomonari-Tuggle. *Synthesis of Cultural Resource Studies of the 'Ewa Plain*. Honolulu: International Archaeological Research Institute, 1997.

Vandercook, John. *King Cane: The Story of Sugar in Hawaii*. Honolulu: Hawaiian Sugar Planters' Association, 1940.

Vowell, Sarah. *Unfamiliar Fishes*. New York: Riverhead Books, 2011.

Wedemeyer, Alice. *The Story of the Mokihana Club of Kauai*. Lihue: Mokihana Club, 1987.

Wenkam, Robert. *Kauai and the Park Country of Hawaii*. San Francisco: Sierra Club Books, 1967.

Wichman, Fredrick B. *Kaua'i: Ancient Place-Names and Their Stories*. Honolulu: University of Hawai'i Press, 1998.

——. *Nā Pua Ali'i o Kaua'i*. Honolulu: University of Hawai'i Press, 2003.

Wilcox, Carol. *Kauai Album*. Lihue: KHS Publications, 1981.

——. *Sugar Water: Hawaii's Plantation Ditches*. Honolulu: University of Hawai'i Press, 1998.

Wilcox School. *Wilcox Elementary School: 1881–1981: Centennial Memory Book*. Lihue: Wilcox School, 1981.

Wilkes, Charles. *Narrative of the United States Exploring Expedition*. 5 vols. Philadelphia: 1850.

Wilson, William H. *The City Beautiful Movement: Creating the North American Landscape*. Baltimore: Johns Hopkins University Press, 1989.

Wist, Benjamin O. *A Century of Public Education in Hawaii*. Honolulu: Hawaii Educational Review, 1940.

Worden, William L. *Cargoes: Matson's First Century in the Pacific*. Honolulu: University of Hawai'i Press, 1981.

Yamafuji, Vee Miyake. *Follow the Rainbow*. Irvine, Calif.: privately published, ca. 1980.

Zalburg, Sanford. *A Spark Is Struck! Jack Hall and the ILWU in Hawaii*. Honolulu: University of Hawai'i Press, 1979.

INDEX

Page numbers in **boldface** type refer to illustrations.

A

D

E

F

G

J

K

L

M

N

O

P

T

U

V

W

Y

Z

He luelue ka ʻupena e kuʻu ai.

The fine-meshed net
is the one to let down
into the sea.

HAWAI'I

PRODUCTION NOTES FOR GRIFFIN

LĪHU'E

Jacket design by Julie Matsuo-Chun.

Text design and composition by

Julie Matsuo-Chun with display type

in Berthold Akzidenz and text type

in Georgia. Printing and binding by

Sheridan Books, Inc. Printed on

70# Sterling Premium Matte, 556 ppi